A Child of One's Own

A Child of One's Own

Parental Stories

RACHEL BOWLBY

OXFORD
UNIVERSITY PRESS

Great Clarendon Street, Oxford, OX2 6DP,
United Kingdom

Oxford University Press is a department of the University of Oxford.
It furthers the University's objective of excellence in research, scholarship,
and education by publishing worldwide. Oxford is a registered trade mark of
Oxford University Press in the UK and in certain other countries

First Edition published in 2013

Impression: 1

British Library Cataloguing in Publication Data

Data available

ISBN 978-0-19-960794-5

Printed in Great Britain by
Clays Ltd, St Ives plc

Contents

Acknowledgements

In writing this book I am grateful for so many conversations with friends and colleagues who have shared their thoughts and stories about parenthood. Special thanks for suggestions, or encouragement, are due to Thomas Baldwin, Gillian Beer, Fran Bigman, Peter Brooks, Lawrence Foley, Sarah Franklin, Elena Gualtieri, Margaret Homans, Anne Ketteman, Sammy Lee, Marie-Christine Lemardeley, Josephine McDonagh, Rhoda McGraw, Jesse Olszynko-Gryn, Matthew Reisz, Ritchie Robertson, Michael Sheringham, and Pat Thane. At UCL, I would like especially to thank Rosemary Ashton, Matthew Beaumont, Gregory Dart, Paul Davis, Philip Horne, Hugh Stevens, Peter Swaab, and Sarah Wintle. Grateful thanks are also owed to my agent Jon Elek; to Jacqueline Baker and Rachel Platt at OUP; and to Jackie Pritchard and Lesley Rhodes for their careful copy-editing and proofreading.

The Leverhulme Trust awarded me a Major Research Fellowship to pursue this project, and I am immensely grateful for that support.

Earlier versions of two of the chapters were previously published in journal articles: 'I Had Barbara' in *differences* 17: 3 (2006), and 'Parental Secrets in Thomas Hardy's *The Mayor of Casterbridge*' in *Comparative Critical Studies* 5: 2–3 (2008), where it formed part of a longer piece entitled ' "Where Ignorance is Bliss": The Folly of Origins in Gray and Hardy'.

Introduction

In 1983, a baby was found one night abandoned in a telephone box; in 2006, a woman aged 62 who had become pregnant through IVF with a donor egg became what the media called 'Britain's oldest mother'. Both these natal events occurred in the same small town— Lewes, in East Sussex. There were just a couple of decades between them, but in other respects they are worlds and centuries apart. The abandoned baby appeared as a strange return to times when motherhood out of wedlock could carry an unbearable stigma or when material circumstances might make it impossible for parents to care for a child. The other birth, to the older woman, could represent one of the more striking possibilities of a new order in which parenthood has come to be seen as a form of personal fulfilment, a valid lifestyle option open to anyone, whatever their age or their marital status or their sexuality This woman, with her husband, had travelled abroad to receive the expensive medical treatment that might possibly enable them both to become parents. The young girl— if she was— had fled from the motherhood she found herself in, leaving her baby to chance.[1] In terms of age the high-tech mother, ironically, could have been the grandmother of the younger one. Capsuled together in a single place, so near and so far, these two stories, as though from the opposite ends of history, bring out utterly different orientations to the prospect of parenthood, the foundling and the 'seekling' each being the result of a fervent need to be, or else not to be, a parent.

Yet between the extremes of casting out and seeking afar is a wide middle ground of ordinary life, one generation after another, in which children have just come along, more or less wanted, without

---

[1] The 'mother of 62' was Patricia Rashbrook, a paediatrician with three adult children; the story of her and her husband (who was 60 and a first-time father) was featured in the *Daily Mail* and other newspapers. The finder of the foundling was Stephen Medcalf, a medievalist at the University of Sussex (close to Lewes). He wrote about the experience much later in 'A Light in the Darkness', *Guardian*, 21 December 2002.

engendering any particular story. Unlike other elementary human experiences, and for all its importance as a daily occupation and preoccupation in people's lives, parenthood has often tended to go without saying: as if we know the story, and the story is not very interesting. Compared to the passions of childhood, parenthood appears as just the counterpart or background: where there is a child, there are or were parents. Compared to the spectacular attachments of erotic and romantic love, it looks like nothing more than a predictable and storyless sequel: where there is a marriage, there will probably be children. In the final chapter of Charlotte Brontë's *Jane Eyre*—the chapter that famously begins with 'Reader, I married him'—the birth of a son to Jane and Mr Rochester slips by in a subordinate clause: 'When his first-born was put into his arms...'[2] Nothing in the narrative led up to it (no thought of a possible child; no mention of a pregnancy), and nothing comes after it (parenthood is not the start of a story).

But despite some appearances, parenthood is not symmetrically related to childhood or dully detachable as an after-event to falling in love or marriage. Childhood refers to a period of life; parenthood is a contingent status. Childhood comes to an end; parenthood goes on.[3] In the basic order of things, a child is originally and forever the child of two parents; but parents may become parents of indefinite numbers of children, appearing at different times in their lives. Children may or may not have siblings, of either sex or both; but genetically at least, every parent has a (single) co-parent, of the other sex. Also parenthood—unlike childhood—is not universal, and while children are never (or never meant to be) parents, every adult has been a child and is thereby in part a post-child, still suffering from or enjoying the reminiscences of what modern times have taken to be the most formative of human life-stages. Parenthood, if it happens, may begin at very different ages, from adolescence to middle age or

---

[2] Charlotte Brontë, *Jane Eyre* (1847), ed. Margaret Smith (Oxford: Oxford University Press, 2000), 451.

[3] But although childhood ends, in lived experience it is a far longer period than it is for the parents watching it. In Dan Jacobson's evocative words, 'We expect our children's childhood to pass as slowly as we remember our own to have done. And so it does—*to them*'; *Time and Time Again: Autobiographies* (London: Andre Deutsch, 1985), 137.

even beyond, and it is widely variable in its significance for the person concerned: sometimes indifferently accepted, sometimes experienced as an imposition; sometimes much wished for, or surprisingly found as a joy. Sometimes it is all of these things to the same person at different times—or with different children. For any parent, perhaps for most, the whole range of possible feelings, from delight to boredom to agony, may come upon them at different points in the long parental life that follows the arrival of a new child. Alternatively, parenthood may sometimes mean no more than a formal status, with little effect on the parent's practical or emotional daily life. In its happiest modes, parental love may be as bindingly passionate as romantic love; and like marriage it involves a long-term attachment to another. But unlike a marriage, it is a relationship whose commitments are expected to diminish as time goes on and the grown child moves on to further lives and loves. And unlike marriage, too, it has always more often than not been both serial and multiple (one child after another).

One aim of this book is to bring out the sheer peculiarity of parenthood and its distinctiveness in relation to the neighbouring attachments that often obscure it. Where there is a child, or where there is a love story, there may very well be an interesting parental story too, if you look with that possibility in mind. By focusing in much of what follows on mainstream literary works that have not been considered from this point of view, I hope to indicate the way that parental stories tend to get sidelined even when they are present with varying degrees of obviousness, and even when they stand apart from the cultural norms.

As well as considering parenthood in its own right, in its differences from other elementary human ties and conditions, the book also seeks to show up a hinterland of antecedent stories and situations for many of the forms of contemporary parenthood that may seem to be quite new. In the last two or three decades, possible parental types have multiplied far beyond the old norm of marital procreation, generating new kinds of likely parental story; and the growing frequency of modes of parenthood that used to be socially unthinkable or biologically impossible brings with it correspondingly changing conditions of public and private narrative. Gay parenthood and chosen single parenthood are the most salient indications

of this, with the neutral 'single parent' of either sex a quite different
figure from the previously stigmatized 'unmarried mother'. The
increasingly common break-up of initial parental couples makes
step-parenting into a common role—as it always used to be, but
through death, not separation. With both spousal and marital longevity in western countries, it may well be that the middle decades
of the twentieth century were the only historical period in western
culture when a 'nuclear' family consisting of two parents (neither
previously partnered), a small number of children, and no one else
living with them (no other relatives or servants) was actually the
commonest form.

Biologically, new reproductive technologies have altered the very
'facts of life' which engender parents as well as children, and here
too there has been a proliferation of new parents or proto-parents,
through surrogacy and egg or sperm donation. For the first time in
human history, fathers can be known with scientifically proven certainty (through DNA testing); but simultaneously, motherhood has
acquired a new indeterminacy: egg donation and some forms of surrogacy both involve two biological mothers. And apart from the
possible divisions within each, the very separation of biological from
social parenthood represents another multiplication of parental
parts—one that was always the case in situations of adoption, but
that now becomes newly prominent in light of the changing pre-
and postnatal conditions of life.

There have also been fundamental changes in the imagined
status of parenthood across the past century, as it became a condition supposed to be actively chosen, for both the married and,
increasingly, the unmarried. Initially, contraception enabled the
negative choice of not (or not now) having children; but the emphasis today is more often on the wishful and positive choice, for individuals as well as for couples, to have a baby, perhaps with the help
of reproductive technologies.[4] Both kinds of choice, the pro and the
contra, also imply a new differentiation between parenthood and

---

[4] Two key dates for the British context: in 1961, oral contraception ('the pill') was
approved for prescription in Family Planning clinics; in 1974—just four years before
the first IVF baby—contraceptive provision was placed under the aegis of the NHS,
with advice and supplies free of charge irrespective of marital status.

sexuality. Contraception separated sex from procreation (as Freud, with historical prescience, had done in theory); reproductive technologies separate procreation from sex. Or: first you could have sex without having to have babies; now you can have babies without having to have sex.

Within this broad demarcation of parenthood as against sexuality, smaller divisions and separations appear. Again, in this subdivision, there is an analogy with Freud's analysis of sexuality as a bundle of component elements which may or may not get connected up as the culturally standard packages of masculine and feminine orientations. The new types and possibilities of parenthood have the effect of showing up distinctions between its biological, social, and legal aspects which rarely come to the fore with a baby born naturally to a married couple. Today, contractual arrangements have to be made to settle prenatally the postnatal status of parties who may have played bodily roles in a baby's production, but who will not have any parental rights or responsibilities once it is born. Sperm donors, egg donors, and surrogate mothers all have to be sorted out from those who will be deemed, in legal terms, the real parents of the postnatal child, one or both or neither of whom—if there are two—may themselves have a biological relationship to it.

All these changes generate new kinds of likely (and unlikely) parental story. New reproductive technologies and their accompanying parental possibilities tend to have the fascination of the fantastic, with an equally striking speed of normalization. In July 1978, the birth of the first 'test-tube baby', Louise Brown, was an international news story; her birth was often compared (in an idiom that now seems nostalgically dated) to the landing of men on the moon.[5] Moon

---

[5] John Brown, the father of Louise, used the immensity of the lunar landing to suggest the smallness of just one little (differently made) baby arriving on this planet: 'New discoveries were being made every day and several years had passed since we'd been to the clinic. "After all," I went on. "Scientists have put a spaceman on the moon." Compared to that, making Les pregnant seemed such a little thing'; Lesley and John Brown, with Sue Freeman, *Our Miracle Called Louise: A Parents' Story* (New York: Paddington Press, 1979), 97. Jacques Testart, one of the team responsible for the birth of the first French IVF baby in 1982, said of couples who were willing to try the new treatment before it had ever worked, 'it was a bit like walking on the moon'; *L'Œuf transparent* (Paris: Flammarion, 1986), 64.

walkings failed to proliferate, but IVF is now seen as a fairly ordinary procedure, even though its success rates have never been high;[6] and controversy occurs not around its medical or ethical justification but around the qualifications of postnatal parents: the 'mother of 62' and rising; the gay male couple or single man 'commissioning' a surrogate mother. Such stories are widely reported in the media, but this is only the more sensational end of a broader cultural concern with the state and significance of parenthood which is relatively new, and is prompted as well by the sense of swiftly shifting or disintegrating norms of both bearing and rearing.

The diminishment of the age-old dissymmetry between mother and father—the known biological mother, to whom a baby is seen to be born; the father in principle uncertain—has a further dimension in the possibility now, through egg donation, of post-menopausal maternity (so that either parent, not just a father, may be old from the start); while in IVF each genetic parent is merely the source of a neutrally named 'gamete'. And the tendency to biological equalization is echoed socially through the growing expectation, promoted by maternity (and paternity) leaves and by flexible working time, that both mother and father have paid jobs and both actively participate in something called 'parenting' (a telling new word). Until recently, modern ideology has tended to make a clear distinction of roles: mothers as homemakers and fathers as providers. Ordinary language also distinguishes between 'mothering' and 'fathering'. To 'mother' someone relates to a social role or emotional attitude, while to 'father' a child is prenatal and has nothing to do with the born child. But now that mother and father are becoming increasingly comparable in both their biological conditions of existence and their presumed postnatal roles, the neutral word 'parent' takes on a new significance. From this point of view, the differences of motherhood and fatherhood verge on or merge

---

[6] Statistics for IVF and related treatments are notoriously difficult to assess—and in many countries, where clinics are private and relatively unregulated, to gather. The goal (for prospective parents) is what is peculiarly called a 'take-home baby'; figures may be made to seem better by giving rates of pregnancy rather than live birth, or full-term birth. In the UK, according to the statistics of the statutory HFEA (Human Fertilisation and Embryology Authority), about one in four treatments (out of 50,000) were successful in 2009—a figure rising to one in three for women under the age of 35.

into a single kind of 'parental' identity. The two parents may even be imagined as a kind of interchangeable dual subject, separately sharing the tasks or pleasures of childcare and outside work, one at a time. Taking this to its logical limit is the hopeful vision of one advocate of equal parenting: 'I hope that future generations of mothers will be able to push open their front doors, crossing fathers on the threshold, as they both move freely between their private and public roles.'[7] Clocking in and out for their alternating and complementary shifts, the two parties to this jobshare may never actually meet.

The book's first chapters consider some of the larger notions that frame contemporary accounts of parenthood. New reproductive technologies—'Changing Conceptions'—have stood out as striking incursions or inventions, but they have also altered the ordinary understanding of the processes that lead to the birth of babies and the designation of parents. Surrogate motherhood has elicited sharper arguments than any other of the new reproductive practices; I suggest some reasons for this, and also describe some antecedents of modern surrogacy in Old Testament stories and in eighteenth-century arguments about wet-nursing. A chapter on choice looks at some of the earlier roles of this confident and rational modern word. The twentieth-century political demand for reproductive choice was the offspring, discursively, of an earlier argument about the right to choose one's own spouse, and the nineteenth-century claim that the exercise of choice is the mark of independent thinking. Chapter 4, with a discussion of William Hogarth's painting 'Moses Brought before Pharaoh's Daughter', describes the eighteenth-century charitable initiative that established the Foundling Hospital in London.

The following chapters look at parental stories to be found for the most part in nineteenth-century novels, most of them well known, but few of them much remembered for a concern with parental emotions and experiences. Collectively these works show up a range of paradigmatic parental situations and orientations, often several in a single work. Parenthood may be actively sought, by would-be adoptive parents (Charles Dickens's *Great Expectations*, Thomas Hardy's *The Mayor of Casterbridge*, Henry James's *What Maisie Knew*)

---

[7] Rebecca Asher, *Shattered: Modern Motherhood and the Illusion of Equality* (London: Harvill Secker, 2011), 213.

or a would-be birth parent (Euripides' *Medea*). It may be unexpected, or unexpectedly embraced (George Eliot's *Silas Marner*, George Moore's *Esther Waters*). It may come into conflict with other attachments (*Medea, What Maisie Knew, Esther Waters*). It may also be rejected or given up, through despair or need or pressure (a word that inadequately invokes all kinds of covert and unspoken social or personal urging); in one form or another, this phenomenon appears in every one of the chapters except the last. Conversely a parent may tenaciously keep a child in the face of the greatest material hardship (*Esther Waters*). Taking on a parental role may be an act of charity—in some forms of adoption (Jane Austen's *Mansfield Park*) or when a foundling is taken in (*Silas Marner*), or both (Henry Fielding's *Tom Jones*). Children may be moved about between different places and people, with successive or multiple parents (*Mansfield Park, What Maisie Knew*), or parental alternation (*Tom Jones, What Maisie Knew*).

The last two chapters take up a question that is implicit throughout the book: that of the secret story, or what is suppressed or unspeakable in any given narrative or argument about parenthood. Secret parents—their relationship unknown to their offspring but sometimes also to themselves—have always featured in literature, through centuries of 'Who's the father?' plotlines going back to Sophocles' *Oedipus the King*.[8] But the new provability of paternity, together with the emergence of new social forms of parenthood, has profoundly changed the landscape of secrets. While some former sources of shame, in particular illegitimacy, may fade away, others are newly generated. Thomas Hardy's *The Mayor of Casterbridge* and Edith Wharton's 'Roman Fever' are concerned with the persistence of parental secrets; they are also, in different ways, about how retelling or returning to a story may give it new meanings in the light of changed times. This is what happens with all the excavations of 'old' parental stories in this book: whether secret or not, they come out looking different in the contexts in which we encounter them now.

---

[8] Or beyond: in Homer's *Odyssey* (book 1, lines 215–16), Telemachus declares that although his mother tells him he is Odysseus' son, really 'no one knows their parentage'. In Sophocles' *Oedipus the King*, it is revealed that Oedipus' original parents are not, as he thought, the mother and father he grew up with, but the woman he married and a stranger he casually murdered.

Several of the novels, as mentioned, describe arrangements in which children are moved about from one parent or surrogate parent to another: moved and then moved back or moved on. There are also definitive moments of handing over or handing on, from one person to another—as in Hogarth's 'Moses Brought before Pharaoh's Daughter'. Chapter 4 discusses this picture in relation to its Old Testament story of equivocal motherhood and to its first situation: painted for the London Foundling Hospital, it evoked a distinctive moment of transition in the life of the children there. Thinking about its suggestiveness in relation to parental stories, I return to this picture in the Afterword at the end of the book.

Calling a book *A Child of One's Own* is bound to evoke Virginia Woolf's famous title. For Woolf, the room of *A Room of One's Own* is a space for privacy and self-expression; it is a chance to be creative—ideally, to write beautiful books. My own title is meant to suggest the change since Woolf's time, when parenthood, and motherhood in particular, could be perceived as an obstacle to superior forms of achievement; whereas now, it is frequently seen as a form of personal fulfilment in its own right.

But there is also, quite close to the surface of *A Room of One's Own*, a particular parental story that is part of its argument. Woolf thinks that women have always been held back from creativity for a mixture of economic and ideological reasons. In a straightforwardly practical sense, 'to have a room of her own, let alone a quiet room or a sound-proof room, was out of the question, unless her parents were exceptionally rich or very noble'.[9] Beyond that, the world was against the idea of a woman writing: 'the effect of discouragement upon the mind of the artist should be measured' (51). In relation to those few women, over the centuries, who have succeeded in doing some writing in spite of such adverse conditions, Woolf notes various flaws—in the case of nineteenth-century novelists, they are 'all the victims of inner strife as their writings prove'. Before that, in the time of Shakespeare, there was no possibility of a woman author at all: 'whatever she had written would have been

---

[9] Virginia Woolf, *A Room of One's Own* (1929; London: Panther, 1984), 51. Further page references will be included in the main text.

twisted and deformed, issuing from a strained and morbid imagination' (49). The ideal is somehow to get a work out which has not been warped in this way.

Woolf says that for anyone, man or woman, to produce a work unmarked by conflict there has to be an enabling tradition of famous 'forerunners' and 'forgotten poets': 'For masterpieces are not single and solitary births' (63). The masterpiece is a baby and the preceding writers are midwives or co-parents. Without that support, 'Everything is against the likelihood that it will come from the writer's mind whole and entire' (50); and 'if anything comes through in spite of all this, it is a miracle, and probably no book is born entire and uncrippled as it was conceived' (51). There is, then, a lapse of more than time from conception—flawless—to birth, with the intervention of disabling conditions unless, 'in spite of all this', there is the miracle baby which has not become damaged on the way. Woolf is preoccupied by the spectacle of deformed progeny, which loom more visibly than the exceptional baby-masterpieces that arrive unblemished. Writing of a message sent to Mussolini which expressed the wish that the new Italian regime 'would soon give birth to a poet worthy of it', she comments:

it is doubtful whether poetry can come of an incubator. Poetry ought to have a mother as well as a father. The Fascist poem, one may fear, will be a horrid little abortion such as one sees in a glass jar in the museum of some county town. Such monsters never live long, it is said.   (98)

Natural pregnancy and conception are necessary for an artistic baby; the planning and artifice of reproductive technologies produce its antithesis, something stillborn and repulsive.[10]

---

[10] At the time of Woolf's writing, there was a small museum in the village of Bramber in what is now West Sussex: an idiosyncratic collection of curiosities called Potter's Museum. Among the exhibits of stuffed and otherwise preserved creatures were a two-headed snake and the foetus of a two-headed lamb. Woolf visited Bramber one day in September 1926, just two years before she gave the lectures that would become *A Room of One's Own*. In her diary she does not mention visiting the museum (what she records is a scene at the village's 'tea garden'), but if she did, before or after her refreshments, it seems likely that what she saw then was what prompted the grotesquely strange image of *in vitro*, *ex utero* monstrosities. See *The Diary of Virginia Woolf*, vol. iii, 1925–30, ed. Anne Olivier Bell (Harmondsworth: Penguin, 1982), 105. I went to the museum in the early 1970s and have never forgotten what I saw.

The picture of natural generation is made more explicit in a passage where Woolf imagines a kind of internal copulation on the part of a writer who combines both sexes in one mind: 'Some collaboration has to take place in the mind between the woman and the man before the art of creation can be accomplished. Some marriage of opposites has to be consummated' (99). Both sexes are needed, because 'without some mixture of the kind the intellect seems to predominate and the other faculties of the mind harden and become barren' (99). When Woolf is speaking of creative writing, this language of natural fertilization and natural birth is insistently present, and it is shadowed by the spectre of its failures in the form of the abortion, the barren, the deformed or crippled.

In equating the creativity of art or writing with parenthood, Woolf is following in a line of rhetorical forefathers that goes back to Plato. In the *Symposium*, Socrates describes a difference between physical and mental generation—for men. Writers are among the supreme examples of the superior creative capacity: 'We'd all prefer to have children of this sort rather than the human kind, and we cast envious glances at good poets like Homer and Hesiod because the kind of children they leave behind are those which earn their parents renown and remembrance.'[11] Men can make the intellectual creations which are so much more valuable, in themselves and as a credit to their parents, than ordinary physical offspring. In Woolf, what she calls the 'woman-manly or man-womanly' is the 'mixture'—within a single person—that is vital to creativity. For Plato, the creative work comes to fruition—literally, the (male) pregnancy is completed—through an inspiring (male) lover who is then a co-parent:

once he's come into contact with an attractive person and become intimate with him, he produces and gives birth to the offspring he's been pregnant with for so long [*ha palai ekuei tiktei kai genna*]. He thinks of his partner all the time, whether or not he's there, and together they share in raising their offspring.[12]

For both Plato and Woolf, what is desirable is a form of parenthood that exceeds—and thereby demotes—the physical reproduction of

[11] Plato, *Symposium*, ed. R. G. Bury (2nd edn. 1932; Cambridge: W. Heffer, 1973), 209c–d; trans. Robin Waterfield (Oxford: Oxford University Press, 1994), 53; tr. mod.

[12] Plato, *Symposium*, 209c; 52.

ordinary mortals. The creative person generates babies that are so much better than the ones that appear in everyday life; but babies is what he (or she) generates, and a parent, intellectual rather than bodily, is what the maker is, in relation to his or her creative productions.

For Socrates, the making of real children in the family way is nothing like as rewarding or praiseworthy as the higher pursuit of intellectual generativity. For Woolf, with a similar logic, the artwork is a superior kind of offspring, with the difference that the having of real babies rather than writerly babies is marked out as having been one of the principal setbacks for creative women throughout history. You could not find four women less like each other than the greatest women writers of the nineteenth century, she says (her quartet is Jane Austen, George Eliot, and Charlotte and Emily Brontë)—'Save for the possibly relevant fact that not one of them had a child' (63). She says 'a' child, not 'children' or 'a large family': even one, it is implied, might interfere with a woman's creative talents in other spheres; and interference or thwarting is the only effect of motherhood that is imagined.

It is interesting too that, unlike Plato's Socrates, Woolf seems to draw on a distinction between conception and birth—on the harmful effects on the baby that a bad pregnancy can produce. For Socrates, there is only the simple statement of an alternative between intellectual and physical gestation. This makes it all the more striking that Woolf separates the two stages of (pure) conception and (tainted) birth. There is the authentic, creative parenthood of the immaculate conception, somehow unmarked by the social atmosphere and conditions that then come to distort or blight or disfigure the genius of the genesis. The conception is not of this world; the eventual baby has been corrupted by its influence.

In Woolf's book, real babies as babies do not count for much; or rather, they count negatively, as a poor exchange for the female imagination that their existence, like other commonplace disadvantages of women's domestic lives, is bound to stifle. But in recent years the having and rearing of children has been given, some of the time, and for some people, a new kind of value. It may be separated from other relationships and it may be sought as a source of creative fulfilment. A child of one's own, desired above all else.

1

Changing Conceptions

Misconceptions. Everything Conceivable. Inconceivable Conceptions. Inconceivable. Inconceivable. Inconceivable.[1] Sometimes it can seem as if any book that has something to do with the having of babies has to establish its credentials by means of the obligatory pun. Naomi Wolf's *Misconceptions* is concerned with the management of pregnancy, Liza Mundy's *Everything Conceivable* with the politics of reproductive technologies; *Inconceivable Conceptions* and one of the *Inconceivable*s are about infertility and reproductive technologies; Carolyn and Sean Savage's *Inconceivable* is the story of how, through a mistake at an IVF clinic, she became pregnant with an embryo belonging to another couple; finally, back in the last millennium, and perhaps the progenitor of all this populous brood, Ben Elton's novel *Inconceivable* is about a couple's attempts to have an IVF baby. The relentless pun, devoid of variation (as if no other word were conceivable), evokes the sheer counter-intuitive amazement at the new ways that babies may come into being. But it also, perhaps less designedly, evokes the inseparability of the facts of life and the stories of life—the beginnings of life in particular.

---

[1] In order, the books listed are: Naomi Wolf, *Misconceptions: Truth, Lies, and the Unexpected on the Journey to Motherhood* (London: Chatto & Windus, 2001); Liza Mundy, *Everything Conceivable: How Assisted Reproduction is Changing Men, Women and the World* (New York: Alfred A. Knopf, 2007); Jane Haynes and Juliet Miller (eds.), *Inconceivable Conceptions: Psychological Aspects of Infertility and Reproductive Technology* (Hove: Brunner-Routledge, 2003); Julia Indichova, *Inconceivable: A Woman's Triumph Over Despair and Statistics* (New York: Broadway Books, 2001); Carolyn and Sean Savage, *Inconceivable: A Medical Mistake, the Baby We Couldn't Keep, and Our Choice to Deliver the Ultimate Gift* (New York: HarperOne, 2011); and Ben Elton's bestselling novel, *Inconceivable* (1999; London: Black Swan, 2000).

For conception has the rhetorical convenience of being open to metaphorical metamorphosis, moving as if by nature between the ultra-biological (the beginning of a new life) and the ultra-intellectual (the mental conception or philosophical concept). The word is already well adapted to show and tell the fluidity of the facts of early life. For conception has changed: it can now be got to happen under previously unknown conditions. Whereas before it was something that occurred invisibly, in the past few decades it has been brought out into the open. It can take place outside the female body; it can be seen; and it has also, from being a private mystery, become a topic of tense public argument and dramatization. When Sperm Met Egg—now in full slow-motion view of the embryologist who helpfully put them in touch.

Conception has changed by changing places, even if it remains, in essence, the conjunction of the two gametes, sperm and ovum, to make the single cell from which an embryo, then a foetus, may develop, and ultimately a baby be born. There is a world of difference between a hidden process that happens within a body, unwitnessed and unregistered, and one that is clinically prepared and tracked in minute detail.[2] This is not to suggest that events that lead to what has now been relegated or promoted to the status of the 'traditional' mode of conception may not involve just as much active intention as those that require the direct manipulation of the ingredients that are fused in the fertilization of egg 'by' sperm. But previously conception was an obscure event, the *sine qua non* that must have occurred before signs of pregnancy began to appear; whereas now its component parts and stages can be separated and reassembled, step by step, in methodical time and visible external space. Conception is no longer always a mysterious moment of origin, a real event but one that can only be imagined and retrospectively inferred. After the collection of eggs and sperm, it is possible to choose precisely which ones to bring together. After fertilizations

---

[2] As the obstetrician William Smellie memorably put it in a book of 1779: 'the *modus* of conception is altogether uncertain, especially in the human species, because opportunities of opening pregnant women so seldom occur'; cited in Thomas Laqueur, *Making Sex: Body and Gender from the Greeks to Freud* (1990; Cambridge, Mass.: Harvard University Press, 1992), 182.

have taken place, it is possible to choose which embryo to implant in the womb. Eggs, or sperm, or embryos, can be frozen for years, before being thawed for 'use'.

Just as it would be wrong to deny the place of method and planning in the pre-conceptional process sometimes referred to as 'trying for' a baby, so it can also be seen that conceptions that happen in a glass dish, rather than in a womb, are not primarily matters of cool scientific observation and fact. Reproductive technologies are the source of fascination and wonder—for those who bring them about and those who benefit from them, and also for those who read or hear about them. Right from the outset, with the very first 'test-tube baby', external conception was a very big news story, reported all over the world; and further developments in reproductive technologies have gone on making headlines and generating controversy, creating new objects of emotional and financial investment, of private hope and disappointment. In particular, these minuscule clusters of cells, the embryos that may be implanted for pregnancy, have become a new kind of human or pre-human being—somehow born before they are born, temporarily present in the world before they are placed in a woman's womb in the hope of pregnancy and birth.[3]

Not all of these creatures get to be 'put back' in the place where in fact they never yet were ('put back' elides the fact that only the egg came from the woman's body). The embryologist, like a personification of Darwinian nature, will 'select' the ones that look likeliest to succeed, if there are enough to choose from; if there are too many to transfer (which may, in some countries now, mean simply more than one),[4] early-stage embryos have to be put

---

[3] As Marilyn Strathern put it in 1994, 'a potentially new legal and social entity had come into the world in the form of the human embryo in the very early stages of development, alive but outside the parental body'; *Reproducing the Future: Essays on Anthropology, Kinship and the New Reproductive Technologies* (Manchester: Manchester University Press, 1994), 4.

[4] In the countries, including the UK, in which reproductive medicine is closely regulated, there has been a growing tendency to limit the number of embryos that may be transferred in order to reduce the chance of multiple pregnancies. Apart from the social and psychological challenges of becoming all at once the parent of two or three babies, let alone more, such pregnancies are more risky to the mother's health and more likely to result in very small, premature babies with much reduced chances

somewhere else. They may be discarded, or they may be 'donated'—either to other prospective parents, or for use in research. They may graduate to a further strange limbo-like existence called cryopreservation—or freezing. By a bizarre twist of unnatural nature, it happens that freezing and thawing minuscule embryos is a relatively simple matter; their use-by limit time is, to date, unknown.[5] (In the UK there is a legal limit of five years on storage time, but in many countries there is none.)

In the United States there are now organizations dedicated to placing donated or 'abandoned' embryos for 'adoption' ('abandoned' meaning, in effect, that bills for storage have not been paid). In 2005 President Bush personally vetoed legislation that would have enabled the use of embryos in stem cell research and was photographed the following year holding a 'Snowflake' baby: one born to an infertile couple after having been 'adopted' when frozen. Worldwide, it is estimated that the number of embryos in storage may now amount to millions, a whole new subpopulation of beings not human, but not not human; like sperm or eggs, lacking the means of development but in principle able to proceed, in the right conditions. A sperm or egg needs an egg or sperm to become an embryo; an embryo, in order to turn into a baby, needs a womb.

For those undergoing fertility treatment, the surplus frozen embryos will usually be few enough in number for them to be thought of individually. The pre-pregnancy or non-pregnancy embryos may figure for their 'parents' as earlier versions of the foetus as seen on an ultrasound scan: they are pre-pre-babies. And just as parental projection can endow the fairly generic ultrasound image with infinite and unique attributes, so some pre-parents cherish photographs of their potential loved ones, giving them interim names appropriate to their current appearance and life situation: Snow White, Frosty, and the like are popular choices for the

of healthy development after birth. For a strong argument against the transfer of multiple embryos, see Bart Fauser and Paul Devroey, with Simon Brown, *Baby-Making* (Oxford: Oxford University Press, 2011).

[5] In *Everything Conceivable* (306), Liza Mundy cites a case of a baby born in 2005 after an embryo had been frozen for thirteen years.

'embies'.[6] From the other side, a boy whose embryo had been frozen when others were transferred was described by his older sister as having been 'let out of the freezer a bit later'. The unfrozen boy, Orlando, came from an embryo that had split into two, and his identical twin had been born—along with the big sister—four years before he was.[7] Conception in this case was followed by a stalling of natural developmental time and also generated a new creation story nicely adapted for harmless sibling rivalry. But the practice of freezing and thawing highlights the way that *in vitro* fertilization in any case almost always requires the next stage of development to be artificially enabled—in this case through the transfer of the blastocyst or pre-embryo to a womb at the point of being ready to receive it.

The 'freezer' option makes a peculiar counterpart to the traditional image of the 'bun in the oven': the reproductive kitchen has been updated to include a relatively new appliance which allows for some long-term control and planning, along the lines of 'Here's one I prepared three years ago'. The frozen embryo is doubly incongruous in relation to natural processes of development. Not only, like all *in vitro* embryos, does it come into existence in the laboratory, not the womb (or the Fallopian tube); but it then goes 'back' to a state of suspended animation from which, in order to get growing again, it would have to be released. That is, it would need to be defrosted before being transferred to a womb, with a further change of environment and a return to real (biological) time. This never-never place and time, the indefinite pause of the cryobank (where no infant howls are heard), has the air (where no air is breathed) of a parallel universe out of mythology or theology, where the souls are cut adrift in some timeless limbo, waiting to be born or not born; or more mundanely, waiting to be unfrozen and possibly transferred. This strange population is not about to take over the earth or to rise in rebellion to protest at its inhuman treatment; but its presence disturbs. The existence of frozen embryos also confers on their

[6] The names are taken from chatroom websites and blog postings. See Beth Kohl, *Embryo Culture: Making Babies in the Twenty-First Century* (New York: Farrar, Straus, Giroux, 2007), 254.

[7] The remark is taken from a Channel 4 'Cutting Edge' documentary directed by Daisy Asquith, about the five children of Barrie and Tony Drewitt-Barlow, *My Weird and Wonderful Family*, broadcast 22 July 2010.

'parents' a new state of indeterminacy. What the twentieth century cheerfully called family planning (or planned parenthood), with some optimistic sense of a reasonable choice, for the first time practicable, of how many and how far apart, here becomes a question about whether and when to give specific pre-children a chance of grown human life—or when to let them go or try to forget about them.

Most commonly the 'leftover' embryos belonging to patients can be counted on the fingers of one hand, but sometimes these beings may be quite numerous, in which case they will place their 'mothers' in a situation much more like that of a father (in unassisted reproduction) than would have been possible—conceivable—before. That is to say, a woman may have provided the eggs for a great number of frozen pre-embryos, in the same way that a man might hypothetically father any number of children, known or unknown to him, in the course of his life. A somewhat surreal instance of this comes up incidentally in a case discussed in Charis Thompson's ethnographic study of IVF patients, *Making Parents*, when no fewer than forty-five embryos were generated from a single egg collection cycle; eventually, on the third attempt at thawing and transferring some of this vast batch, a pregnancy resulted. All in one go, a virtual, monofamilial village population had been brought into existence which it would barely be possible for one woman to gestate and give birth to even if she were somehow pregnant throughout her fertile life.

This story is present in Thompson's book not because of the high number of embryos produced, but because of the unlikely relationships of the parental protagonists, three in all. The eggs were generated by one woman for another, older one—her mother. The sperm came from the mother's second husband. Thompson is interested in the attempt to stave off any suggestion of relational perversity by the mother's emphasis on her daughter's similarity to her genetically, so that the daughter's eggs, in this logic, made a natural match as a good substitution for hers. Nothing was said of the daughter–stepfather connection, or of the curious fact that resulting children would be genetically fathered by one of the mother's husbands and grandfathered by the other. Altogether, as many relational doublings or conflations are produced by this scenario as in the Oedipus story, when siblings and parents may be one and the same person. In this instance, the daughter was both mother and sister to the children who might be born; their postnatal and gestating mother was also their grandmother. For the daughter, as well as the mother, there seemed to be no difficulty in ruling out or rationalizing the peculiar aspects of the scenario when thinking about the goal of making a single baby for the new couple. But the long-term existence of all those embryos was 'unsettling' to the daughter. Rather than moving on into what was visibly the mother's pregnancy and the mother's baby, they were remaining in time, and in the outside world, as 'the conjoined gametes of the daughter and the stepfather'.[8]

The embryo (or pre-embryo) has come out as a newly separable entity: something which, by its extra-uterine existence in the world, appears to push back the timeline of pre-personhood and the conditions of pre-parenthood. It is surrounded by debates about its moral status and possible rights, in many of the same ways as the foetus has been for many decades in abortion arguments. It has given new impetus to pro-life anti-abortion advocates, because unlike the foetus, whose mother may wish it gone from her body, an embryo has always been willingly and hopefully generated for at least one prospective parent. And with its capacity for regeneration after freezing, the embryo is in some respects more not less open to arguments for its preservation than the foetus—even though, consisting of just a few cells, it is an earlier form of life. The embryo floats free of a potentially reluctant or rejecting mother; it has all the time in the world to wait to grow into a baby, unlike the foetus for which or whom it is now or never. But any case for the status of the embryo then has an a fortiori effect on arguments surrounding the foetus: if this thing so much simpler and further back in the line of development has a right to be kept in existence, then all the more must that be true of the pre-human entity that is further advanced.

In their newly visible and extra-corporeal existence, embryos have altered the perception of the foetus. But the foetus' own status had already been subject to redefinitions as a result of its own newfound visibility and availability for prenatal medical intervention. While

---

[8] Charis Thompson, *Making Parents: The Ontological Choreography of Reproductive Technologies* (Cambridge, Mass.: MIT Press, 2005), 163.

the possibility of conception outside the body has changed the way that we think about the beginnings of pregnancy, it has not affected the way that most people go about making babies, when they want to and when their bodies can. Ultrasound technology, on the other hand, has altered the routines and rituals of every pregnancy in developed countries. And by a nice conjunction of reproductive technological events, ultrasound actually made one of its first media appearances in relation to the birth of the first IVF baby.[9] The *Guardian* explained at the time:

When Mrs Brown was presented with her long-awaited child today it was not the first time she had seen her. Earlier this month she saw the fully formed baby in her womb with the help of an ultrasonic scanner.[10]

Before long, it would become normal for any foetus to be seen by its mother before birth in this way, and checked for abnormalities by the medical experts—just like a test-tube baby. The various scans at different stages of a pregnancy have also become special events which may be witnessed by close friends or family. Like a smaller-scale rehearsal for the birth, the scan is an occasion for anxiety, relief, and celebration. It is when everyone gets to see or be told that the baby is apparently all right. These first appearances of the baby in the world, before it emerges from its mother's body, can also be recorded and remembered with photographs. So even while it is still in the womb, the baby now has an externally visible existence—on the screen, and in the photos which preserve that image.[11]

---

[9] Diagnostic ultrasound technology had been in development since the 1950s; one of its prime movers was Ian Donald, Regius Professor of Midwifery at Edinburgh, who had become interested in radio and sonar during wartime service.

[10] David Beresford, 'Test-Tube Mother has Girl', *Guardian*, 26 July 1978.

[11] Independently of medical technology, a further reproductive event which has become differently visible is what used to be called the confinement, including the birth itself. Since it has become expected, rather than the reverse, for fathers to be present, they are witnesses to a birth that was previously known (or not known) to them only in more removed ways. Men now have their own labour stories. And deliveries are accessible for anyone to watch—in their thousands on YouTube, or on the Channel 4 documentary series *One Born Every Minute* (since 2010) which frames the presentation of a birth with the story of the awaiting parents.

Ultrasound scans, as well as some tests commonly required or recommended during pregnancy, deliver definite or probable pieces of information about a baby which were previously hidden from view or from knowledge until its birth. In particular, as scanning has become standard, so has the habit of finding out the sex of the baby. It is now more common to know than not to know whether what you are expecting is a boy or a girl, and not to seek to know, or to ask not to know, can be regarded as eccentric, calling for justification. 'It's a girl!' 'It's a boy!' as postnatal exclamations have presumably declined, but without that implying any fall in human beings' preoccupation with differentiating their kind into two sexes.

Like other existential phenomena in the progress of pregnancy, this one concerning the norms of antenatal sex-knowledge has undergone rapid change. In the 1985 edition of his manual on pregnancy and childcare, Hugh Jolly mentions the issue, at this stage in relation to amniocentesis not ultrasound, and makes an unequivocal judgement: 'knowing the sex beforehand is not helpful, especially if the fetus is not the sex for which the parents had hoped.' And he was wrong in his prescriptive points about the trends of future practices: 'It is therefore increasingly the practice for laboratories not to report the sex so that the obstetrician or midwife is left in ignorance and cannot tell you if asked.'[12] No longer, in most cases, do parents-to-be (and those around them) wonder about the sex of the child, or think of possible names for both boys and girls. Thus a significant element of uncertainty—or possibility—has gone. The effect of knowing the sex, when it is known, is to change the imaginative conception of the nature of the child to come: no longer simply a baby-to-be, but pretty definitely either a boy or a girl, perhaps with clothes and equipment to be chosen in colour-coded accordance.

This further novelty of ultrasound technology—not just seeing the baby but seeing it as a baby boy or girl—was also mentioned in the reporting of the birth of Louise Brown: 'Doctors have also known the sex of the child, but at her own request Mrs Brown was not told until the birth.'[13] In the first years of ultrasound, choosing not to

---

[12] Hugh Jolly, *Book of Child Care*, 3rd edn. (1985; London: Unwin Paperbacks, 1986), 10.

[13] Beresford, 'Test-Tube Mother'.

know, or being refused the knowledge, was common, as Hugh Jolly
both implied and prescribed in relation to amniocentesis; it is only
quite recently that finding out has become the norm. But whichever
the decision, to know or not to know a foetus' sex has become,
through ultrasound, another choice that prenatal parents have to
make—whereas previously, throughout human history, it had been
simply a matter for speculation, perhaps for fervent or secret hopes
or hopes not. The likelihood of this knowledge being acquired also
means, paradoxically, that an unborn baby now has, in effect, three
possible gender identities: boy, girl, or 'don't know'.

Quite apart from its diagnostic and informational uses, ultrasound changes the view of pregnancy; it makes the foetus more of
a recognizable soon-to-be baby, and less of a hidden, interior being
perceptible only through its creeping movements and (earlier on in
the twentieth century) through an amplified heartbeat heard at an
antenatal check-up.[14] Another alteration in the pre-birth order of
things has come about through the availability of over-the-counter
pregnancy tests. In the 1970s pregnancy testing 'kits', your own
little lab at home, were marketed for the first time, making it possible for women to find out this information in private, and without
medical involvement.[15] Like the ultrasound scan, the pregnancy test
is a new technology providing something like a visible, external
indication of pregnancy: the image on the screen or the famous
'thin blue line'. But whereas the scan introduces a new scene of
shared prenatal experience, the home test may well be a solitary
moment in the bathroom, to be communicated (if it is) only afterwards. A (scientifically) 'positive' result can be positive or negative
for the person in an equally divided way. Advertising for pregnancy
tests has regularly used facial images of feminine serenity that might

[14] Feminist debates about abortion rights since the 1980s have been much
concerned with the politics of foetal visibility. See for instance Rosalind Pollack
Petchesky, 'Foetal Images: The Power of Visual Culture in the Politics of Reproduction', in Michelle Stanworth (ed.), *Reproductive Technologies: Gender, Motherhood and
Medicine* (Cambridge: Polity Press, 1987), 57–80.

[15] As Linda L. Layne points out in a critique of the assumption that such tests are
beneficial to women, this privacy may well be offset by different forms of public visibility, at the moment of purchase or at home; 'The Home Pregnancy Test: A Feminist
Technology?', *Women's Studies Quarterly* 37: 1–2 (Spring–Summer 2009): 61–79.

actually apply to either result: calm relief (she's not) or anticipation (she is); for obvious reasons, advertisements did not use the correspondingly unhappy image of the woman who has found out the result she did not want: distress (she is) or disappointment (she's not).

Early pregnancy testing also changes the experience of miscarriage. The beginning of bleeding a few weeks after the last period will now be experienced and known as an early miscarriage if there has been a positive pregnancy test. Before early testing, this would have been understood as a late period, perhaps something more, but without further clarification. In this way, the provision of knowledge has increased the potential for sadness when the pregnancy was much wished for—and this has happened independently of anything different in the development of embryos themselves.

In other respects, pregnancy has arguably remained the stubbornly intractable element in the sequence of biological occurrences that lead to the arrival of a baby. Although the creature within may now be seen and imagined in different ways, and may even be subject to prenatal medical interventions, it still has to stay where it is, in the womb, for a definite length of time. No human baby has yet come into the world that did not emerge from a female (or partly female) human body.[16] That passage, even though the infant may have started life as an embryo on the outside, before being placed into the womb, remains the recognized point of 'birth', with its defining date and place in the official identity facts of the resulting person's life.

This is not to say that it might not be possible to get pregnancy to happen elsewhere or otherwise. Cross-species gestation has been carried out between non-human animals,[17] and the transfer of just-conceived embryos from one uterus to another is a practice derived from veterinary medicine that was occasionally tried on women in

---

[16] The qualification is to allow for the case of the American transgender man Thomas Beatie, who gave birth to three children between 2008 and 2010; he had retained his original female reproductive organs so as to be able to do this.

[17] Successful cross-species gestation, from a rabbit to a hare, was reported in 1890 by a young Cambridge researcher called Walter Heape; see e.g. Robert Winston, *A Child Against All Odds* (London: Bantam, 2006), 81–2.

the early years of IVF.[18] Male pregnancy has been a long-standing fantasy, imagined as a replication of the usual female environment, with the provision of a womb-equivalent and the requisite conduits for the transmission of food and waste. There are biblical and mythical stories of male pregnancy. In Greek mythology, Zeus is both father and mother to Dionysus, prenatally reimplanted in his thigh when the baby's mother, Semele, is fatally struck by lightning sent by Zeus' jealous wife, Hera. On another occasion, Zeus is able to offer a safe womb to another of his children, Athene, who is born from his head—again, after it becomes necessary for her to be removed from her mother's womb. In the Bible, male motherhood is so primary as to conflate and abolish the separation of mother and father at all. Adam is some sort of parent to Eve, who is formed from a part of his middle body. He is mother (Eve is from his body) or father (he is male) or neither and both, in a *sui generis* case of single parenthood (the only possibility, since there is only one person in the world). This peculiar reproductive procedure is prior, in the Genesis story, to the beginnings of normal human sexual reproduction—involving a man, a woman, and sex—when Adam and Eve have children together and Eve is the one who bears them. In the beginning was the variant; only later, and only by mistake—as a result of the Fall—does the 'traditional' method of making babies get started.

Adam's first offspring is not conceived—or is conceived only in the mind of God, who ordains the creative extraction of the body part that will be Eve. There is no joining of two separate elements derived from two different progenitors—and no moment of implantation of a future baby in a bodily place of gestation. Instead, the rib is non-reproductively part of the pre-Eve Adam: it has its place in

---

[18] The method of embryo transfer from one womb to another is described in Jacques Testart, *L'Œuf transparent* (Paris: Flammarion, 1986), 42–3 and in René Frydman, *L'Irrésistible désir de naissance* (Paris: PUF, 1986), 100. Testart and Frydman are two of the trio responsible for the birth of the first French IVF baby in 1982, 'Amandine'. Frydman decided to cease offering this treatment when, after failing to find a tiny embryo in the womb of a woman conceiving for her sister, he felt he saw in her eyes the terror of turning out to be pregnant with her brother-in-law's baby (if an embryo was there, but had been missed and so not taken out for transplantation); *Irrésistible*, 145.

his own anatomy and leaves him permanently one rib down when it is taken away. Adam is passive throughout the process. In a sort of primitive version of a full-anaesthetic Caesarean, God comes when he is asleep, and takes away the rib to make it into a woman; the repair of the wound (though not the initial incision) is carefully noted in Genesis.[19] Although the child-producing body is his, in this respect Adam is physically distanced from the birth. Bleary-eyed, as it were, he is presented with the newly formed creature, and recognizes her as his own. But just as this story docs without a conception and a pregnancy (there is no period during which a seed—or rib— slowly grows), so it also dispenses with the period of postnatal maturation. Eve is an adult already, not a dependent newborn. The being whom Adam sees when he wakes up is his ready-made companion, not a nurture-needing baby.

Eve is made, not born a woman. It is a bone not a human being that is taken from Adam's body by the divine midwife, who then does the overnight transformative work. But it is crucial that Eve should be created from a part of Adam in order that the two of them should be, in their union, 'one flesh'. They will grow back together as man and woman. In the making of Eve there is neither sex nor conception nor pregnancy nor birth—and yet she is indisputably derived from the body of another human, a physical parent: a case of involuntary assisted reproduction.

The birth of Jesus offers another story whose strangeness can cast light on normal expectations. Here there is a conception, a pregnancy, and a birth, but there is no sexual connection between the mother and the father. Today science has not yet succeeded in cloning from a piece of the ribcage, but fertilization *in vitro*, rather than in the body, makes it not just possible but unavoidable that conception occurs without sex. Conception may also today be immaculate in a more banal sense, in that great emphasis is placed on the necessity for an ultra-hygienic environment in the clinic where the medically enabled conjunction takes place—with sperm, for instance, 'washed' and examined for defects or potential; by

---

[19] In the King James version, Genesis 2: 21: 'And the Lord God caused a deep sleep to fall upon Adam, and he slept: and he took one of his ribs, and closed up the flesh instead thereof.'

comparison, the usual circumstances of non-medical conception fall some way short of best practice. Through IVF, a virgin birth is a real possibility, not a counter-realistic theological dogma.

Although it involves no sexual event, the story of how Mary came to be pregnant has other aspects in common with classical myths of the babies born to hapless nymphs or young girls after encounters with passing gods. A god turns up; later, a baby is delivered and perhaps abandoned (there is always a pregnancy; or, at least, the only stories told are ones in which pregnancy follows). Euripides' dramas take apart this narrative convention by featuring challenges to the stories of women who claim that they were divinely impregnated. So Creusa, in the *Ion*, who gave birth in secret to a boy after Apollo raped her, is gently questioned as to whether she might have made up the story to cover herself for a sexual misdemeanour. In the *Bacchae*, the sister of Semele, the mother of Dionysus, defends her memory. Semele claimed to have been ravished by Zeus and was blasted by Hera's lightning—with the consequence, as described above, of the foetal Dionysus' third trimester being spent in his father's refurbished upper leg.

In the case of Mary and Jesus, God takes on the role of the reproductive doctor who impregnates the woman with the seed of a future birth. This is a version of artificial insemination, but it is also like embryo transfer. For conception in the sense of the joining of two particles, egg and sperm, or the fertilization of one by the other, is a relatively recent arrival in the area of reproductive beliefs. Since the seventeenth century, the identification of mammalian ovaries, then follicles, then individual ova, together with the separate but comparable functions of spermatozoa, has progressively (but unevenly) altered the conceptualization of baby beginnings, ultimately paving the theoretical way for so many of the reproductive reconfigurations that became thinkable and practicable in the final decades of the twentieth century.[20] Conception did not used to be seen

[20] In *Making Sex*, Thomas Laqueur engagingly demonstrates the interlocking of cultural, sexual, and reproductive models of the differences of the sexes in different periods. Before equal genetic contribution was established there was great variation in the assignment of functions to male or female reproductive elements: 'no consensus as to what sperm and egg actually were or did, until the turn of the nineteenth century' (173).

as the conjoining of male and female gametes, but as the beginning of the future baby's development *in utero*. Without the perspective of modern genetics, even-handedly and arithmetically assigning exactly twenty-three chromosomes each to the otherwise different ovum and sperm, the transmission of maternal qualities might be imagined as taking place in other ways, such as the symbiosis of pregnancy or the milk of a mother or wet-nurse.[21]

In retrospect, the identification of eggs as a female counterpart to sperm can be seen to have set up the frame of thinking that makes it possible to think of a child as having two 'biological' mothers—one who supplies the egg and one who becomes pregnant. Once the female maternal function is regarded as twofold it can also, potentially, be divided between the bodies of two different women, as happens with egg donation and 'full' surrogacy (in which the egg used is not from the gestating woman). In almost every real-life pregnancy, including most cases of IVF (when the eggs extracted to create the embryo are those of the woman who will subsequently bear the child), these two mothers are still one and the same. But there is a theoretical distinction between them which was inaugurated long before the invention of the new reproductive technologies, which bear it out. And while the representation of the two gametes as separate, equal, and comparable elements works in the direction of making a woman seem more like a man, a mother more like a father, the fact of pregnancy works against that by continuing to show the other difference of female from male biological parenthood.

The possible splitting of biological maternity between two women has also had the effect of creating an uncomfortably unequal division of labour and prestige in the field of reproductive medicine. This can be seen most clearly in the United States where in many states both surrogate mothers and egg donors can be paid, and egg donors may receive higher sums than the women who go through the many months of pregnancy. The qualifications expected of each are very different. Egg donor prices are higher according to features

---

[21] For an eighteenth-century argument against wet-nursing, partly on the grounds of the bad influence of the wrong woman's milk on a baby's character, see Chapter 2, 54–64.

such as the educational level or physical attractiveness of the candidate, fully displayed on website catalogues; 'gestational carriers' need mainly to be sound in body and decent-sounding in character, with a proven record of problem-free pregnancy. A new kind of class division follows, with surrogates typically being women who are currently raising children of their own, while egg donors might be young women in college whose debts will be greatly reduced by the payment of the fee which their top-level eggs can command.

There is also, increasingly, a globalization dimension to this issue. Individuals or couples from outside the United States may seek to make use of American donors and surrogates in order to bypass restrictive laws or limited availability in countries such as the UK where these services are compensated only by expenses.[22] The resulting 'reproductive tourism', whereby patients go abroad to find the treatments or the donors or surrogates that they cannot get legally or affordably in their own country, also applies to smaller countries which may have looser laws or cheaper provision than is available in highly regulated countries like Britain and France. India is rapidly becoming a centre for lower-cost reproductive medicine. One of the most reputable British IVF clinics, Bourn Hall, is setting up branches there and in the Middle East; high standards can be maintained, but prices are much lower than in the home country. The 2009 documentary film *Google Baby* showed how one Indian clinic is involved in an elaborate outsourcing arrangement initiated by an Israeli entrepreneur, the father of a baby born using a surrogate and egg from America. He saw a market opportunity for cost reduction by geographically separating the sources of the two female components. In his cynically imaginative distribution, sperm, egg, and womb come from Israel, the USA, and India: embryos using donor eggs and the sperm of prospective fathers (from Israel) are created in America, then taken in portable vats to India. There they are transferred to the womb of a surrogate mother whose progress through the pregnancy is monitored and controlled by her confinement in the clinic for the entire period, along with others in the same

---

[22] A further restriction on what is referred to as 'supply' has been the removal of anonymity for donors in the UK since 2005. Donor-conceived children now have the right, at the age of 18, to find out identifying information about their donor parents.

situation. In the Indian clinic there are occasional visits from the woman's husband and child or children. After the baby's delivery, by Caesarean, the future parents come to take it 'home' to wherever they may have come from to pick it up.[23]

Mettre au monde is the everyday expression in French for what English calls giving birth; this familiar 'bringing a baby into the world' acquires a new inflection in the extended global reach of reproductive tourism. Extraordinary geographical journeys are undertaken by would-be parents, who travel to countries where it is cheaper or legally easier to make use of particular treatments (journeys are also necessarily involved in transnational adoptions). But this new world of distance delivering is not confined to exceptional pregnancies in which the intending parents are in one place and the pregnant woman in another. In the tale of the stork that was supposedly told to children puzzled by the sudden arrival of a new baby in the family, the baby comes from elsewhere, a gift of the gods or an ominous delivery from an unknown source. Wanted or not, the new being is a demanding guest who takes up permanent residence after its carrier has deposited it. But way back then, in the days of the stork story, the facts of early life were quite otherwise. The baby did not come from another place. Most often it was conceived and born at home, in the same bed and the same room; it grew 'inside', unseen and unheard through the months of pregnancy, its presence only conjectured or surmised. Today, a baby is usually, not exceptionally, delivered in another place than home. If it is made with medical assistance, it will also be conceived somewhere else. The aim of every prospective parent is to acquire what is called in the fertility trade a 'take-home baby'. The point of this expression is to differentiate the desired final outcome from all the separate points of progress and potential difficulty on the way to having a child. Conception may not occur, or may not be followed by an established pregnancy; a pregnancy may cease at any point before term. The take-home baby, starting its post-birth development normally, is the goal. But the phrase also casually acknowledges that it is not at home that the baby will first have made its appearance; as in the

---

[23] *Google Baby*, directed by Zippi Brand Frank, first broadcast in the USA, was shown in the UK on Channel 4, 31 May 2011.

stork myth, it is only when it is already in the world that it is brought there, having begun its life elsewhere.

That babies now typically start off somewhere else and only later arrive in their future home is clearest in the case of the baby born with the help of reproductive technologies, whose conception takes place away, if not far, from home. (The one exception, some of the time, is artificial insemination—the so-called 'turkey-baster baby'.) But distance occurs on a smaller scale in almost every instance. In the last half century it has become the norm for almost all babies in western countries to be delivered in hospital. And this is the end-point of the various now standard modes of externalization and separation which are part of the typical antenatal pattern. A pregnancy will be monitored outside the home from an early stage. The foetus will be seen on a screen: the baby appears, but appears 'over there', the focus of all eyes, not where it actually is.

Real space is travelled when you go off and get or have a baby somewhere else, but there are other ways too in which the modern baby is set at a distance, as an object towards which a 'journey' needs to be made before the point of (its) arrival. The 'IVF journey', uncertain at every stage, is well signposted in its progression from initial consultations and tests through the many stages or stopping points of a given attempt—a single journey within the larger and longer journey of the overall aim. For each cycle, there are the different points of progression or halt: when follicles are counted and eggs, if any, retrieved; when sperm are obtained; when fertilization of one or more eggs takes place, if it does; when the resulting pre-embryos develop or fail to; when embryo transfer does or does not result in a positive pregnancy test two weeks later; when pregnancy continues to develop; and, finally, if and when a healthy baby is born.

The much-mapped itinerary of this journey is fraught with the potential for difficulty and disappointment, even as it promises, if the end is reached, the greatest possible sense of arrival at a destination. But the standard route towards having a baby, while much simpler by comparison, is not a million miles away in terms of the way it is imagined and represented. Expecting a baby—that unusual guest—is not something that arises as though by marital nature, as it seemingly might have done before family 'planning'. By the end of the twentieth century, there was the curious expression 'trying for a baby': meaning not so much having sex as refraining from contraception. Of course, pregnancies may still be unchosen or 'unplanned', in the idiom made to match the norm of contraceptive use and reliability; and they may also, and even if intended, be unwanted in the event. But that does not alter the broader expectation: that a pregnancy will most often be the result of a deliberate course of action (or an active inaction: no contraception); that it is both unsurprising (as previously it would almost always have been after marriage) and also intended (since if not, it can be prevented).

In May 2012 the organization that sets policy guidelines for the British NHS issued new draft guidelines on infertility treatment, recommending that IVF should be available to women up to the age of 42, and to same-sex couples.[24] Media responses focused mainly on the raising (by three years) of the age limit. But the opening up, if only in principle, of funding for reproductive technologies to same-sex couples marks a far more significant change than the adjustment of an existing criterion. Biologically, a same-sex couple could never have generated a baby on their own. Their non-reproductiveness as a couple is a given, not a physical defect that might be treatable. It may well be—it is much more likely than not—that neither partner is individually infertile. This new dispensation is not related to a healthy biological capacity belonging to the patient or patients which medical intervention can hopefully either restore or make up for; 'assisted' reproduction here necessarily—not in relation to a contingent defect—requires the use of bodily elements (gametes or womb, donor or surrogate) from someone other than the couple.

It is possible to reconstruct a medical logic for the progressive naturalization of gay parenthood within reproductive medicine. In the simplest form of IVF (simplest in that there are no special contractual or medical third-party arrangements involved), the gametes

[24] See NICE [National Institute for Health and Clinical Excellence] guideline, 'Fertility: Assessment and Treatment for People with Fertility Problems', draft update (May 2012), 18, 35. Though the phrase used is 'same-sex couples', in practice only women are implied since the treatments mentioned are IVF and IUI (intrauterine insemination).

are from the two intending parents, and the pregnant woman is the future mother of the baby. The process replicates what would otherwise have happened naturally, without intervention. But sperm or egg donation, and surrogacy, all methods used in the treatment of heterosexual couples, involve the substitution of gametes or uterus in order to achieve an equivalent outcome. This scenario can be seen as maintaining the nature-enabled family unit, with a little outside help. But the logic of substitution then allows for the possibility of making a gay parental couple along the same lines. The process is the same: one or two of the three required elements for making a baby is missing, but can be supplied.

In this connection it is interesting to see that there has been a linguistic shift, over the reproductive technology years, from one A to another. The word 'artificial' is abandoned for its implications of falseness, of being against nature; 'assisted' is more benign, more therapeutic, and less passive: the patient or client becomes a parent with a little help. Similarly the first reproductive technology, once known as artificial insemination, is now much more commonly referred to as donor insemination. The change here does more, in fact, than move the suggestion from the non-natural (here, meaning not through sexual intercourse) to the generous ('donor', like 'assisted', introducing a helper figure). It presumes that the sperm is not that of the future father. But in earlier discussions of the process, this was not the case. In the 1950s a Church of England report on grounds for marriage annulment several times mentions the issue of artificial insemination (in relation to the prior question of whether other grounds for annulment still hold when children have been born to a marriage). The semen used is taken to be that of the husband; the process is used when there has been 'imperfect intercourse'. And 'the case of artificial insemination with the seed of some other man' is presented as an exception, placed in parentheses, to this already exceptional practice.[25]

---

[25] *The Church and the Law of Nullity of Marriage*, Report of a Commission appointed by the Archbishops of Canterbury and York in 1949 (London: SPCK, 1955), 39. The Report also refers to *fecundatio ab extra*, when there is no penetration. In fact, fertilization naturally occurs 'from the outside' in that the necessary sperm is not generated within the conceiving woman; but the association of a reproductive technology with externalization seems to anticipate later developments.

The use of other people's sperm or eggs has some similarities with the transfer of organs from one human body to another; the same vocabulary of donation is used in both cases, though there are also many differences (organ donation does not create a new person but keeps an existing one going).[26] But another aspect of infertility treatment is entirely idiosyncratic: the patient is most often something called a couple.[27] Two-bodied patients are not to be found in any other branch of medicine. Nor is it the case in other fields that treatment may be given to patients not suffering from the malfunction that is being remedied. But this is what happens as a matter of course when a couple is treated and only one of them has something wrong (or neither has anything findably wrong, so-called 'unexplained infertility'). This double peculiarity of the default infertility treatment—that the patient is a couple, that patients may have no impairment—then facilitates a natural transfer to the gay couple: incapable, by themselves, of having children, but probably reproductively healthy when considered as two individual bodies.

These distinctive features of infertility treatment—the substitution of missing functions, and the two-person patient—mean that a non-heterosexual couple can come to fit its paradigm. This facilitates the ethical shift that the new policy guidelines imply: that the family-seeking entity, while it may still be a pair, does not have to be one that consists of individuals of the two biological sexes, otherwise known in this context as the mother and father. Assistance is reasonable even when there may be nothing amiss in the patients' reproductive capacities. The grounds for the policy are not medical but ethical and humanitarian: that any long-term adult couple should be allowed to seek to have children of their own.[28]

[26] For a discussion of some of the emotional, ethical, and cultural issues involved in sperm and egg donation see Joan Raphael-Leff, 'The Gift of Gametes: Unconscious Motivation, Commodification and Problematics of Geneaology', *Feminist Review* 94: 1 (March 2010): 117–37.

[27] In a psychoanalytic critique of reproductive technologies, the French psychoanalyst Michel Tort draws attention to the peculiarity of the couple-subject presumed to be one in its conscious and unconscious desires; see *Le Désir froid: Procréation artificielle et crise des repères symboliques* (Paris: Editions La Découverte, 1992), 146, 198.

[28] For a critique of the desire for a 'biological' child, see Karin Lesnik-Oberstein, *On Having an Own Child: Reproductive Technologies and the Cultural Construction of Childhood* (London: Karnac, 2008).

In this new world, being of one sex rather than the other is no bar to the choice of a pre-parental mate. What is biologically missing can be supplied, and parents can be brought into being by whatever available means. Amid all of these changes in parental norms there remains, though, one small piece of the picture which—at least until now—has stayed the same. You may take them away from the bodies they come from and then put them back into someone else's; you may artificially help them on their way or pick out the ones that look likeliest to succeed; but still, in order to make a baby you will have to bring together a male and a female gamete, one of each kind. The sperm and the egg, poor things, have been left behind in the forward march of modern couplings. The egg still makes its stately progress down the Fallopian tube, waiting hopefully and with dignity just as it has done since time immemorial. The sperm, the lucky sperm, the one in a million, still makes for the egg across a crowded womb, to the exclusion of all the others. Even when the process is happening outside the female body, and even when the sperm in question is one that has been specially selected, not part of an indefinite horde, the encounter still occurs in the same way and with the same result. The pair become one. As soon as the sperm has entered the egg, they are inseparable forever and have lost their individual identities. They can only be an indivisible couple, and they can only be (or have been) one of each sex. They are perfectly matched, quintessentially heterosexual, and quite oblivious to the fluid world around them in which sexes and bodies combine and uncombine without any sense of natural reproductive destiny. The gametes can only marry (that is their etymological and biological nature), and who they marry can only be one of the other sex. In glass or in bodies, that is what they are put on this earth to do—and they do it if they can.

2

Surrogates and Other Mothers

In the most basic description, a surrogate mother is a woman who becomes pregnant on behalf of another person or persons.[1] She will become a mother: she will give birth to a baby. And she will not become a mother: she will not be its postnatal parent. What makes a woman a surrogate mother is not, or not only, the particular sequence of giving birth and giving up, of having a baby and not then becoming its mother: that applies equally to situations of adoption and fostering. The distinctive feature of surrogacy is that the pregnancy itself is initiated for the benefit of those who want and plan to be a baby's parents after it is born, and who may be genetically its parents too, one or both of them. Thus surrogate motherhood is surrounded and conditioned by the simultaneous existence, before and throughout the pregnancy, of other designated parties— usually but not always two of them—who are the future parents of the baby or babies who will result from the pregnancy. Of course this is true of most pregnancies, whenever there is someone apart from the mother who is expected to be the baby's co-parent after the birth. But surrogacy is marked out by the double requirement that future parents, or a future parent, must have been specified before conception; and that the pregnant woman herself is not one of them.

[1] A sign of the potential for confusion in these matters, the definition currently offered (July 2012) in the online *Oxford English Dictionary* defines a surrogate as 'A woman whose pregnancy arises from the implantation in her womb of a fertilized egg or embryo from another woman'. That rules out the surrogate whose own egg is used, and also fails to specify the crucial condition: that the pregnancy is undertaken on behalf of others. The first citation given, from June 1978, pre-dates even the first IVF baby, let alone the use of donor eggs; so it cannot in any case be applied to this definition, which is in fact a description of IVF using an egg that is not the (pregnant) mother's.

Like other practices associated with new reproductive technologies, surrogacy has had its own rapid history, both in terms of the sociology of its occurrence—who does it, for whom, and where— and also in terms of its biological conditions; and this history has been closely bound up with modifications in the surrounding terminology. In the first stage, the surrogate mother generally became pregnant via artificial insemination with the prospective father's sperm. In the past two or three decades, the commoner practice has been for the embryo to be produced *in vitro*, if possible using the gametes of both intended parents (when there are two, and when there is one of each sex). The first set-up is now often referred to as 'classical' or 'traditional' surrogacy—'as though it came over with the Pilgrims', as the American feminist Katha Pollitt mordantly wrote in 1990.[2] This 'classical' method, worthy but superseded, is then contrasted with what is (somewhat counter-intuitively) called 'full' surrogacy, meaning that the pregnant woman was not the source of the egg from which the embryo was made. Full, in other words, means empty from a genetic point of view. The less of a biological link to the surrogate mother—or gestational carrier—the more natural, by this logic, her disconnection from the baby after its birth; whereas with old-style or 'partial' surrogacy, the surrogate is fully the biological mother, providing both womb and egg. Not only, then, do we have the difference, implied in the name, between surrogate motherhood and some other kind, but surrogacy has its own subdivisions too, with full surrogacy falling at the opposite extreme from something that should now perhaps be thought of as 'full' motherhood. The very name of surrogacy, whatever its form, impacts upon every understanding of motherhood—both making it questionable in new ways, and also giving a new kind of value to what may now be regarded as the real thing. In this situation, still by a very long way the usual situation, the supplier of the egg, the pregnant woman, and the post-birth mother are all the same person. But as this description suggests, even in its hypothetical wholeness, that original form of maternity is marked by the new ones, being broken down into component elements now seen to be potentially distributed between more than one individual.

[2] Katha Pollitt, 'When is a Mother not a Mother?', *Nation*, 31 December 1990, 842.

Though modern surrogacy did not begin as a new technology, its development at the same time as IVF meant that it was regularly regarded as if that was what it was. Before IVF, and before surrogacy had a name and a public image, it was perfectly possible, though probably not common, for a woman to bear a child for others—whether through artificial insemination or through no technology at all. An article about surrogacy written in the early years of its political prominence begins with this deliberately striking anecdote:

Ten years ago a friend of ours was pregnant for somebody else. In this case the somebody else was her boy-friend, who was also the begetter of the child. They were not sharing a home.... [H]e acquired sole custody of the child. It all went rather smoothly.[3]

Surrogacy, at that previous point, had no name; there is no way of knowing how many instances there may have been of informal arrangements in which a woman had a baby in order for someone else to have a baby. But in practice, a real as opposed to an imagined link with the new technologies did develop, as IVF had the effect of separating biological maternity into two distinct functions, gestation and egg provision. IVF involves the transfer of an embryo or embryos into the body of a to-be-pregnant woman who may or may not have been the source of the eggs. Surrogacy could henceforth be more surrogate than before ('full' surrogacy), because it had become possible to generate babies genetically unrelated to their birth mother. But the surrogacy difference is not determined by either biological relationship or a specific new technology; it is primarily about the social circumstances of the pregnancy, and that was what gave it its shock values.

In this context, it is notable that, unlike 'the surrogate mother', no debatable or mediatized category of the 'IVF mother' emerged—despite the complete novelty of the technical procedure and the public fascination it aroused. With IVF, attention was focused on

[3] Juliette Zipper and Selma Sevenhuijsen, 'Surrogacy: Feminist Notions of Motherhood Reconsidered', in Michelle Stanworth (ed.), *Reproductive Technologies: Gender, Motherhood and Medicine* (Cambridge: Polity Press, 1987), 118.

the extraordinary baby and the science that had brought her into being. The point about the mother, or the parents, was that they were to be seen as just an ordinary couple, who had longed for a baby, and had now been granted one through a feat of modern medicine. Somewhat in line with the aura of masculine achievement, IVF babies were considered a matter of national pride, and different countries marked their 'firsts' (the first first, of course, let us never forget, was British). For instance, *Le Monde* ran a long commemorative magazine feature on the occasion of the twenty-fifth anniversary of the birth of French baby Amandine in 1982.[4] The story was all about the three men who together achieved this miraculous French infant. But the mother? Or the mother and father? Barely a mention. It is interesting too that Amandine, in the French mythology, is always Amandine; whereas in Britain Louise Brown is plain Louise Brown—ordinary baby, ordinary family, as opposed to the princess-like French name, floating free of any workaday surname or identifiable parents. One of the 'creators' of little Amandine ironically recounted how, on the long solitary nights in the laboratory when he would be dutifully watching the Petri dish, he would dream of the fairytale baby—always a girl, he jokes—who might some day come after all this hope and waiting.[5]

So the IVF mother had and has no special image when, as the first IVF parents all were, she is part of a married couple longing for a baby, and happily enabled, with brilliant medical assistance, to achieve a pregnancy. The figure of the surrogate mother is entirely different. Whether she is celebrated or condemned, whether she is seen as mercenary or exploited or saintly, the surrogate is almost never regarded with indifference. As an object of fascination she is not unlike the post-menopausal mother, another figure of extreme maternity, who has appeared in the past ten years or so. 'Appeared'

---

[4] 'Amandine, premier bébé-éprouvette', *Le Monde 2*, 17 February 2007, 53–61.

[5] Jacques Testart, *L'Œuf transparent* (Paris: Flammarion, 1986), 57: 'Alone with this living thing, at the end of the night, I often dreamt that there perhaps was "our" first child and that right now, it was coming into being for the first time. Never did I think it would be a boy; quite obviously, I knew it was female. Some of them were privately named after existing beautiful women.' It is curious, in this context, that all four of the first national IVF firsts—Britain, Australia, the United States, and France—*were* girls.

in the sense of acquiring a strong presence in the media and, concomitantly, in public and private debate about the ethical and social implications of new reproductive technologies. The post-menopausal birth mother goes against or beyond nature. She may also be going against or beyond the law, when there are age restrictions on access to IVF; and sometimes quite literally going to another jurisdiction where it is possible for a woman past childbearing age to pay for treatment.

In some respects, the differences between these two situations could hardly be more extreme. The very old mother is determined to be pregnant with a baby of her own, even though her infertility is to be expected and her pregnancy defies the natural female life-cycle. The surrogate mother, on the other hand, will probably be a youngish woman of unassisted aptitude for pregnancy (there are exceptions, such as the occasional grandmother who carries a child on behalf of her daughter). For the post-menopausal mother, there is no saving grace of possible altruism: she is definitely doing it for herself.[6] But both categories of pregnancy, the surrogate and the elderly, can be presented as unnatural, even grotesque: bearing a child to whom you will not be a mother, or bearing a child to whom you insist on being a mother, beyond the age of motherhood set by nature (or by nature's modern mechanical metaphor, the 'biological clock'). A related element in the portrayal of both surrogate and much older mothers has to do with the sheer visibility of pregnancy. She's pregnant—but the baby is not hers! She looks like a granny—but she's pregnant! No media story of an elderly mother is complete without its photo of the unfresh face above the pregnant torso, like one of those contrivedly incongruous portraits in a game of Consequences. The pregnant body has always been the carrier, potentially, of scandalous connotations, and this continues in new forms in cultures in which out-of-wedlock motherhood is no longer a source of shame.

Very often, this much older woman—the one who is shown up in the media—turns out to be specified as the 'mother of 62': this was the case for the English Patricia Rashbrook, whose baby was born

---

[6] Patricia Rashbrook, however, who already had grown children of her own, justified the wish for a baby as wanting to give 'the gift of fatherhood' to her second husband; quoted in 'Britain's Oldest Mother', *Daily Mail*, 8 July 2006, 2.

in 2006, and for the Italian Rosanna Della Corte whose baby was born in 1994. A third 62-year-old, and unlike the other two a 'first-time' mother, was Jeanine Salomone, from the south of France, who gave birth to a baby in 2001. Of course, these women are not quite the only ones of their limited kind.[7] But 62 seems to be the number that puts the woman definitively over the biological or ideological threshold. At sixty-something, it is impossible according to all known precedent that there could have been a natural conception, without the use of another woman's egg to produce the embryo.[8] The mother over 60 is sufficiently monstrous, patently out of the natural order, to make her story worth showing.

The surrogate mother is also subject to very different representations from the egg donor, like her a woman who gives or sells her reproductive capacities to enable others to become parents. The egg donor has to undergo the same invasive procedure to 'harvest' her eggs as an IVF patient, but once the eggs have been obtained, her job is done, and she is also assumed to be capable of an emotional detachment equivalent to her actual separation from the minuscule follicles that have been removed from her body. Gametes are not babies, even if they are necessary to make them; any pre-menopausal woman who is not pregnant loses an egg every month, in any case. Also egg removal, however complex and debilitating a process, can be private: unlike the situation of the surrogate, it does not entail months of being publicly seen in a physically (pre-)maternal state. The egg donor may be represented as overpaid, or underpaid, or altruistic; she may be thanked or not for taking on the considerable medical risks of the process of extraction; but unlike the surrogate she is not seen as weird, or pathologized.

---

[7] Several women have given birth when they were even older than 62: Adriana Iliescu, a Romanian woman of 66 (baby born 2005); Maria del Carmen Bousada, from Spain, whose twins were born in 2006 when she was 66 (she died three years later); Elizabeth Munro (Adeney), an English businesswoman who gave birth in 2009, like Bousada a few days before her sixty-seventh birthday. Lastly, the Indian Omkari Panwar was 70 when twins were born to her in 2008.

[8] This was demonstrated negatively by the further case of Elizabeth Buttle, the Welsh sheep farmer who was said in 1997 to have produced a baby in the natural way at 60—they're a rugged race up on those hills—but later turned out to have had IVF treatment with an egg donor after all.

In general, surrogacy always seems to be open to negative associations that do not apply to egg or sperm donation. Unlike the clinical setting of the other processes, surrogacy goes on as part of the woman's normal existence. There is a real home and a real woman's daily life taking place for many months; for the commissioning couple this may come to represent the long-term anxiety of an uncontrolled environment. Smoking, alcohol, and diet are all seen as potential problems. There is also the risk that the woman may have sex with her own husband or partner—and thereby conceive the wrong baby (this happened in 2004 with Britain's most prolific 'serial' surrogate, Carole Horlock). None of these sordid possibilities applies to the egg donor, who is squeaky clean almost by definition. With her there are no worrying long months of potentially harmful behaviour. She cannot damage her eggs—they are what they are. And the extraction takes place in a sterilized environment, nothing to do with the woman's own lifestyle. Even the sperm donor comes out looking like a safer prospect than the surrogate. To be sure, the actual production process is fairly artisanal. But again, it usually takes place in a clinic or hospital; there is a reassuringly sterile container; and the results will be tested for defects and 'washed'—a word often placed in slightly mysterious inverted commas, but that conjures up soothing visions of homely suds.

Yet another figure related to the surrogate is the birth mother who gives up her child for adoption; that too, like surrogacy, is a legal rather than a biological procedure. But women who relinquish their babies for adoption probably did not became pregnant on purpose whereas surrogate mothers, by definition, did. This is a point worth emphasizing for its sheer paradoxical oddity: that a group of women whose babies are planned, in a sense much stronger than when the word is applied to an ordinary hoped-for pregnancy, have no intention of becoming mothers to the children to whom they give birth.

Surrogacy brings out further anomalies of category and label. The woman who is delivered of a baby is called its birth mother—to be distinguished from an adoptive mother and also, now, from a genetic mother, since the ovum may have come from someone else. Yet no one speaks of the egg-providing woman as either an 'egg mother' or, for that matter, a surrogate (in that she takes on a biological maternal role for a baby to whom she will not be the mother). Instead, the woman from whose ovum the baby is made is referred to as either the (egg) donor or the genetic mother—the second always when this is also the woman who will be the baby's postnatal mother, the first when that is not the case. An 'egg donor' appears as emotionally and physically detached from the end result. The term 'genetic mother', referring to the same individual, but in a different relation to their product, grants a version of parenthood, but also takes a clinical distance from the idea of physical involvement. 'Genetic' seems technical, as if naturally belonging in the laboratory rather than the body—already extracted and abstracted from the woman. In relation to a donor, this sense of non-involvement may well be partly derived from the association of the word with sperm and blood donation, two practices that preceded egg collection historically. Sperm and blood are infinitely renewable for the donor, and can be got from the body with a minimum of intervention. Eggs are a finite and age-limited resource which must be artificially stimulated to emerge from the innermost recesses of the body beyond their regular rate of just one each month.

It may also be noted that surrogate mothers are never referred to as 'baby donors'. And yet a baby is manifestly the product involved—the physical being that is visibly and symbolically given, somewhat more sizeably and conclusively than an egg or a sperm. 'Baby donor' grates: there would be a risk in suggesting so crudely that that is the transaction involved—or in implying that the baby was, in the first place, the surrogate's to give—or keep. Instead, the surrogate's role must be represented as transitory and enabling.[9] What the surrogate gives is not a baby but the chance of parenthood. Or—and this is usually the official representation in the calculation of 'reasonable expenses'—it is the gift of the priceless

---

[9] 'It is one woman helping another woman': the sentence was repeatedly spoken by the Indian fertility doctor Nayana Patel featured in Zippi Brand Frank's documentary film *Google Baby* (2009) about the globalization of a baby-making industry. 'One woman helping another woman' is meant reciprocally: one woman gets to be a mother and the other gets to buy a house. The place of the middlewoman (the doctor) is elided to create a picture of sisterly support; also unspoken is the social inequality of the different situations.

work of pregnancy, which the future parents cannot for whatever reason undertake for themselves. A surrogate 'gives' birth.

Often, today, the reason that parents-to-be seek a surrogate is that neither of them is a woman. The phrase 'gestational carrier' is much better suited to cases when there are no female intending parents, because 'surrogate mother' implies that eventually a real one is going to take over—and could also suggest that a mother is something that might be necessary to a child. One effect of the increasing normalization of gay parenthood has been to make arguments against new reproductive arrangements, including surrogacy, come to appear conservative; previously it was the other way round, with the new technologies figuring as an extension of the patriarchal control of women.[10] From this perspective, to object to women becoming pregnant in order for men to have babies is to deny that men on their own, or gay men, can be adequate parents. Or it is to fall back on an outdated essentialism which would insist that because, to date, only female bodies give birth to babies, therefore women are meant to rear them; or, in relation to single parents and gay couples, that because a baby is made from the products of both male and female bodies, sperm plus egg, therefore it should be raised by a man and a woman together. In this context, it is all the more striking that a wish for biological parenthood should feature so strongly in the demand for children on the part of both individuals and gay couples (of both sexes). Nature, in other words, provides the point of reference even when it is impossible that nature, in the particular case, could provide the baby.

Where there is no future female parent involved, then you need both an egg and a womb to assemble your own biological baby. Since there are bodies, called women, which can supply both, it might seem obvious that this was the simplest prenatal method from a technical point of view. But in practice, the pregnancy and egg

---

[10] Critiques from the first years of new reproductive technologies include Rita Arditti, Renate Duelli Klein, and Shelley Minden (eds.), *Test-Tube Women: What Future for Motherhood?* (London: Pandora, 1984); Gena Corea, *The Mother Machine: Reproductive Technologies from Artificial Insemination to Artificial Wombs* (1985; London: Women's Press, 1988), Michelle Stanworth (ed.), *Reproductive Technologies: Gender, Motherhood and Medicine* (Cambridge: Polity Press, 1987).

functions are most commonly fulfilled by different women; the American websites that specifically appeal to prospective gay male parents do not suggest any other way. That means, incidentally, more income for the agencies involved; but it also means that there is no one woman who has been the bodily mother, and who might then be unequivocally seen—by herself, or later, by the child—as a natural or rightful parent of the baby.

In Britain, Ian Mucklejohn has become a well-known example of a father who is bringing up children specifically created as his and his alone. A single man in possession of a good fortune, he was in want of a family (but not of a wife) and was able to pay many thousands of pounds for the services of a surrogate and a donor, both American. The result, on the first attempt, was triplets (four embryos had been implanted).[11] Another much publicized case, this one involving dual, gay fatherhood, is that of the Drewitt-Barlows, Tony and Barrie, who have (to date) five children produced by way of Californian donors and surrogates and who, like Mucklejohn, are regularly featured in the *Daily Mail* (they were also the subject of a 2010 Channel 4 documentary, *My Weird and Wonderful Family*). Today these exotic male stories involving parenthood via surrogacy have taken over from the surrogacy sensations of the 1980s which were focused on the women involved: the 'Baby M' case in the United States, and Kim Cotton, the first British surrogate mother, in 1985.[12]

'Gestational carrier', now a common American usage, represents a forceful semantic attempt to distinguish what the pregnant woman does or is from any suggestion of a parental identity or parental

[11] See Ian Mucklejohn, *And Then There Were Three* (London: Gibson Square, 2005).

[12] On these two cases, see Phyllis Chesler, *Sacred Bond: The Legacy of Baby M* (1988; London: Virago, 1990), and Kim Cotton and Denise Winn, *Baby Cotton: For Love and Money* (London: Dorling Kindersley, 1985). The 'Baby M' case was a custody battle that ensued when Mary Beth Whitehead, ('traditional') surrogate for Bill Stern and his wife Betsy, decided she could not part with the baby after the birth; controversy focused on the legal status of a surrogacy contract, the rights of birth mothers, and economic needs and means (Whitehead's family was working-class, the Sterns were middle-class professionals). Kim Cotton had been paid £6,500 by an American surrogacy agency, and in Britain controversy was mainly about the remuneration. The case was instrumental in the passing of legislation in 1985 restricting surrogacy payments to expenses. Such legislation had been recommended by the Warnock Report on reproductive technologies of 1984, in which surrogacy had been an object of special censure.

rights. A donor does give. But a carrier? Well, a carrier transports, just like American Airlines; and given the deliberate use of the newer designation in the United States (it is not, for instance, current in Britain), this might seem especially appropriate. For various reasons—the lack of regulation of surrogacy in many states, the presence of clinics and other businesses dedicated to every facet of reproductive medicine, and the marketing of surrogacy services via media that are now globally accessible—America has generally been the country of choice for non-Americans as well as Americans seeking a surrogate pregnancy. (This primacy is changing as other countries, notably India and some European states, increasingly offer cheaper deals.) But the gestational carrier does not in the end convey the baby to its parents. However much or little involvement commissioning parents from abroad may have with 'their' surrogate or carrier, they will need, at the end, to fly to the point of delivery and receive the baby she has produced for them. This, in the most melodramatic form, was the situation facing Jeanine Salomone, the French woman who gave birth (in France in 2001 at the age of 62)—and then flew to Los Angeles days after her child's arrival to collect a second baby, simultaneously gestated by an American surrogate mother. Her own delivery had been brought forward in order not to clash with the Californian birth.[13]

The expression 'gestational carrier' avoids the suggestion that the woman concerned is any sort of mother. In French there has been a terminological shift from *mère porteuse*, bearing or carrying mother, to *la gestation pour autrui*, gestation for another, which is used by those seeking to make the practice acceptable (surrogacy in France is illegal). The word 'mother' is dropped, while the addition of *pour autrui* introduces an element of relationship to the intended parents rather than (as with a *mère porteuse*) to the intended child.[14] The English

---

[13] On the Salomone case, see Jeanine Salomone, with Isabelle Léouffre, *Je l'ai tant voulu: Maman à 62 ans* (Paris: J.-C. Lattès, 2002). The two women were impregnated at the same time to double the chances of a last attempt; three embryos were implanted in each, so that six new babies at once for the late-seeking Salomone was not an inconceivable prospect.

[14] The phrase echoes *père pour autrui*, 'father for another', used much earlier in relation to donor insemination; see e.g. René Frydman, *L'Irrésistible Désir de naissance* (Paris: PUF, 1986), 124.

'surrogate mother' is awkward as it so directly calls out for a definition of a non-surrogate mother and raises the question of primary or authentic motherhood. But this is precisely what has come about in any case through the practical separation of womb and eggs in the processes of *in vitro* fertilization. Before the existence of egg donation and embryo transfer, the question would have been merely theoretical, because the two functions always occurred in the same body. At an earlier historical stage, before the identification of the ovum as a female seed, it would not have made any sense.

If a child can have two 'biological' mothers, then the issue of the priority of one to the other can be raised. Women with either type of biological involvement can feel they are the real mother—or alternatively, as is the case with most surrogates and most egg donors, they can legally as well as practically concede or assert that they are not. Those who become pregnant with a donor egg will talk about pregnancy being the authentic, long-term aspect of biological motherhood, while the egg is just a tiny starter element. Those whose own eggs are used to make an embryo whose pregnancy their own body cannot support will focus on the fact that the other woman is only a carrier (or a babysitter, an incubator, or any number of other friendly metaphors); the baby will look like them and continue the traits of them and their family. This is not an issue that can be decided: one woman's sense of authentic motherhood is just that; and the same is true for an experience of non-motherhood. But surrogacy and reproductive technologies have created these new situations that lead to the wish to identify one part of the female generative process as the overriding maternal qualification—while the other is not.[15]

Surrogacy and egg and sperm donation can all be represented as enabling services, prior to the intended parents taking over their child. But surrogacy has developed something more than this. A frequently offered rationale is that it lets a woman repeat a

[15] Examples of such processes of personal naturalization are found in ethnographic studies of the use of reproductive technologies (by both gay and straight couples) as well as in media testimonies. See in particular Gay Becker, *The Elusive Embryo: How Women and Men Approach New Reproductive Technologies* (Berkeley: University of California Press, 2000); Laura Mamo, *Queering Reproduction: Achieving Pregnancy in the Age of Technoscience* (Durham, NC: Duke University Press, 2007); and Charis Thompson, *Making Parents: The Ontological Choreography of Reproductive Technologies* Cambridge, Mass.: MIT Press, 2005.

uniquely pleasurable past experience while not having to live with the usual sequel. In a standard line of American agency website profiles, 'I love being pregnant—but my family is complete'. Pregnancy is isolated as a separate state which, while it excludes future motherhood (of this baby), is positively valorized as feminine. Jill Hawkins is a single woman from Brighton without children of her own who, like the proverbial long-suffering nineteenth-century wife, has been having and losing babies in rapid succession for much of the past twenty years. In *Daily Mail* interviews, as regular as her pregnancies, she has several times declared that she has just had her 'last' baby; but it never has been, yet. 'I find being pregnant very fulfilling. I'm a naturally giving person and to be able to give babies away is what I do.'[16] The combination was almost unimaginable a few decades ago. 'What would we think of a person who discarded her intentionally conceived child at birth, claiming that the only part of parenthood she enjoys is pregnancy?' asked the philosopher Onora O'Neill in an article of 1979.[17]

The practicable division of biological motherhood into two separate elements is historically unprecedented. But the processes of conception and pregnancy always contained these distinct components of the starter ingredients and the gestating environment. And in one way the (relatively) new duality and uncertainty of motherhood simply brings out into the open a theoretical plurality that has always been a feature of maternal—and more broadly of parental—situations. Between birth and bringing up there is a gap; nothing in

[16] Arthur Martin, 'Addicted to Pregnancy: The Surrogate Mother, 47, Who's Expecting Babies Number NINE and TEN', *Daily Mail*, 27 February 2012; the twins were born prematurely, after severe complications, at the end of June 2012. Hawkins is unique in not having had children of her own before embarking on surrogacy. According to Kim Cotton (*Archive on 4: A Life Less Ordinary*, BBC Radio 4, 4 June 2011), an exception was made for her owing to the strength of her desire, from the outset, to do surrogacy. Cotton had founded the non-profit organization COTS (Childlessness Overcome Through Surrogacy) after having been vilified for her own paid pregnancy as Britain's first contractual surrogate.

[17] Onora O'Neill, 'Begetting, Bearing, and Rearing', in O'Neill and William Ruddick (eds.), *Having Children: Philosophical and Legal Reflections on Parenthood* (New York: Oxford University Press, 1979), 30. Of many hypothetical actions or behaviours in relation to real or possible children that the article mentions, this is the only one to attract the appeal to an obvious consensus that is implicit in the rhetorical question.

nature ensures or requires that the same woman will both bear and be a (postnatal) mother to a baby. (Still less is there any natural sequence to ensure that a man whose sperm engenders a baby will take up whatever paternal place his society expects or grants.) Until the middle of the twentieth century in developed countries, and still in many places in the world, it was not unlikely that a woman would die either during or shortly after childbirth. For all kinds of reasons, to do with poverty or social values or their inclinations, however defined, mothers may be unwilling or unable to take on the role and identity of mother—or discouraged, even prevented from doing so, as was the case for very many young unwed mothers in the middle decades of the twentieth century, expected to hand over their babies for adoption, and without cultural or economic support for a decision to keep them.[18]

In France there exists a unique category of maternal non-identity called *l'accouchement sous X*: anonymous labour and delivery. Under this provision a pregnant woman has the right to receive hospital care during her confinement without giving her name at any point; afterwards she leaves without the baby, which in most cases is soon adopted.[19] *L'accouchement sous X* is the limit point of a legally and

---

[18] 'Mother and baby' homes where young women spent the last months of pregnancy, so that their condition would not be seen at home, were common in Britain, Ireland, France, and other western countries; see the interviews describing the experiences of American women who were taken away, and whose babies were taken away from them, in Ann Fessler, *The Girls Who Went Away: The Hidden History of Women Who Surrendered Children for Adoption in the Decades Before 'Roe v. Wade'* (New York: Penguin Press, 2006).

[19] This is an extreme case of the relinquishment on the part of the birth mother associated with any voluntary adoption. It was legally formalized in 1939, partly as a pro-natalist measure to discourage women from seeking abortions or from abandoning their babies: in this sense it was a continuation of the long-standing charitable, and later governmental, provision for foundlings, *les enfants trouvés*. Social changes—notably contraception, the legalization of abortion, and the ordinariness of unwed motherhood—have greatly reduced the take-up of *l'accouchement sous X* (in the same way that they have more broadly diminished the number of babies given up for adoption in western countries); the annual rate is now just a few hundred (out of a birth rate in the region of 800,000), down from around 10,000 a year in the 1970s. Today the continuing possibility of *l'accouchement sous X* is strongly contested—not least by representatives of those who have been directly concerned; an association

medically sanctioned form of non-motherhood on the part of a woman whose body has, in fact, gestated and given birth. It differs from surrogacy arrangements in that the pregnancy is (presumably) unwanted—allowing for all the diversity and ambivalence that that word can simplify—and no other woman (or man) is waiting to take over the baby, once delivered, as their own. But the two situations are similar in that in both cases a woman gives birth but has refused in advance the legal and social status of mother.

The legal specialist Marcela Iacub has drawn attention to what now appear as French historical precedents for modern forms of birth-mother non-motherhood. Lawsuits from the nineteenth century provide evidence of the clandestine practice of supposition. This involved a simulation of natural motherhood, when a couple received a baby not born to the wife, and pretended that it had been. Usually the birth mother would be unmarried and vulnerable, needing to hide her pregnancy as much as the adopting mother needed to hide her lack of one. Typically such cases came to light only if an inheritance was challenged much later by a relative alleging that the couple's child was not really theirs; and strikingly, even when the evidence then indicated that the accusation was justified, courts would nonetheless tend to rule that the child was the rightful heir, on the grounds that he or she had been brought up as, and understood to be, the parents' own child (the legal criterion is *la possession d'état*). The judgement, in other words, did not depend on the biological but on the social relationship.[20]

that assists mothers and their children in seeking one another was founded in 2002. Both women who gave birth and those who were born in this way may come to regret that no trace of the birth mother's identity was left (which distinguishes this scenario from other kinds of adoption). Though anonymous labour is still possible in France, mothers are now encouraged to leave confidential records of their identity and letters to their children; around 30% do. On the arguments surrounding the practice see Nathalie Perrier, *Faut-il supprimer l'accouchement sous X?* (Paris: Editions du Rocher, 2008).

[20] See Marcela Iacub, *L'Empire du ventre: Pour une autre histoire de la maternité* (Paris: Fayard, 2004). Stephen Cretney describes the English case of an heir to a Yorkshire estate supposedly born during his mother's unexplained absence in California in 1910. Members of the family hired private detectives and were eventually successful in securing a conviction for fraud; Cretney, *Family Law in the Twentieth Century: A History*

In the diverse situations of surrogacy, adoption, supposition, and *l'accouchement sous X*, it is manifestly the surrounding legal and social environment that makes a mother, not the fact that a woman's body has produced a baby. But this, of course, says nothing about what it might mean emotionally, in different situations, for a woman to give birth to a baby to whom she does not then become the mother. In the aftermath of the big story of 'Baby M', Helena Ragoné conducted an ethnographic study of surrogate mothers and their commissioning couples in American clinics. She describes a process of normalization whereby behaviours and reactions are channelled in ways that are meant to render them both liveable and ordinary: 'Programs, because they are engaged in a process of normalizing the surrogate mother experience for both their couples and their surrogates, use inclusive, colloquial language, describing their surrogates as "great gals who want to give something to someone else" and their couples as "regular folks who want a baby just like everyone else".'[21] This is the template into which surrogacy should fit: one of business and decency as usual. It is deliberately set against the wilder representations of high-flying dramas of loss and love that 'Baby M' brought out—as well

(Oxford: Oxford University Press, 2003), 529–30. There is an instance of supposition in Euripides' *Phoenician Women*, described by the birth mother of the child concerned: Oedipus. Euripides has Jocasta recount the events surrounding his birth somewhat differently from how they come out in Sophocles' version. For this Euripidean Jocasta, Laius is unequivocally the one solely responsible for the conception of Oedipus (risky because of the threatening oracle) and for his exposure as a newborn. The baby is said to have been given to the queen of Corinth rather than to her husband or both of them, and 'She took the one born of my pain and labour, put him to her breast, and persuaded her husband that she had given birth'; Euripides, *Fabulae*, vol. iii, ed. Gilbert Murray (2nd edn. 1913; Oxford: Oxford University Press, 1954), *Phoenissae*, lines 30–1. The addition (by a Jocasta now many years on from both these events and the revelation of Oedipus' subsequent marriage to her: this Jocasta did not kill herself) has the effect of pitting the two women competitively against each other as rivals for being the baby's mother. Jocasta also separates both the couples: Merope deceives Polybus, and Jocasta has no responsibility for Oedipus' engendering or exposure.

[21] Helena Ragoné, *Surrogate Motherhood: Conception in the Heart* (Boulder, Colo.: Westview Press, 1994), 43.

as against the more mundane pathologization of the participants in surrogacy arrangements.[22]

Discussions of surrogacy often point out that unlike egg donation—which only became practicable in the wake of IVF—it has a long history; it is one of those extreme reproductive practices, like the exposure of newborn babies (see Chapter 4), which is submerged because of the absence or distortion of historical record. There are two clear instances in Genesis, one of which has been regularly mentioned since the first years of contemporary surrogacy—both as a form of legitimation and for the opposite reason, to point out that biblical credentials are hardly relevant to present-day ethical concerns. As it happens, neither of these stories is remotely a happy one.[23] Both involve strong feelings of jealousy between women—the wife and the surrogate in one, and two sisters in the other. In the milder case surrogacy solves nothing and in the other, the one that is always referenced, it turns out very badly.

In the first and more famous story, Abraham and Sarah (at this point named Abram and Sarai) are very old and still childless. Sarai suggests to her husband that her servant Hagar could be used to bear a child—for her, as she specifies: 'Since Yahweh has kept me from having children, go to my slave-girl. Perhaps I shall get children through her' (Genesis 16: 2). The idea is hers, the children are said to be for her. A pregnancy begins, but then Hagar becomes contemptuous of Sarai, and Sarai complains to Abram, who gives her permission to deal with Hagar as she sees fit; after which 'Sarai treated her so badly that she ran away from her' (16: 6). At this

---

[22] In 1987, the sociologist Françoise Laborie made an interesting case for surrogacy as simpler for the intending mother than IVF, because it avoids all the laborious treatments and likely failures of that procedure. She does not consider 'full' surrogacy (which requires IVF), and argues instead that 'in this method of procreation, there is nothing medical or technological; you only need a syringe to inseminate the carrying mother and, since she is fertile, success—the birth of a baby—is very likely'; Laborie, 'Les Intérim-mères (à propos des mères porteuses)', in Geneviève Delaisi de Parseval with Jacqueline Bigeargal (eds.), *Objectif bébé—Une nouvelle science: La bébologie* (1985; Paris: Autrement, 1987), 116.

[23] In passing, a surrogacy story appears in the *Odyssey* (book 4, lines 11–15), with no particular emphasis: Menelaus had his son Megapenthes with a slave-girl since his wife Helen had no more children after giving birth to their daughter Hermione.

stage the narrative leaves Sarai and Abram and follows Hagar into the wilderness, where it is left for Yahweh to pick up the pieces. His messenger meets up with Hagar, finds out the problem from her point of view, and tells her to go home and submit to Sarai, with the promise of countless descendants. In the end, 'Hagar bore Abram a son, and Abram gave to the son that Hagar bore the name Ishmael' (16: 15–16). By naming him, Abram takes on the full role of father; the boy is effectively his and Hagar's, and Sarai, the commissioning parent, is out of the picture.

There is a somewhat unexpected sequel when Sarah, following a divine promise (which she laughs at) and easily beating all the elderly twenty-first-century *primigravidae*, gives birth to a baby well into her nineties. But then she becomes jealous when she sees Ishmael playing with her own son Isaac. 'This slave-girl's son is not to share the inheritance with my son Isaac', she says; and 'This greatly distressed Abraham because of his son' (21: 11–12). Ishmael is still his son, even now he has had one with Sarah. But he does send Hagar away after God has reassured him that he will look after Ishmael's future.

In this story, Hagar the surrogate comes to treat the child as fully hers, initially through rivalry with the would-be mother. The two women's conflict is not directly to do with the child that is born: Sarah never tries to claim Ishmael for herself, and she gets a child of her own in the end. This is more like a tale of the pitfalls or futility of surrogacy than a vindication of it. The best that can be said, ignoring the feelings and reactions of all the individuals concerned, is that the overarching theological perspective makes the story one that ultimately has its own good ends: in this grander public narrative, what matters is that Isaac's two sons, including the one born by surrogacy, go on to fulfil particular roles in history.

The other Genesis surrogacy story is not one that gets cited in that connection, perhaps because, in the manner of parental stories, it is eclipsed by the drama of love and marriage that precedes it. In this, Jacob falls for Rachel, works for her father for seven years to marry her, but is then tricked when the father substitutes her elder sister, Leah, on the day; Jacob then works another seven years to get the wife he originally wanted. Leah is herself a kind of surrogate, as a stand-in for someone else. But the sisters' childbearing histories, which follow, are equally confused and comparative. After the second marriage (but not, curiously, during the seven years of marriage before that), it is Leah, not Rachel, who has a series of sons. Their birth is attributed to Yahweh's sympathy for Leah's secondary position, but it is also interpreted by Leah herself as a bargaining point for securing the love of her husband, which is her primary objective—not, as it was for Sarai, the having of children for herself:

Yahweh saw that Leah was neglected, so he opened her womb, while Rachel remained barren. Leah conceived and gave birth to a son whom she named Reuben. 'Because' she said 'Yahweh has seen my misery; now my husband will love me'. Again she conceived and gave birth to a son, saying, 'Yahweh has heard that I was neglected, so he has given me this one too.' (Genesis 29: 31–3)

There follow two more conceptions and two more sons, 'Then she had no more children' (Genesis 29: 35). But the birth of the four sons has more effect on Rachel than on Jacob:

Rachel, seeing that she herself gave Jacob no children, became jealous of her sister. And she said to Jacob, 'Give me children, or I shall die!' This made Jacob angry with Rachel, and he retorted, 'Am I in God's place? It is he who has refused you motherhood.' So she said, 'Here is my slave-girl, Bilhah. Sleep with her so that she may give birth on my knees; through her, then, I too shall have children!' (Genesis 30: 1–4)

As with Sarai, surrogacy is suggested as a remedy for a woman's infertility; as with Leah, the motivation for having a baby at all is rivalry.

At first, things seem to turn out reasonably well for Rachel, given that her aim is to get even with her sister. Bilhah has two sons; 'Then Rachel said, "I have fought God's fight with my sister, and I have won"' (30: 8). But the battle is not over yet: 'Now Leah, seeing that she had no more children, took her slave-girl Zilpah and gave her to Jacob as a wife' (30: 9–10); she bears two sons. Both sisters have now produced children for their husband by means of servant surrogates, and they have reached a kind of stalemate. The next event is a tussle over an aphrodisiac or fertility

drug called mandrakes, supplied by Leah's son Reuben. Leah
eventually secures an arrangement whereby Rachel will let her
have Jacob for a night if she gives Rachel the mandrakes. This is
serious trading: when he comes home from work, Leah says: ' "You
must come to me, for I have hired you at the price of my son's
mandrakes". So he slept with her that night' (30: 16). Leah duly has
another son, and then another, and finally a seventh child (in addition to the two sons born to Zilpah)—a daughter called Dinah. This
is too much—and acknowledged as such: 'Then God remembered
Rachel; he heard her and opened her womb'; at last, she gives birth
to a son, 'saying "God has taken away my shame"' (30: 22–3).

In the Leah and Rachel story (it seems better to call it that, since
Jacob's role becomes wholly passive in the postmarital episodes),
surrogacy is one card to play in an ongoing inter-wife, inter-sisterly
competition. The procreational competitiveness is not officially connected to the initial long period—fourteen years—when Jacob was
working to marry Rachel. Nothing is said then of the sisters' rivalry,
even though the only events of this period involve both Jacob and
their father putting one of the two before the other. When it comes
to the years when both are married, competition is assumed and
having children becomes a new currency in which Leah can get
more than the sister who is preferred to her by their joint husband.
Surrogacy is unremarkable. Unlike the Hagar story, we are not told
of the surrogate mothers' feelings at any point. But by the same
token surrogacy is neither a solution nor a disaster; it brings neither
completion nor calamity for anyone. And as a strategy, it is simply
self-perpetuating: one sister's use of the practice leads to the other
one doing the same thing.

Once extremely common, a now more or less obsolete form of
surrogate motherhood is the practice of wet-nursing. This does
not fit the modern boundary between pre- and postnatal parenthood, the first 'biological' and the second not. The wet-nurse, in
breastfeeding another woman's baby, feeds it from her own body
in the same way as a surrogate birth mother does. Arguments
over the importance of maternal breastfeeding have been going
on for the past 300 years, at least. The alternative today, though,
is not another mother—a wet-nurse—but a bottle. Formula milk

is a thing of the twentieth century, and was preceded by other beverages thought suitable for an infant without a mother, or a surrogate to take her breastfeeding place. Pip's older sister in *Great Expectations* has, as it is often repeated, brought him up 'by hand'— without the help of a wet-nurse. In 1911, a manual for well-off women gives instructions for successful breastfeeding and then has a subsection headed 'Bringing up by Hand' which mentions, but dismisses, the option of a wet-nurse, still a theoretical possibility.[24] Wet-nursing is also a cross-class phenomenon, as mothers who had to earn a living for themselves and their children were obliged to leave a baby with a wet-nurse, sometimes as a boarder, when they went to work. This is the situation dramatized, with painfully detailed accounting of the negligible difference between her own earnings and her payments to the wet-nurse, in George Moore's novel of 1894, *Esther Waters* (see Chapter 10).

In the eighteenth century, when it was standard practice for women to delegate the job of nursing the baby, forceful arguments against it began to be voiced. Rousseau's hugely influential *Emile* (1758) starts off with a warm account of how mothers should nurse their own babies and generally have the care of them up to the age of 7, at which point—if they are boys—they will be transferred to a full-time male personal tutor. Rousseau's case for maternal primary care is made in terms of nature and health: for the baby to be fed by its own mother, not by some other woman, is natural—and therefore good—in the same way as freeing it of restrictive clothing, another of his concerns.[25]

[24] The section begins: 'When it is quite impossible for a mother to nurse her baby, it will be necessary that the little one be brought up by hand. There is the alternative, of course, of engaging a "wet nurse," but this is not always advisable, for many reasons. The milk used should be the special "nursery milk," which is always sent from the dairies in sealed bottles'; Florence R. Jack and Rita Strauss (eds.), *The Woman's Book: Contains Everything a Woman Ought to Know* (London: T. C. & E. C. Jack, 1911), 477.

[25] Given his advocacy and influence on questions of childrearing in relation to both parents, it is extraordinary that Rousseau's own five children, with his companion Thérèse Levasseur, were all handed over at birth to the Paris foundling hospital— where their chance of survival, as he may or may not have known, was extremely low, and where the education they would receive if they survived to receive it was minimal. Thérèse's part in this decision is not known.

Half a century before Rousseau, Richard Steele in 1711 made a not dissimilar case in the English *Spectator* 'to exhort the People with the utmost Vehemence to let the Children suck their own Mother'.[26] In his letter (signed 'Mr Spectator', like all the journal's articles), he states 'that of all the Abuses that ever you have as yet endeavoured to reform, certainly not one wanted so much your Assistance as the Abuse in nursing of Children' (287). The case made is worth considering in some detail, because it reveals a longer history to today's thinking about a division of biological motherhood into two and a division of mothers into the real one and the surrogate.

There are two strands to Steele's argument. First, that wet-nurses are bound to be bad, and will damage the babies as a result; and second, that mothers are perfectly fit for the job and ought to do it 'both for the benefit of Mother and Child' (289). The case is partly pragmatic, but also draws on ideas of what is natural or not natural. Wet-nurses are less than adequate for several reasons—intrinsic to themselves, and also relative to the superior qualities of the birth mother:

It is unmerciful to see that a Woman endowed with all the Perfections and Blessings of Nature, can, as soon as she is delivered, turn off her innocent, tender, and helpless Infant, and give it up to a Woman that is (ten thousand to one) neither in Health nor good Condition, neither sound in Mind nor Body, that has neither Honour, nor Reputation, neither Love nor Pity for the poor Babe, but more Regard for the Money than for the whole Child, and never will take further Care of it than what by all the Encouragement of Money and Presents she is forced to. (287)

The nurse is bound to be in poor condition physically, socially, and emotionally by comparison with the mother of all perfections; she is bad to her good, in a stereotypical division. And she is only doing it for the money ('and Presents'). The mercenary objection may seem to be separate from the negative personal qualities—or only linked

---

[26] [Richard Steele], *The Spectator*, no. 246, Wednesday 12 December 1711, in Joseph Addison and Richard Steele, *The Spectator*, ed. G. Gregory Smith, vol. ii (London: J. M. Dent, [1907]), 289. Further page references will be given within the main text.

to them by rhetorical association—but it turns out that there is a fundamental connection, which emerges at interview:

The first Question that is generally asked a young Woman that wants to be a Nurse, why she should be a Nurse to other People's Children; is answered by her having an ill Husband, and that she must make Shift to live. I think now this very Answer is enough to give any Body a Shock if duly considered; for an ill Husband may, or ten to one if he does not, bring home to his Wife an ill Distemper, or at least Vexations and Disturbance. Besides, as she takes the Child out of meer Necessity, her Food will be accordingly, or else very coarse at best. (288)

It is not only that the wife has to be the breadwinner, but that the sick (and unemployed) husband will 'bring home' bad qualities that affect her and thereby the baby. It is interesting all the same that Steele chooses to make the moral infection secondary, via the husband: the nurse herself is not in this case to blame.

Whether they emanate straight from the nurse or have come from the difficult husband, the bad qualities of bad milk are moral and mental as well as physical, and they are taken in directly by the baby: 'The Power of a Nurse over a Child, by infusing into it with her Milk her Qualities and Disposition, is sufficiently and daily observed' (287). That the qualities and disposition are bad is not just because of the nurse's necessitous situation and the husband-induced 'Vexations and Disturbance' of her home environment. It is also because of a basic difference between natural and non-natural which is indicated by way of a popular and ancient fable. The nurse will not do more than she has to (to get her pay and presents), because she is

like *Æsop*'s Earth, which would not nurse the Plant of another Ground, altho' never so much improved, by Reason that Plant was not of its own Production. And since another's Child is no more natural to a Nurse than a Plant to a strange and different Ground, how can it be supposed that the Child should thrive? And if it thrives, must it not imbibe the gross Humours and Qualities of the Nurse, like a Plant in a different Ground, or like a Graft upon a different Stock? (287)

The place of nature moves about from one maternal 'Ground' to another, and the argument only works if the nurse's 'Humours and

Qualities' are necessarily 'gross'. In the initial analogy with the
Aesop fable, it is the baby (the 'Plant') which is alien for the nurse
('Ground'). This risks making the nurse the original mother, and so
in the next sentence there is a subtle shift of perspective such that
the Ground (or nurse) ends up 'strange and different' from the Plant
(or baby) as the natural starting point. The nurse is put back into
the secondary place, and now her inevitably and irredeemably negative features—even though, in an almost accidental subordinate
clause, it is acknowledged that they may after all enable the child to
'thrive'—are brought out as a new kind of danger. The secondary
or surrogate mother is risky because if the baby thrives, it thrives
with her (bad) nature, which is passed on ('imbibe') as surely as any
twenty-first-century genes were ever transmitted from parent to
child. Nurturing contributes to the natural growing of the baby;
there is no distinction in this regard between prenatal and postnatal
motherhood, no fixing of 'biological' parenthood in relation to what
the initially procreating parents put in.

What the surrogate 'nurse' mother can do to the baby does not
bear thinking about. Steele has a plentiful supply of negative classical examples to hand, including the would-be historical cases of
extra-shocking Roman emperors. There is Nero's nurse 'very much
addicted to Drinking, which Habit *Nero* received from his Nurse'
(288); and then there is Caligula's nurse, who

used to moisten the Nipples of her Breast frequently with Blood, to make
Caligula take the better Hold of them; which, says *Diodorus*, was the Cause
that made him so blood-thirsty and cruel all his Life-time after, that he not
only committed frequent Murder by his own Hand, but likewise wish'd that
all human Kind wore but one Neck, that he might have the Pleasure to cut
it off. (288)

This consummate horror is not to be thought of as off the scale.
'Such like Degeneracies', Steele goes on, 'astonish the Parents, not
knowing after whom the Child can take, seeing the one to incline to
Stealing, another Drinking, Cruelty, Stupidity; yet all these are not
minded: Nay, it is easie to demonstrate, that a Child, although it be
born from the best of Parents, may be corrupted by an ill-tempered
Nurse' (288). In general the nurse, in her role as a second mother
and second source of nature for the child, is almost bound to cause

harm. Steele makes one quick reservation for 'some Cases of Necessity where a Mother cannot give suck, and then out of two Evils the least must be chosen'—but he does not estimate the likelihood of this eventuality very high: 'I am sure in a thousand there is hardly one real Instance' (289).

Steele's second strand of argument focuses on the positive aspects of mother-sucking, and here several points are made. First, that it is good, not bad, for the health of the mother, who 'grows stronger by it'. Then, that it is good for the children, who 'will be like Giants, whereas otherwise they are but living Shadows and like unripe Fruit': it is a choice between over- and underdevelopment. Third, that 'if a Woman is strong enough to bring forth a Child, she is beyond all Doubt strong enough to nurse it afterwards' (289): it is physically demanding work, but then so is labour, and breast-feeding should be seen as a continuation of that effort, to which the mother has already proved herself equal by going through childbirth.

Having run through these preliminary arguments about bodily well-being, Steele then takes up a different line:

But I cannot well leave this Subject as yet; for it seems to me very unnatural that a Woman that has fed a Child as Part of her self for nine Months should have no Desire to nurse it farther, when brought to Light and before her Eyes, and when by its Cry it implores her Assistance and the Office of a Mother. Do not the very cruellest of Brutes tend their young Ones with all the Care and Delight imaginable? For how can she be called a Mother that will not nurse its young Ones? The Earth is called the Mother of all things, not because she produces, but because she maintains and nurses what she produces. The Generation of the Infant is the Effect of Desire, but the Care of it argues Virtue and Choice. (289)

This plea for the mother to act as a natural mother—or to go on being the natural mother that she has been until the birth—involves an appeal to all sorts of disparate qualities. On the one hand, it is 'unnatural' not to want to continue the intimate nurturance that she has been providing for the prenatal months; and this is the good nature—good for the young and a source of 'Delight' for the mother—that can be found in even 'the cruellest of Brutes'. On the other hand, unlike getting pregnant, the second stage of nursing 'argues Virtue and Choice': it implies a responsible human agent, rather than an acquiescent animal. The two aspects are skilfully joined together in the analogy with 'the Earth'. The real mother, it turns out, is the one who 'maintains and nurses'—who puts in the postnatal care while still being par excellence natural.

This passage also stresses the significance of mother as a name to be earned and a duty to be fulfilled, and again there is the blending of arguments from nature and from merit. The baby, now out in the world, 'by its cry' 'implores her Assistance and the Office of a Mother'. To be 'called a Mother'—a phrase that is repeated—you have to nurse your young ones. At all events, deserving the name of mother depends on feeding the baby after its birth—not on a fixed entitlement that would come from having happened to generate it. The mother becomes the mother through what she actively does after the baby is born. And implicitly, she does not deserve that name if she delegates her natural nurturing to another woman.

In the 'Virtue and Choice' of the nursing mother we may also see in embryo the beginning of a parental noun that was destined to have a long and varied history in these reproductive discussions. 'Virtue' did not survive the journey—it is not a word that springs to mind in relation to our contemporary discussions about good parental behaviour. But 'choice' has gone from strength to discursive strength, working backwards from this early manifestation in relation to the nurturance of a born child to highlight instead a possibility of decision about babies not yet in existence: the choice to have or not have them, the choice to continue to grow them or not. Such prenatal points of choice—of seeking or not seeking, keeping or not keeping a pregnancy—for the most part fell outside the domain of the publicly thinkable in the *Spectator*'s time. And Steele's 'Choice'—with Virtue at its side—is not, as would be the later incarnations, to do with a woman's own rights or wishes so much as with what should properly be done by a mother for her child. Choice has not yet become a question of 'empowering' an individual who may or may not want to be, in addition, a mother; but the seeds, all the same, of its subsequent prominence may well be being sown in this early suggestion that a good mother, as opposed to a fecklessly thoughtless one, is a mother by choice.

Steele goes to and fro between his various charges against the two unnatural and second-rate mothers: the wet-nurse and the non-nursing birth mother. While he stresses the point that a baby will be bound to take in the undesirable qualities of whoever is nursing it, he does not, interestingly, consider the further issue: that the child who has been busy imbibing its nurse's nature may also regard that woman as its mother. This is a prospect that concerns Rousseau in making his own case for maternal breastfeeding. For the mother, says Rousseau, an inconvenient aspect of having some-one else nurse her baby is that of 'seeing her child loving another woman as much and more than her; of feeling that the tenderness he preserves for his own mother is a favour, and that that which he has for his adoptive mother is a duty: for do I not owe a son's attachment where I have found the care of a mother?'[27] Rousseau then suggests that the usual solution to this produces a greater problem:

The way that this disadvantage is remedied is to instil in children a con-tempt for their wet-nurses by treating them like nothing more than servants. When their work is over, the child is taken away, or the nurse is dismissed; by not being made welcome when she visits, she is put off from coming to see her foster-child. By the time a few years have passed he no longer sees her and he no longer knows her. A mother who thinks she is substituting for her and repairing her neglect by her cruelty is wrong. Instead of making a loving son out of a foster-child turned away from nature [*dénaturé*], she is training him to be ungrateful; she is teaching him how, one day, to despise the woman who gave birth to him as he does the one who nourished him with her milk.[28]

'A mother who thinks she is substituting for her [*qui croit se sub-stituer à elle*]': the nurse, who originally took the mother's place, is now herself in the primary position and the mother is a surrogate of the surrogate. Trying to push the wet-nurse away will not bring about the desired replacement (of the replacement), or the resto-ration of the birth mother as the mother. On the contrary, the treatment of the one who is now, effectively, the mother will even-

[27] Jean-Jacques Rousseau, *Emile ou de l'éducation* (1758; Paris: Garnier-Flammarion, 1966), 47.

[28] Rousseau, *Emile*, 47.

tually have a knock-on effect on the child's understanding of mothers in general—or of any woman whom he is called upon to think of as a mother.

Rousseau's argument is meant to dissuade mothers from delegating the nursing of their babies, and he begins by homing in on the individual situation, with the threat that the child will eventually despise the original mother precisely because she makes an attempt to regain her position by casting the other one out. But he goes much further than this, making the issue of proper motherhood into nothing less than the key to social order. With the practice of wet-nursing, everything falls apart:

> Do you want to bring everyone back to their first duties? Begin with mothers: you will be amazed by the changes you produce. Everything happens in stages as a result of this first depravity: the whole moral order is changed; nature is extinguished in every heart; the interiors of houses feel less alive; there is no longer the spectacle of a growing family to attach husbands and make visitors respectful; there is less respect for a mother whose children are not seen; families are no longer living in the same place; habit no longer reinforces the ties of blood; there are no more fathers or mothers or children or brothers or sisters; all of them hardly know each other; how could they love each other? Each of them thinks only of themselves. When the home is just a sad solitude, you really do have to go and cheer yourself up elsewhere.[29]

The world depends on a stability of home that can be seen as such, as a reviving 'spectacle' for the returning husband; it all breaks down in a hysterical list of collapses if mothers refuse to fulfil the duty of mothers.

For Rousseau, just as the effects of surrogate mothering amount to the disintegration of the whole 'moral order', so the proper performance of that role is the foundation of its restoration:

> But if mothers would deign to feed their children, then customs will be reformed by themselves, and the feelings of nature will awaken in every heart; the State will be repopulated: this first point, this point alone, will bring everything together. The attraction of domestic life is the best counterpoint to bad customs. The stress of children, which is thought to be too

[29] Rousseau, *Emile*, 47.

much, becomes pleasant; it makes the mother and father more necessary and more dear to one another; it tightens the matrimonial bond between them.[30]

From the fulfilment of the first natural bond of mother and infant, all other familial ties and social practices follow suit, including the tie between the parents as a couple, which is given a separate status but also made dependent on the mother–children tie.

Mary Wollstonecraft, following Rousseau in her own strong advocacy of maternal breastfeeding, picks up the same image of a domestic 'delight' centred on the nursing mother, as a picture for the husband:

Cold would be the heart of a husband, were he not rendered unnatural by early debauchery, who did not feel more delight at seeing his child suckled by its mother, than the most artful wanton tricks could ever raise; yet this natural way of cementing the matrimonial tie, and twisting esteem with fonder recollections, wealth leads women to spurn.[31]

The man is called a husband not a father. The sight of the nursing mother is not only a picture of nature; it is a natural agent in 'cementing' a marriage—something which, like Rousseau, Wollstonecraft is presenting as a distinct and laudable end. Rousseau's husband bonds better with his wife when she nurses the children herself, and he fails to be attached to his family in the absence of the breastfeeding mother; Wollstonecraft's husband too is specifically affirmed in his connection to his wife as a wife, in 'the matrimonial tie', well away from 'debauchery' and 'wanton tricks'. As her paragraph expands, Wollstonecraft puts herself in the place of the spectator of this family, watching the husband's happy return:

I have seen her prepare herself and children, with only the luxury of cleanliness, to receive her husband, who returning weary home in the evening found smiling babes and a clean hearth. My heart has loitered in the midst of the group, and has even throbbed with sympathetic emotion, when the scraping of the well known foot has raised a pleasing tumult.[32]

[30] Rousseau, *Emile*, 47–8.

[31] Mary Wollstonecraft, *A Vindication of the Rights of Woman* (1792), ed. Janet Todd (Oxford: Oxford University Press, 1993), 223.

[32] Wollstonecraft, *Vindication*, 223.

The imagery of these passages in Rousseau and Wollstonecraft is well on the way to the modern self-contained 'nuclear' family. Wollstonecraft cuts down the number of those present (the mother has 'perhaps, merely a servant maid to take off her hands the servile part of the household business'[33]), and she has the husband coming home from some outside employment to complete the scene. In this small world, there is room for just one mother figure, and it is vital that she should be established as who she rightfully and naturally is in her children's order of things. Rousseau's unsuckling mother, in simple contrast, is responsible for all the ills to which the domestic and the larger social order can be laid open. Once the first substitution has happened with the first surrogate motherhood, nothing remains in its natural place.

Rousseau and Wollstonecraft make their case by appealing to the smaller and larger 'natural' orders of home, family, and state, all of which at their different levels will be disturbed, if not altogether overthrown, by the unbalancing effects of putting a child out to nurse. Bring back natural mothers, and you ensure the maintenance of every level of harmony. Steele's *Spectator* piece, in its way, is more radical in its implications because it unsteadies the very notion of nature as it is to be applied to mothers (or perhaps, because it works with a notion of the natural that has not yet acquired the place it would have for Rousseau and then for Wollstonecraft). Long before modern gestational surrogacy and egg donation, there was already a potential division of natural mothers into two.

[33] Wollstonecraft, *Vindication*, 223.

3

Reproductive Choice

A Prehistory

In *Civilization and its Discontents* (1930), Freud offers a striking image for the origin of cohabiting couples:

One may suppose that the founding of families was connected with the fact that a moment came when the need for genital satisfaction no longer made its appearance like a guest who drops in suddenly, and, after his departure, is heard of no more for a long time, but instead took up its quarters as a permanent lodger. When this happened, the male acquired a motive for keeping the female, or speaking more generally, his sexual objects, near him; while the female, who did not want to be separated from her helpless young, was obliged, in their interests, to remain with the stronger male.[1]

At the outset, according to this little explanatory myth, there was a disconnection between sexuality and parenthood, which divide along gender lines. Sex is what he has to do and nurturing is what she has to do. Neither has a choice about the matter. Living together is a convenient arrangement which suits both these needs, like a match in response to a pair of personal ads. It provides a place where he can get sex at any time and where she can look after her children.

The babies appear in the passage as a given, like the periodic genital forces propelling the male; there is no suggestion of any link between the two kinds of demand on (and by) the man and the woman. In the beginning, there was sex (for men) and there were

---

[1] Freud, *Civilization and its Discontents* (1930), *Standard Edition of the Complete Works of Sigmund Freud*, trans. James Strachey, 24 vols. (London: Hogarth Press, 1955–74), xxi. 99.

babies (for women). And while the idea of settling down, of 'permanent' residence, does appear in what Freud says, it is not in relation to the stability of a home environment for living with a spouse or raising children. The unexpected guest who later becomes the live-in lodger is not a person but a physical urge. Freud's analogy does away with the customary association of marriage and children with domesticity, and the suggestion that often accompanies it, that sexual desire is something not always or easily accommodated in the home. Family life in this vision is a secondary effect of the domestic arrangements that are made first of all for the sake of male sexual demands that refuse to go away.

Another common association that waits in the wings of Freud's image is the idea of pregnancy as a temporary lodging, and also—as here with the genital demands on the man—as a form of hospitality that the guest cannot fail to take up and the host cannot fail to offer, at least initially. Pregnancy is something that happens to both the 'host' female and the foetus, whether or not the woman invited it. This guest has not asked to be lodged—or to be dislodged either, if it stays inside long enough to be 'born'. But here, again, Freud seems to turn away from the more obvious imagistic expectations, as if to consolidate the otherwise incongruous marriage of convenience that he is proposing. In some respects this asymmetrical union of two individuals with entirely different needs does follow the conventional story as told by the nineteenth-century evolutionary anthropology that forms one background to Freud's thinking. The family in Freud's account is structurally and chronologically prior to other forms of social community. But the gap between the man and the woman is so extreme as to make them effectively different species whose needs have nothing to do with one another. Sexual instincts are not mentioned in connection with the woman, though she is there as the means of satisfaction for those of the man. Fatherhood would seem to be something unknown or of no interest to the man; the woman is the parent, and parenting is exclusively and inescapably what she does.

Ordinary English language makes a similar kind of radical distinction between parents. Fathering a child has to do with the results of sex; it is biological and pre-dates the born child's need for a parent of any human description. Mothering, on the other hand, implies a kind of attitude or attention which need not involve the woman's own children. A man may be found to have fathered a child, meaning that the child is biologically his; but this fact has nothing to do with any relationship he may or may not have had to it after the sexual act which started its life. A woman may be said to mother a person who has no relation to her. But the biological basis of fathering and the social basis of mothering in fact go against the habitual division of ideas about parenthood. In the classical separation of parental functions, the bodily tie is associated with mothers— who are pregnant, who give birth, who breastfeed and cuddle. Fathers are fathers in name, and by law: fatherhood is accepted or bestowed as a matter of social legitimacy rather than natural connection. Fathers are fathers also, in this line of thinking, through their exercise of social authority and their provision of material means of support for mothers and children.

After the moment of pragmatic domestication, Freud's compressed history continues by talking about an ever-widening distinction between maternal and masculine roles, with men situated at a symbolic and actual distance from the home. The men participate in an increasingly complex cultural community, while the mothers (that is, all the women) remain just where they were at the initial moment, forever holding the babies.[2] Freud offered different accounts of the conditions of parenthood, for men and for women, and it is quite surprising that this anthropological vignette should have been written during a period when he was also, in other essays, thinking about female sexual development and questioning the idea that a desire for motherhood comes naturally to women.

In its sharp differentiation of men from women—or men from mothers, which is what women are—the passage deliberately evokes a prehistoric time. But looked at from another angle it may be seen as peculiarly modern in its separation of sexuality from reproduction. At the time that Freud was writing, contraception was beginning to make it possible for sex to be separated off from the likelihood or risk of pregnancy. Then, in a second more recent stage, it has become possible through reproductive technologies for babies to be conceived without sex having taken place. Initially a

---

[2] Freud, *Civilization*, 103–4.

remedy for infertility affecting married couples, and thus replicating the conditions in which pregnancy could have occurred by nature, reproductive technologies have increasingly come to serve as a means for individuals or same-sex couples—who could never have reproduced without 'assistance'—to become the parents of children of their own. And this both reflects and contributes to a various and complicated familial picture in which the long-term (heterosexual) married couple who conceive and rear their own children is one of many possible parental situations.

In the 1920s and 1930s, the increasing availability and reliability of contraceptive devices was beginning to make the having of children into a decision separate from marriage: couples could choose not to have children yet, or even at all, and to 'space' their pregnancies.[3] The negative choice—no children, no pregnancy—came to suit (and also to prompt) the changing sexual norms of the second half of the twentieth century, especially after the invention of the contraceptive pill.[4] Contraception also went with the second-wave feminist demand for women to have the right to choose not to be mothers, or not to be pregnant. The 1960s slogan 'a woman's right to choose' encompassed both contraception and abortion. But while choice has remained as a focal word, the emphasis has shifted in recent decades to the positive choice to become a parent, whatever a person's age or sexual orientation or marital status. Wanting to

---

[3] On earlier developments in the promotion (and contestation) of 'family limitation', see Richard Allen Soloway, *Birth Control and the Population Question in England, 1877–1950* (Chapel Hill: University of North Carolina Press, 1982). Kate Fisher's *Birth Control, Sex and Marriage in Britain 1918–1960* (Oxford: Oxford University Press, 2006) shows through detailed interviews that while the use of contraceptive devices (other than the age-old strategies of *coitus interruptus* or abstention) did much increase during the inter-war period, this was not accompanied by a shift, at the level of couples' private discussions, to a model of long-term planning and rational choice. But the active promotion of such forethought, together with the greater obtainability of contraceptive means, inevitably changed the frame for the spoken and unspoken negotiations of reproductive possibilities for individuals and couples.

[4] In *Call the Midwife: A True Story of the East End in the 1950s* (2002; London: Phoenix, 2006), Jennifer Worth describes the impact of the pill on a working-class community where earlier methods of birth control had been little used: 'In the late 1950s we had eighty to a hundred deliveries a month on our books. In 1963 the number had dropped to four or five a month. Now that is some social change!' (5).

have a child of your own can be seen as analogous to many other kinds of personal choice that individuals are invited to make in both everyday and existential ways. Choice is a sign of autonomy and control: of the person who knows, as a person should, what they want, or don't want, and may reasonably seek or avoid it.

In his essay *On Liberty* (1859), John Stuart Mill gives a central place to a notion of individual choice, but sees it as a questioning of cultural norms: 'The human faculties of perception, judgement, discriminative feeling, mental activity, and even moral preference are exercised only in making a choice. He who does anything because it is the custom makes no choice.'[5] Mill is scornful towards unthinking followers of the behavioural fashion: 'He who lets the world, or his own portion of it, choose his plan of life for him has no need of any other faculty than the ape-like one of imitation' (123). Choices which break away from what is prescribed or expected Mill calls 'experiments of living'; he sees these as contributing to the 'diversity' (120) which is to be generally encouraged: 'As it is useful that while mankind are imperfect there should be different opinions, so it is that there should be different experiments of living' (120).

'Experiments of living' is irresistibly appealing, like an early advertisement for the counter-cultural lifestyles and alternative family forms of the later twentieth century. This makes it all the more interesting that Mill mentions as a special case the choice of having children. That he gives this as a choice at all is also somewhat remarkable at a time when in practice, the choice to have no children, or no more children, was not securely attainable (so that actively choosing to have them would seem superfluous); and when there was as yet no common idea that two people might choose to marry without at the same time expecting or accepting that children were likely to follow in due course. Of having children, Mill says this:

The fact itself, of causing the existence of a human being, is one of the most responsible actions in the range of human life. To undertake this responsibility—to bestow a life which may be either a curse or a blessing—unless the being on whom it is bestowed will have at least the ordinary chances of a desirable existence, is a crime against that being. (179)

---

[5] John Stuart Mill, *On Liberty* (1859), ed. Gertrude Himmelfarb (London: Penguin, 1982), 122. Further page references will be given within the main text.

Mill does not suggest a right to life for an imagined future child, so much as a right not to be born in adverse circumstances. The potential harm does not stop with the child, but takes on Malthusian concerns for collective welfare and diminished resources as Mill also considers the effect of having children as socially and economically selfish: 'in a country, either overpeopled or threatened with being so, to produce children, beyond a very small number, with the effect of reducing the reward of labour by their competition is a serious offence against all who live by the remuneration of their labour' (179).

Children form a special type of choice in another respect as well. Or rather, they form a special case within what is already a special case, that of marriage and divorce, which Mill discusses in the context of the right to withdraw from a contract. He is disagreeing with the argument (put forward by Wilhelm von Humboldt) that contracts that involve personal relations should be time-limited and in any case open to dissolution at the wish of either party; and that marriage, above all, should be immediately terminable at the behest of either spouse because it requires that 'the feelings of both the parties are in harmony with it'. Things are not so simple:

When a person, either by express promise or by conduct, has encouraged another to rely on his continuing to act in a certain way—to build expectations and calculations, and stake any part of his plan of life upon that supposition—a new series of moral obligations arises on his part towards that person, which may possibly be overruled, but cannot be ignored. And again, if the relation between two contracting parties has been followed by consequences to others; if it has placed third parties in any peculiar position, or, as in the case of marriage, has even called third parties into existence, obligations arise on the part of both the contracting parties towards those third persons, the fulfilment of which, or at all events the mode of fulfilment, must be greatly affected by the continuance or disruption of the relations between the original parties to the contract.   (174)

Mill goes on to show the complications of (in his wonderfully defamiliarized, pseudo-legal phrase) calling third parties into existence, by pointing not only to the rights of those third parties but also to the continuing claims, even when there are children involved, of the two parties whose separate rights to call their marriage out of existence Humboldt had implicitly championed. Although he takes issue with

Humboldt's ignoring of marriage's unusual contractual status, given its responsibilities for other parties it has itself created, Mill objects to the way that divorce 'is usually discussed as if the interest of children was everything, and that of grown persons nothing' (175).

In *On Liberty* uncustomary forms of parental plan or practice are not mentioned as possible 'experiments of living' (the tantalizing phrase is in fact not followed by any examples at all); but today these would be likely to figure in any notional list of distinctive life choices. None the less Mill's stress on the significance and responsibility of having children—of the bestowing of life, for better or worse—is notable at a time when the question of whether to become a parent was not, as such, one that was normally separable from the question of whether or not to be married (and conversely). This is visible too in the passage from *Civilisation and its Discontents*, where the cohabitation of men and women assumes the co-presence of children.

A nice illustration of how having children continued into the twentieth century to be regarded as a matter of marital course can be found in a compendious publication of 1911 called *The Woman's Book*. Running to over 700 big pages, and subtitled *Contains Everything A Woman Ought to Know*, this ample volume is packed with useful information of many kinds, some of it quite progressive. It is aimed at the middle-class woman running a household with servants, but it also includes facts about new possibilities for women's professional life and it insists, for instance, that girls' education should be regarded as having as much importance as boys'. The editors' Preface makes it clear that the book is consciously untraditional: 'While...we cannot appreciate too highly the value of the work done by the domestic woman, it is absurd to regard that as woman's only sphere.'[6] There is a chapter called 'Women in Politics' which makes a strong and unapologetic case for female suffrage, at the time when campaigning was at its height in Britain:

Women, like men, have the desire to expand their realm of intelligence, to take part in the affairs of the world, which bear upon their lives, and the restraint and force of mere tradition, prejudice, or caste, have become intoler-

---

[6] Florence B. Jack and Rita Strauss (eds.), *The Woman's Book: Contains Everything a Woman Ought to Know* (London: T. C. and E. C. Jack), vi. Further page references will be given within the main text.

able to them. Women want freer lives because they want freer development; they want more capable minds and increased capacities for grappling with the increasing difficulties of modern civilisation.   (697)

The argument is put in a language of expansion and restraint that recalls the phrasing of Mary Wollstonecraft, or for that matter Mill— and perhaps remembers Jane Eyre's ruminations on Rochester's rooftop.[7] Women, 'like men', have capacities and desires which fail to find an outlet in the present restrictive organization of culture; they seek a wider world. The next paragraph mentions both Wollstonecraft and Mill by name, making the case that 'The agitation for women's rights is no new thing' (697): a tradition for the rejection of tradition. Mill's emphasis on the need to refuse a reliance on custom for custom's sake—the prompt for the 'experiments of living'—is more than affirmed here, with 'mere tradition, prejudice, or caste' making tradition something obviously questionable, and associated with consciously negative terms. But a new element in this dismissal of tradition is the appeal to the 'increasing difficulties of modern civilisation'. The world in which the new woman is to find her freedom is different and requires special skills for its negotiation.

Given this framework of modern change and complexity, it may seem surprising to find that when *The Woman's Book* has a chapter called 'The Child', it begins like this:

Very soon in the married lives of most young wives comes a time when the knowledge is brought home to them that they are to be called upon to fulfil woman's noblest mission—the mission of motherhood.   (466)

It is quite consistent with the tradition of feminist thought that goes back to Wollstonecraft to think of motherhood positively, as a privileged aspect of being a woman whose centrality in women's lives should not prevent their enjoyment of other kinds of recognition

---

[7] 'Women are supposed to be very calm generally: but women feel just as men feel; they need exercise for their faculties, and a field for their efforts as much as their brothers do; they suffer from too rigid a restraint, too absolute a stagnation, precisely as men would suffer; and it is narrow-minded in their more privileged fellow-creatures to say that they ought to confine themselves to making puddings and knitting stockings, to playing on the piano and embroidering bags'; Charlotte Brontë, *Jane Eyre* (1847), ed. Margaret Smith (Oxford: Oxford University Press, 2000), 109.

and fulfilment as well. But what is striking in the sentence from 1911 is the combination of coyly unphysical phrasing with the absence of any sense that their coming motherhood is anything that the wives (or anyone else) have willed or initiated. Motherhood is delivered as a mission and calling; women do not go out of their way to find (or avoid) it, but rather 'the knowledge is brought home to them'.

For a book with a consciously forward-looking mission of its own, the body's absence from this moment of maternal enlightenment is also noticeable. This is not a pregnancy so much as an annunciation; and it is not sex—or 'biology'—that makes babies, but marriage. (It makes some sort of sense in this context that the word 'natural' was used in the past to refer to illegitimate children, as opposed to those born within a marriage. The very notion of legitimacy stresses a legal not a biological foundation for the family—to the point that the natural can even be identified, by name, with the non-marital.) Only seven years later, Marie Stopes would publish the first of many editions of *Married Love*, her book about contraception and sex; her first 'Mothers' Clinic' opened in 1921. From the 1920s, contraception was being energetically promoted (though it was not yet widely available) by activist doctors like Stopes and Helena Wright. Before long, it would not seem reasonable to speak of the onset of pregnancy after marriage as a matter of course—something that simply comes to pass, and probably 'Very soon'. 'Family planning' would start to take its place among the ordinary discourses surrounding marriage and parenthood. The arrival of children would no longer be the default expectation of the recently married; but would become a more or less organized event, a positive choice to be made.[8]

The Woman's Book implicitly prescribes the proper time for pregnancy by its reference to early married lives, but even without the possibilities of private planning introduced by contraception, cultural specifications might be—at least officially—quite precise. In the fourth century BCE, Aristotle's *Politics* is definite in laying down prescriptive suggestions for procreative practice that cover

---

[8] Letters sent to Marie Stopes in the years following the publication of *Married Love* testify poignantly to the sufferings of all kinds experienced by those unable not to go on having more and more children. See Ruth Hall (ed.), *Dear Dr Stopes: Sex in the 1920s* (1978; Harmondsworth: Penguin, 1981).

everything from the age of marriage for men and women to the professionals who should be consulted before starting a family. A twenty-year gap between husband and wife is recommended so that both will reach the end of their reproductive years (50 for women, 70 for men) at the same moment. Also, attention should be given to the difference of ages between parents and children: too great, and they will be of no use to each other in their old and young age, respectively; too young, and there will not be sufficient distance for sons to respect their fathers as they should. Aristotle summarizes the advice available about the timing of pregnancies and the health of the parents:

We have spoken now about the time of life when marriage should take place, but not about the periods of the year best suited for sexual intercourse. However, the common practice of choosing the winter season is satisfactory. In addition those contemplating child-bearing [*ten teknopoiian*] should seek the advice of doctors and scientists; the former can give the requisite information about periods in the life of the body, the latter about weather conditions; they recommend a time of northerly winds rather than southerly. On the question of what kind of physical condition is most advantageous for parents, those who want more detailed information must seek it in manuals on the rearing of children [*tes paidonomias*]; for our present purpose the following outline will suffice. Athletic fitness does not provide the best condition either for a citizen or for health in the production of offspring.[9]

Aristotle goes on to give more information about the right physical conditions for setting about reproduction: not too fit, not too unfit, but somewhere sensibly in between; and 'these provisions are applicable to men and women alike'.[10] Parenthood is meant to occur only in the appropriate circumstances, which start from the marriage of the appropriately age-matched individuals and go on to encompass lifestyle, fitness, season, and weather. The parents should be prepared. And they should know what they need to know, both from reading and from finding out the views of experts on the body and the natural world. So reproduction is both assisted and artificial.

[9] Aristotle, *Politica*, 1335a–b; *The Politics*, trans. T. A. Sinclair (Harmondsworth: Penguin, 1962), 293–4.

[10] Aristotle, *Politica*, 1335b; *Politics*, 294.

There are others, apart from the prospective parents, to monitor it; and there are special rules to be followed for how it should happen.

Starting with marriage itself, there have always been conventions, sometimes legally enforced, that surround the making and rearing of babies in a given society: in that sense families have always been planned and in different ways 'policed' by their culture.[11] But the normalization of contraceptive practices brought notions of choice and plan to the fore. Behind the advocacy of contraception in the first half of the twentieth century were two supplementary ideas. First, that it was beneficial for a woman's own health and her children's welfare for babies to come in smaller numbers and at longer intervals. And second, that the sexual relationship between husband and wife was something to be fostered and enjoyed for its own sake, and without the anxiety caused by the possibility of pregnancy when that was not desired.[12] By the time that the contraceptive pill became symbolic of a new sexually 'permissive' world in the 1960s, the focus was moving away from the married couple, quietly learning to delay or—in the new inter-war vocabulary—'space' their children. These changes were as radical in their own sphere as the mainstream normalization of non-marital sex.

The difference of perspective can be seen by returning to Mill. *The Subjection of Women* (1869) set out to challenge everything relating to established practices: 'So true is it that unnatural generally means only uncustomary, and that everything which is usual appears natural.'[13] Mill goes out of his way to point out that of all the hierarchies of human inequality, the one that divides the sexes is the most deeply entrenched and thus likely to seem the most natural

---

[11] See Jacques Donzelot, *La Police des familles* (Paris: Editions de Minuit, 1977) for a critique of the developing forms of state intervention in family life in France since the mid-eighteenth century.

[12] See Marie Carmichael Stopes, *Married Love: A New Contribution to the Solution of Sex Difficulties* (1918; 11th edn. London: G. P. Putnam's Sons, Ltd, 1923); Helena Wright, *The Sex Factor in Marriage: A Book for Those Who Are or Who Are About to be Married* (1930; London: Williams & Northgate Ltd, 1933); see also Christina Simmons, *Making Marriage Modern: Women's Sexuality from the Progressive Era to World War II* (New York: Oxford University Press, 2009).

[13] Mill, *The Subjection of Women* (1869; London: Dent, 1974), 230. Further page references will be given within the main text.

and the least open to question. Yet even so, the one aspect of
women's and men's lives that he does not see as being potentially
variable—as being, in his terms, a contingent custom—is the marital
'division of labour' (264). Within this arrangement, it is taken for
granted that women will manage the household and take responsibility for the children's upbringing:

If, in addition to the physical suffering of bearing children, and the whole
responsibility of their care and education in early years, the wife undertakes
the careful and economical application of the husband's earnings to the
general comfort of the family; she takes not only her fair share, but usually
the larger share, of the bodily and mental exertion required by their joint
existence. (264)

So obvious is it that there are children, and that it is their mother
who sees to them in the first years, that both of these points can slip
by as a given, before thinking about the household management
which is considered to be more of an issue. But even if Mill does not
feel a need to make an argument for the existing separation of functions it is significant that he includes in his list of wifely labours the
'suffering' associated with childbearing and that he measures the
contributions of each spouse in terms of work—of 'bodily and mental
exertion'. If she earns money, it is because he is 'forcing her to work,
and leaving the support of the family to her efforts, while he spends
most of his time in drinking and idleness' (264); a caretaking father,
as opposed to a financial provider, is not considered, any more than
a marriage which has not given rise to offspring.

Mill does however consider the effect on women of various forms
of unchosen childlessness. He is elaborating on the theory that nothing is more important, for both men and women, than having 'a
worthy outlet for the active faculties' (314), which is normally what
motherhood supplies:

Women who have the cares of a family, and while they have the cares of a
family, have this outlet, and it generally suffices for them: but what of the
greatly increasing number of women, who have had no opportunity of
exercising the vocation which they are mocked by telling them is their
proper one? What of the women whose children have been lost to them by
death or distance, or have grown up, married, and formed homes of their
own? (314)

Here Mill might seem to be scorning the assumption that motherhood is women's proper calling, though in fact he is pointing out that marriage and the family it hopefully brings are not available to all women. But what the passage also does is to yoke together very different forms of involuntary childlessness, from never having been able to marry (or, therefore, to have children) in the first place, to losing existing children in both extreme and ordinary ways. In 'no opportunity' there may also be an allusion not just to not finding a husband, but to being married and not having children. The last situation—that children just grow up and leave home—reads like an early articulation of the empty nest syndrome, and is notably presented as one of a range of different positions of female childlessness (rather than simply the final phase of a normal female life). Mill's point is that the post-mother has lost her role: having children is first and foremost a matter of the 'outlet' that gives a person a sense of a life worth living.

Mill goes on to make a moving comparison between the retirements of men and women, complicated for both but for women largely unacknowledged as a 'parallel case':

There are abundant examples of men who, after a life engrossed by business, retire with a competency to the enjoyment, as they hope, of rest, but to whom, as they are unable to acquire new interests and excitements that can replace the old, the change to a life of inactivity brings ennui, melancholy, and premature death. Yet no one thinks of the parallel case of so many worthy and devoted women, who, having paid what they are told is their debt to society—having brought up a family blamelessly to manhood and womanhood—having kept a house as long as they had a house needing to be kept—are deserted by the sole occupation for which they have fitted themselves. (314)

But even though their place in women's lives is by his own representation so large, and their bringing up a matter of social duty, references to children in Mill's book about women's 'subjection' are strikingly few. Implicitly, only their absence is a problem; and for as long as they are around and needing a mother's care, they typically provide the means of her happiness, an equivalent outlet to that provided for her husband by his work.

Yet while he does not envisage a marriage in which children are not intended, in one way Mill's view of ongoing changes in the institution does look forward to an arrangement in which having children might seem like an unnecessary supplement to a self-sufficient unit of companionship, intimacy, and shared desires. He refers to 'the ideal of marriage', which involves 'two persons of cultivated faculties, identical in opinions and purposes, between whom there exists the best kind of equality, similarity of powers and capacities' (311); to such a dream unit, in the second half of the twentieth century, the prospect of children, or of more children, might well figure as an impediment to other kinds of joint project. For the young married couple at the centre of Richard Yates's novel *Revolutionary Road* (1961), leaving the sub-urbs and going to Paris to find themselves is the hope and wish that having another child would surely curtail, they think. They seek an authentic fulfilment through the rejection of social expec-tations (that you settle down in a good neighbourhood and stead-ily raise the family). The couple is the agent of the defiance of convention, which at this stage is represented primarily by the burden of babies: you run away from suburban life (and children) as a duo.

But if the married couple can be imagined as a romantic unit whose *raison d'être* is not to be sought in its connections to family, then there is room for a tension to be manifested between on the one hand the bond between the two adults and on the other the subsequent and separate bonds between (each) parent and (each) child. In effect, there is more than one couple—two couples, at least, in competition with one another. In *A Vindication of the Rights of Woman* (1792), Mary Wollstonecraft is already describing this sce-nario in making an argument about the side-effects of 'an unhappy marriage' (at a time when divorce is not a realistic option, she uses the phrase without special emphasis). Far from being detrimental to the children, she suggests, such a situation may be positively benefi-cial: 'I will go still further, and advance, without dreaming of a para-dox, that an unhappy marriage is often very advantageous to a family, and that the neglected wife is, in general, the best mother.' Conversely, a marriage that maintains its initial erotic charge is a bad thing for the children: 'a master and mistress of a family ought not to continue to love each other with passion,' she forbiddingly pronounces.[14]

Wollstonecraft's argument is remarkable in any number of ways—most of all perhaps in what looks almost like a recommendation of marital unhappiness as an aid to good parenting. Modern assumptions tend to be the opposite: that bad marriages are bad for children, and would be helped if the parents could manage to get back a bit of their lost desire and 'rekindle' the relationship. But these issues are commonplaces of contemporary discussions about the stability or break-up of parental relationships, and in that sense Wollstonecraft, in raising them as such, is at the beginning of a modern preoccupation with the dynamics of different and potentially conflicting attachments within a small family. For Wollstonecraft, erotic and parental feelings are necessarily disjunctive. Later thinking would continue to place these two passions in separate compartments, but might see them as mutually supportive rather than the reverse—or more likely, might see the deterioration of one kind of relationship as likely to hurt the other kind too.

Implicitly, in Wollstonecraft's domestic world, there is only so much love available for a person to give out, and if the spouse is enjoying too much of it there will be none to spare: a wife unloving as a wife can better give love to her children. In either case, what is fundamental is the primary attachment to one other, which Wollstonecraft sees as an essential human attribute. Arguing against Rousseau (as she loves to do), she insists that humans are not naturally solitary, and that this is a result of the prolonged period of dependence in infant life: 'he disputes whether man be a gregarious animal, though the long and helpless state of infancy seems to point him out as particularly impelled to pair' (79). It is an argument that would be made psychoanalytically in the twentieth century: that the human baby is unlike other mammals in what is effectively its premature birth; and that this situation of early helplessness has profound and lifelong consequences for the psychology of the grown-up

[14] Mary Wollstonecraft, *A Vindication of the Rights of Woman* (1792), ed. Janet Todd (Oxford: Oxford University Press, 1994), 97, 96. Further references will be given in the main text.

creature that develops.[15] What Wollstonecraft stresses is that the
intensity and inescapability of the initial bond between mother and
baby creates a two-person template that the person is bound to try
to re-establish or recover—in the playful alliteration of 'particularly
impelled to pair'. Like Freud, Wollstonecraft sees the first attachments as prototypes of later ones, which the adult cannot but seek—
'impelled'—to repeat. For the adult there is no differentiation, from
this point of view, between being part of a spousal couple and being
(as a parent) part of a parent–child couple, since both, in their own
ways, are re-findings of the first happy pairing. And depending on
how they are represented or experienced, one type of connection
may seem either detrimental or beneficial to the constancy of the
other one.

Aristotle may have been the first thinker to point to a primacy
of pair-bonding in human beings. Like Wollstonecraft, he states
this almost as a zoological fact about this particular species, but
with man and woman, not infant and mother, as the paradigm
instance:

The love between husband and wife is considered to be naturally inherent
in them. For man is by nature a pairing rather than a social creature [*anthrô-
pos gar tè phusei sunduastikon mallon è politikon*], inasmuch as the family is an

---

[15] Freud would focus on the difficulty for 'His Majesty the Baby' of learning that
he is not at the centre of the world, as the early experience of being—as all babies
must be—waited on hand and foot would have suggested to him; Freud, 'On Narcissism: An Introduction', *Standard Edition*, xiv. 91; *Gesammelte Werke*, 18 vols. (1951–87;
Frankfurt am Main: Fischer Taschenbuch Verlag, 1999), x. 167. The reference to
'"His Majesty the Baby", as we once fancied ourselves'—with the stand-out royal
phrase splendidly in English in the German text—is followed by a shift to the parental perspective: 'The child shall fulfil those wishful dreams of the parents which they
have never carried out.... Parental love [*Elternliebe*], which is so moving and at bottom
so childish, is nothing but the parents' narcissism born again.' The same point about
human prematurity is made in relation to physical rather than psychological development by Jennifer Worth in *Call the Midwife* (39): 'I have a theory that all human
babies are born prematurely. Given the human life span—three score years and
ten—to be comparable with other animals of similar longevity, human gestation
should be about two years. But the human head is so big by the age of two that no
woman could deliver it. So our babies are born prematurely, in a state of utter
helplessness.'

older and more necessary thing than the state, and procreation [*teknopoiia*] is a characteristic more commonly shared with the animals.[16]

It is by way of their (animal-like) child-making—their *teknopoiia*— that humans come to couple up; and it is natural to them to do so.[17] Aristotle sees a mutually reinforcing relationship between children-making and couple-maintaining. He enumerates various ways in which human mating, unlike that of other animals, has benefits beyond reproduction because of the complementary cohabiting qualities of the man and the woman. This seems to relegate children-making to a straightforwardly animal function, subordinate to the two-person coexistence; but there is also a contribution made by the children to the strength of the couple:

Children too, it is agreed, are a bond [*sundesmos*] between parents, which is why the childless [*hoi ateknoi*] break up more quickly. For the children are an asset common to them both, and common possession is cohesive [*sunechei dè to koinon*].[18]

A similar logic appears in Jay McInerney's New York novel *The Good Life*, set in the aftermath of 9/11 in the context of a failing marriage: 'He wasn't even sure if he loved her anymore or if, except for a daughter, they had anything in common.'[19] More broadly, the metaphor of children as the cement, or glue, of a couple relationship has stuck—being often used now to suggest that a baby will securely 'seal' a new partnership, particularly when one or both parents have other children already.

Wollstonecraft's focus on the personal attachment of the married couple, whether for good or ill, may be seen in retrospect to contain the ideological seeds of a possible disengagement of marriage from procreation. If the primary concern of marriage is the attachment between the couple, rather than the formation of a family, then

[16] Aristotle, *Ethics*, trans. J. A. K. Thomson (1955; Harmondsworth: Penguin, 1986), 280; *Ethica Nicomachea*, ed. I. Bywater (Oxford: Oxford University Press, 1894), 1162a.

[17] That the ancient Greeks thought of the pair as distinct from the group or the individual is well indicated by the existence in their language of a separate 'dual' number, between singular and plural, with its own different noun and verb endings.

[18] Aristotle, *Ethics*, 281, trans. mod.; *Ethica Nicomachea*, 1162a.

[19] Jay McInerney, *The Good Life* (London: Bloomsbury, 2006), 172.

children can become a separate issue, perhaps of secondary importance. And long before it became associated with having or not
having children, the question of choice was being polemically linked
to marriage. In Henry Fielding's novel *Tom Jones* (1749), one character challenges another: 'How often have I heard you say, that
children should always be suffered to choose for themselves?'—that
is, not to be subject to their parents' choice of a spouse on their
behalf.[20] This is earlier explained as meaning a choice that should
have to do with love and affection:

'I have, therefore, always thought it unreasonable in parents to desire to
choose for their children on this occasion, since to force affection is an
impossible attempt; nay, so much doth love abhor force, that I know not
whether, through an unfortunate but incurable perverseness in our natures,
it may not be even impatient of persuasion.'[21]

Similarly Wollstonecraft argues, in the context of the possible benefits of 'early attachments', that 'it will be a long time, I fear, before
the world will be so far enlightened that parents...shall allow [their
children] to choose companions for life themselves' (254). A husband
or wife—and there is no distinction, from this point of view—is a
'companion' whom only their own prospective companion can
'choose', and vice versa; the deciding of a marriage is not, or should
no longer be, a matter for the existing families of the future partners. Or specifically, for the parents: it is notable that both Fielding
and Wollstonecraft not only isolate them from other family members who might be thought to have an interest of whatever kind in
a marriage that is in prospect, but also represent them as dual subjects (it is not suggested that their views might differ from one
another). Novels of the time abound in dramatizations of the conflict
between marrying for love and marrying according to familial needs
or demands.[22] The normalization of the love-match is one indication

[20] Henry Fielding, *Tom Jones* (1749), ed. John Bender and Simon Stern (Oxford:
Oxford University Press, 1996), 684.

[21] Fielding, *Tom Jones*, 680.

[22] On this preoccupation in eighteenth-century English novels, see Ruth Perry,
Novel Relations: The Transformation of Kinship in English Literature and Culture, 1748–1818
(Cambridge: Cambridge University Press, 2004).

of the beginning of the period in which close relationships have increasingly come to be envisaged in terms of personal choice.

The growing emphasis on the right of individuals to choose their own partner both raises the value of the marital relationship and downgrades the significance of having children. Written in the heat of post-Revolutionary arguments in France about marriage and divorce, with radically liberalizing legislation enacted in 1792, Suzanne Necker's *Réflexions sur le divorce* (1802) contributed to the counter-movement which would culminate in the much more restrictive Code Napoléon of 1804. Necker's short book against divorce indicates a developing distinction between the marital bond and the children that may follow from it. It is not a reason for divorce, Necker says, that there are no children in a given marriage—because children are not the first object of marriage. Otherwise, people would be no different from animals, who reproduce because that is in their nature. 'If the primary purpose of marriage, as of life, is the happiness of the individual, not the multiplication of the species, then infertility [*la stérilité*] can no longer be put forward as an argument for divorce.'[23] Instead, marriage is founded on friendship, *l'amitié conjugale* (104).

Despite a clear Christian framework, Necker does not put the needs of family or community before those of the man or woman she neutrally describes as an 'individual', entitled as such to a companionate happiness that marriage is suited to provide. This is not to say that children are not considered. Necker notes that 'a large family [*famille nombreuse*], the fruit of a faithful and long union, prolongs our being indefinitely' (64). But even here, it is implied that the pleasurable perpetuation would be meaningless without the accompanying long marriage; the advantage that many children bring is not so much to do with a different or additional kind of relationship as with their extension of the parents' own lives. Later on, they may provide grandchildren: 'having received their birth from us, they will in their turn enable us to be born again' (34). Children may also be pleasing because of their likeness to oneself or

---

[23] Madame Necker, *Réflexions sur le divorce* (Paris: Pougens, 1802), 16. Further references will be given within the main text.

to one's spouse, and incidentally, for a father, because of their love-enhancing proof of a wife's fidelity:

Nature, thus becoming the guarantee and interpreter of conjugal love, enjoys consecrating the chaste sentiments of a faithful wife with her inimitable brush; and all the looks a tender father gives to sons that resemble him fall again on their mother with a renewed gentleness. (35)[24]

Children serve as a confirmation of a good marriage; they are not represented as a separate source or object of personal attachment, for either parent—let alone, as in Wollstonecraft, as an alternative outlet for affections unused or wrongly used in the marriage.

Children do have a secondary but distinct role in Necker's argument—and partly, as with later perspectives, because of the damage that might be done to them by their parents' separation. The image of Medea stabbing her two children because Jason has left her for another woman is used as the (extreme) illustration of the possible ill effects that can ensue. But what this proves, for Necker, is still the primacy of the tie between the two parents: the story provides 'a terrible image of the effects of divorce, and of the indifference or even hatred it can inspire for the offspring [*fruits*] of a love that no longer exists!' (38). More commonly, parents who have parted are likely to lose interest in their children: 'There is no doubt...that the children of a mother and father who have become strangers to one another through divorce are no longer so close to their parents' hearts, nor so essential to their happiness' (46).

Necker does take into consideration some definite differences between the sexes; but these amount to complementary personality traits—principally, that women are sympathetic, 'better suited than men to sharing and diminishing the bitter things in life', while men give them support (29); or that men love glory, while

---

[24] The same image of nature's production of an exact copy—here a reprint—that ratifies the genuineness of the wife occurs at the end of Shakespeare's *The Winter's Tale*: 'Your mother was most true to wedlock, Prince; | For she did print your royal father off, | Conceiving you' (Shakespeare, *The Winter's Tale*, ed. Ernest Schanzer (London: Penguin, 1986), Act 5, scene 1, lines 123–5).

women are good at 'pointing the way and judging the winners' (11). Far from the notion of a primitive separation of maternal women and periodically lustful men, coming together for mutual convenience, Necker's model is one of soulmates—'Marriage joins together our scattered affections; it places two souls in a common life' (11).

The clear subordination of children as a marital objective, and the corresponding promotion of the couple's own attachment, is also apparent, as we have seen, in Wollstonecraft's *Vindication*. Like Necker, Wollstonecraft advocates the lifelong value of marital friendship; but whereas Necker stresses the desirability of having someone with whom to share your later years, Wollstonecraft is more interested in arguing for the advantages of early marriage, allowing 'children ... to choose companions for life themselves'. For both sexes spouses are 'companions', and 'for life'; an 'early attachment' is a means of moral stabilization for characters who might otherwise be at risk. Children, for these children, are not the point; it is their personal 'choice' of each other that is paramount.

Wollstonecraft denounces the woman who conducts her life as if she was 'born only to procreate and rot' (133). Necker says that infertility in a first marriage is not a ground for divorce, 'nature's principal aim, in the institution of marriage, being the happiness of the two spouses, with the reproduction of their being only a secondary aim' (15). When having children is a matter of biology—'the multiplication of the species', or procreating and rotting, as every plant or animal does—it is unworthy of the human individual. It makes sense, within this framework, for the notion of choice to be extended from marriage to parenthood, and for children-choosing to become a further option after spouse-choosing. Eventually, in our own time, children have become a choice apart—but the 'biological' child, far from suggesting parental capitulation to mere species-life, is now the child of choice.

Postscript

The model of (rational) choice, of an individual 'right to choose' in matters of childbearing, has had huge political importance but it has also the disadvantage of simplification when tangled up with the real complexities of decisions to do with having or not having children. To 'choose for themselves' in the matter of spouses is surely better than having that choice made by others; but the political need to claim rights of self-determination has come at the cost of not acknowledging that some choices cannot be straightforward or may turn out to have consequences that were unforeseeable or unimagined at the time. We speak of a choice in relation to having children as if it always involved, for any one person, a single mind. There ought to be, as one contributor to an anthology called *Why Children?* put it in 1980, 'a right to ambivalence'.[25] Certainly the 'gut feeling' of unequivocal sureness is good for any decision, reproductive or not: it evokes an experience free from the divisions and distresses that mar a choice that is other than clear to the chooser. But even a reproductive choice felt as simple and wholehearted in this way may be met with the countering force of rejection from a potential co-parent, or from the social environment in which the would-be or would-not-be parent finds herself or himself. The aftermath of a 'choice' to have or not have, to keep or not keep a baby may well echo on into long-after times of partial or huge regrets, resentments, or guilt. These are the secret stories not often or easily told, that may be unspeakable for the bearer or deliberately left behind; their weight may vary as the culture changes or the person grows older, and sometimes, at a much later time, in a much different context from the moment of choice, they come out.[26]

[25] Kathy West, in Stephanie Dowrick and Sibyl Grundberg (eds.), *Why Children?* (London: Women's Press, 1980), 179.

[26] Perhaps the most visible recent example of how the stories of choice may change over time, both for the person and in relation to the surrounding culture, is that of teenage women who gave up babies for adoption in the middle decades of the twentieth century—with, in effect, no active choice and no counselling—for the benefit of childless couples who, in the standard argument, could give their children a better prospective life. See the remarkable interviews with American women presented in Ann Fessler, *The Girls Who Went Away: The Hidden History of Women Who Surrendered Children for Adoption in the Decades Before* 'Roe v. Wade' (New York: Penguin Press, 2006).

4

Foundling Fathers and Mothers

A baby is abandoned by parents who cannot or will not give it a life; by good fortune it is rescued; eventually, it goes on to achieve great things. In some such sequence, this foundling story has been powerful and perennial, all the more so in that it is so far from likely reality in cultures in which, for whatever reasons, the abandonment of infants has been common.[1] The typical story is focused on the future of the found child—not on the parents on either side, abandoning or adoptive. Two famous ancient foundling stories are those of Moses and Oedipus. Each involves a rescued baby boy who later becomes a great man, but the reasons for parents leaving the child to his fate are very different.

In Exodus, Moses is hidden by his mother in the bulrushes in the hope that he may escape the death that has been decreed for newborn Hebrew boys; the baby is then found by the punitive Pharaoh's own daughter, and she decides to keep him as her own child. She has him looked after by a wet-nurse who, unknown to her, is none other than his own real mother. In abandoning him, Moses' mother does what she can to give her baby a chance of being saved—and she succeeds not just in that, but in being able to be a mother to him after all. She becomes, in effect, a surrogate surrogate mother—not really a surrogate, because she is his birth mother as well as his wet-nurse; not really his mother, because her position is surreptitious and delegated, and she must hand him over to his adopting mother once he has been weaned.

---

[1] For many examples of foundling stories and foundlings' own stories (but not the parents') in different cultures and historical periods, including the present, see Kate Adie, *Nobody's Child: Who Are You When You Don't Know Your Past?* (London: Hodder, 2005).

Oedipus' parents, in Sophocles' play, are not under political pressure to do what they do with their baby son; Laius, the father, is himself the ruler of Thebes. The baby is given to a servant to be exposed on the mountainside, out of fear of an oracle that has said he will grow up to murder his father and have children with his mother. Unlike Moses, this baby is meant by its parents to die. But thanks to the disobedience of the servant, who passes the baby on to someone else instead of exposing it as instructed, Oedipus is eventually adopted, by a childless royal couple in another country. The murderous evasive action of the original parents then sets in train the possibility, after all, of the terrible foreseen future. By the time that Oedipus comes to kill a stranger and then to marry and have children, he has no way of knowing that the man and woman concerned are his own parents.

The modes of abandonment of Moses and Oedipus are very different. With Oedipus, the baby is got rid of for fear of what he may do to the parents. That he is saved is not down to them, but to caring intermediaries who act as foster-parents on the way to his eventual adoption by a couple who are childless. With Moses, the baby is given every chance of being saved. He is wrapped up and put in a basket, and his older sister waits to see what will happen; then, at the moment when he has been found, it is she who comes forward with her convenient recommendation of a wet-nurse. Oedipus' adoptive parents are situated at the opposite extreme from the murderousness of his birth parents (or at least, of his father, Laius): later, Oedipus recalls his father Polybus' great love for him and attributes it to his previous childlessness. In light of the later historical likelihoods of abandoned babies, it is also notable that the parents of both Moses and Oedipus are established couples: here is no desperate young girl who has secretly had a baby. And there is no poverty: Oedipus is even the first-born son of the ruler of the city of Thebes.

In most foundling stories, whatever the outcome or the initial reasons for the parents—or one of them, or someone else—deserting the child, the focus is on a singular case and a personal dilemma or crisis. The story is presented as exceptional. Moses' abandonment is based on a political necessity (to give the boy a chance against what would otherwise be his death if he remained with his

family), yet it is unique (this baby will be Moses). But infant exposure can also be ordinary—as it probably was in Greece in the time
of Sophocles, and as it has been for instance in China through the
enforcement since the late 1970s of the national policy of one child
per family for population control.[2] In the seventeenth and eighteenth centuries, the large-scale abandonment of babies in many
European cities was recognized as a social issue that required remedial action, and charitable institutions were founded or expanded
to provide some minimal care. In most places Catholic organizations were the leading authorities; the Paris Hôpital des Enfants
Trouvés owed its development in the seventeenth century to the
initiative of a priest, Vincent de Paul. In London the establishment
in the mid-eighteenth century of the Foundling Hospital was in
great part a result of the exertions of one man, Captain Thomas
Coram, who took on a kind of general parental duty of care and
persuaded others to do the same.

Coram was a former mariner, who returned to live permanently
in England in middle age. He had been appalled, as he walked into
the centre of London, to see how many dead and dying infants were
left by the roadside, and he determined to take action. Without a
family himself, he loved being with children. In a letter of 1733, he
wrote about some German families he befriended when they were
stuck in Dover waiting to emigrate to America, casting himself as an
amiable avuncular figure:

I carry the Children a few apples, and sometimes give them a few plumbs,
a pound of malaga Raisins which costs 3d fills them with above 5 pounds
worth of Love for me. They shew it by a Dawn of Joy in their faces as soon
as they see me coming.[3]

The sweetness of small gifts, the detail of the fruits, the weights and
prices, and the return in the children's gratitude: it is a picture of
himself as one who loves to bestow happiness. Coram worked for

[2] The most extensive historical study of abandonment in a given culture is John
Boswell, *The Kindness of Strangers: The Abandonment of Children in Western Europe from Late
Antiquity to the Renaissance* (New York: Pantheon, 1988).

[3] Quoted in Ruth K. McClure, *Coram's Children: The London Foundling Hospital in the
Eighteenth Century* (New Haven: Yale University Press, 1981), 24.

nearly two decades to secure the support and funding and institutional framework that culminated in the admission of the Foundling
Hospital's first infants in 1741. A Royal Charter had been granted
by George II in 1739, and the king personally gave £2,000 towards
the building of the Chapel when the Hospital later moved to its own
substantial grounds.

On the night the Hospital first opened, in temporary accommo-
dation, thirty babies were admitted, eighteen boys and twelve girls;
after that there was no more room. The women turned away were
implored not to 'Drop any of their Children in the Streets where
they most probably must Perish', but to wait for more places to
become available.[4] To abandon or not to be able to abandon a baby
might be equally painful, as the minutes written up the day after
poignantly record:

On this Occasion the Expressions of Grief of the Women whose Children
could not be admitted were Scarcely more observable than those of some
of the Women who parted with their Children, so that a more moving
Scene can't well be imagined.[5]

This note also brings in a second group, apart from the abandoning
and would-be abandoning mothers, for whom the women's distress
is a 'Scene', 'observable' to those who are in a different situation
but moved by what they witness. These more fortunate spectators
form another set of those involved in the pathetic event; the report
is already distinguishing them at the beginning of the evening,
before the eight o'clock opening time, when there were 'a great
number of People crowding about the door, many with Children
and others for Curiosity'.[6] The presence of the curious on this first
night is not accidental, for the new institution depended on just
such sympathy on the part of people who would have the means to
help it financially. It had been an inspired initiative of Coram's to
seek out the signatures of aristocratic women on his petition for a
Royal Charter.

[4] Foundling Hospital Daily Committee Minutes, 26 March 1741, quoted in
McClure, *Coram's Children*, 50.

[5] Kit Wedd, *The Foundling Museum* (London: The Foundling Museum, 2004), 15.

[6] Quoted in McClure, *Coram's Children*, 49.

From the beginning of its history—and at the beginning of each infant's own life there—the hospital presented a stirring spectacle of maternal emotion. Even the method of selection, developed later on, was painfully conducive to dramatic tension. One by one, women with their babies came up to draw a coloured ball from a bag. A white one meant admission, pending medical tests; black meant rejection; red meant a stand-by position, in case a white-ball baby was not accepted (as happened if they were found to be too sickly or more than two months old). As well as the drama of this initiatory event, the Hospital presented more ordinary scenes: it was also open to visitors who came to see the children going about their daily routine. And there was a second kind of uplifting experience on offer when the new buildings were finished on what was then the outskirts of London, in Bloomsbury. Members of polite society were able to enjoy cultural benefits as well as the sight of the children. There were concert performances, with Handel among the contributors. Paintings were donated by leading artists of the time, who also acquired a much needed London exhibition space. William Hogarth—like Coram a childless married man—was a very active supporter of the new institution; he was one of its Governors and gave works of his own, including a portrait of Coram himself, to be hung in its gallery.[7] So the institution played a quite different second role, providing cultural resources to practitioners and audiences of the higher classes who would then give their works or their money in aid of the primary project.

The children themselves were objects of support and sympathy to their benefactors, but they were not given the educational or other means to grow into members of the cultured society that moved within the walls of where they lived. At the age of 10 or 11, they were sent out into the working world as apprentices; the girls became servants and the boys learned trades or became soldiers or sailors. A secondary justification for the founding and funding of the institution at all was the idea that children, as future workers, provided a national resource that would otherwise go to waste. In 1737, in the text of his petition to the king, Coram had argued that 'such a

---

[7] On Hogarth's involvement with the Hospital see Jenny Uglow, *Hogarth: A Life and a World* (London: Faber, 1997), esp. chapter 16.

Foundation under good Management, would not only save the lives of many of Your Majesty's Subjects, but be a means of rendering them useful to the Publick, either in the Sea or Land Services'.

The children's destiny was to be respectable, humble, and publicly useful. In the moral climate of the time, it would have been difficult to attract support for a venture that appeared to be seeking to offer more than that to young people who were usually illegitimate as well as poor. But their expectations could sometimes seem grander, not only because of the unique environment in which they were being brought up. In the first years of the Hospital's existence, children were regularly baptized with names (including surnames) that were those of the Hospital's Governors, who formally acted as godparents. There was many a young Thomas or Eunice Coram, or William Hogarth, or an aristocratic-sounding Marlborough or Plantaganet. But there were instances later when those who had been so named claimed kinship with those who had adopted them as godchildren in this nominal way. This was not what had been intended, and the practice was discontinued, with infants instead given ordinary names—or else famous names whose primary owners were not likely to be troubled by their new namesakes: William Shakespeare, John Milton, or Michelangelo. Two girls were named after characters in Fielding's *Tom Jones*. The institutional parenthood, however well intentioned, was not individualized for either the benefactors or the beneficiaries.

In one important sense, the infants taken into the Foundling Hospital were not technically foundlings. They had not been left somewhere and picked up by good luck, but were brought in deliberately by mothers (or someone connected with a mother) who might otherwise have been driven to desert them. The Hospital was founded with a view to putting an end to the practice of exposure; it was a kind of halfway house, giving the possibility of a continuing life to babies whose parents had no means of nurturing them. It also held out the chance that parents might one day be able to take back their offspring if their circumstances became easier. To this end, relinquishing mothers were issued with a formal document which could be used in the future to identify and reclaim their children (it could also be used, if they were challenged, as proof that they had not murdered them). Parents also left tokens and letters for their children to find when older. As well as giving the child something to know their love by, these could also serve a practical purpose of future identification. A sheet of paper ripped in two or a piece of ribbon that could be matched: such things symbolized a sense of being like something torn in half but still capable, one day, of being put back together.[8]

The fragile threads of a possible means of reconnection were all the more vital in that mothers gave up their babies anonymously—and babies were baptized and given new names upon their admission. Both the formal anonymity and the leaving behind of personal tokens of identification occurred in the foundling institutions which existed in other European cities such as Lisbon, Florence, and Amsterdam, whose practices—well researched in the preparatory period—had provided templates for the running of the new London hospital. In its existing form, the Paris Hôpital des Enfants Trouvés dated from 1670; in the eighteenth century, the number of babies exposed in Paris was over 5,000 a year, rising twice in the early 1770s to over 7,000.[9] In the nineteenth century an arrangement called the *tour* came into use in Paris and elsewhere in continental Europe. This was a rotating cylindrical device which enabled a person to deposit a baby outside the hospital building; the *tour* then swung round and the bundle, perhaps with a note and some trinkets to be found in its wrappings, was picked up by receiving hands on the other side.

When the London hospital opened, the numbers of prospective babies were far too many to accommodate if there was to be a realistic chance of healthy life for those they took in; mortality rates for babies admitted to other such institutions were such that few, despite their formal rescue, survived a year. The London hospital was built

---

[8] Surviving tokens and trinkets are conserved, and can be seen, at the Foundling Museum in London, on the site of the old Hospital; as can others from the Paris Hôpital des Enfants Trouvés at the Musée de l'Assistance Publique de Paris. On the ribbons and other textile tokens in the London collection, see John Styles, *Threads of Feeling: The London Foundling Hospital's Textile Tokens, 1740–1770* (London: Foundling Museum, 2010).

[9] The figures are taken from a table compiled by Jacques Tenon for his *Mémoires sur les hôpitaux de Paris*, published in 1788; see the catalogue of the Musée de l'Assistance Publique de Paris (Paris, 2004), 41.

to house just under 400 children at any one time; in having a selective admissions policy it departed from the practices of all its European equivalents. A formal system of appraisal vetted wet-nurses and apprentice employers, and children also received the best available medical care during their years in London. In this respect— and partly thanks to the smaller numbers—standards of welfare were much superior to those in the comparable institutions on the Continent. There was however one brief period at the end of the 1750s when open access was tried by the London hospital, because government funding was granted on that condition.[10] With numbers far beyond capacity, the mortality rate rose to 70 per cent (from 30 per cent, which was not, at the time, thought excessive). Babies were dispatched from all parts of the country to London, many dying on the way; six regional hospitals were then planned to meet the need that had been revealed.[11]

In this period of the founding of foundling hospitals, there was no expectation that infants taken in might be given to childless couples; this was nothing like the moral climate of the twentieth century in which illegitimate children would be (anonymously) adopted by infertile married couples to be raised as their own, and often with a change of social class.[12] But very occasionally, experiments might be made. In 1769 Thomas Day, an avid reader of Rousseau's *Emile*, plucked two likely girls from the offshoot Shrewsbury foundling hospitals, one from Shrewsbury, with a view to having them educated

[10] During the six years of 1750 to 1755, before the period of the General Reception which began in June 1756, just over 2,500 babies were brought to the Hospital and fewer than 800 accepted—a rate of admissions below one in three.

[11] The building of the branch foundling hospital in Shrewsbury had a curious history. It was projected, like the London hospital, on quite a grand scale, on a site above the town. Belatedly finished in 1765 after lengthy funding difficulties, for the same reason it had to close only a few years later. In the mid-1780s the building was bought for a bargain price by the town's five parishes and converted to a 'House of Industry', later officially a workhouse. In a final twist, it was sold in 1871 to Shrewsbury School and converted into facilities for some of the well-parented boys attending that establishment—a function it still performs.

[12] On the modern history of adoption see for instance Jenny Keating, *A Child for Keeps: The History of Adoption in England, 1918–45* (London: Palgrave Macmillan, 2008); Barbara Melosh, *Strangers and Kin: The American Way of Adoption* (Cambridge, Mass.: Harvard University Press, 2002).

up as future wife material for himself (he planned to choose only one, however); this scheme bore some resemblance to that of 'Jean-Jacques', the private tutor of Rousseau's fictional Emile, who picks out the perfect country girl for his young man's wife, even courting her on his behalf. Day's plan involved a conscious merging of paternal and husbandly roles—or an open acknowledgement that in some respects there was no difference, since both have authority over and responsibility for the female in their care.[13]

But although there was no intention that children at the Foundling Hospital would move on to become part of a small-scale family, or that within the institution, special carers would be assigned to them individually, this was effectively what did happen in their first years. The babies taken in at under two months were initially sent to wet-nurses outside London. These were usually the wives of labourers and artisans, and the children lived as part of their families before being returned for their later childhood to the London institution. When they were apprenticed a few years later, it was sometimes possible, when warm attachments had been formed, for them to go back to their foster-families: not unlike an informal adoption.

The charitable care of Governors and lady supporters (all the Governors were men) did not extend to individual connections with the children: in this sense, the different social levels were clearly separated. But one of the paintings given for exhibition offered a powerful image of love and redemption through the saving adoption of a child across social and political divisions. Coram had chosen a representation of baby Moses in his basket for the seal of the new hospital. Hogarth's painting in 1746 of 'Moses Brought before Pharaoh's Daughter', which was hung on the wall of the Hospital's Court Room, portrays the second moment of relinquishment in the

---

[13] On Thomas Day and the girl he named Sabrina Sidney see Jenny Uglow, *The Lunar Men: The Friends Who Made the Future, 1730–1810* (London: Faber, 2002), 185–8. In another rampant blurring of the distinction between the paternal and the husbandly, Elizabeth Inchbald's novel *A Simple Story* (1791) creates wildly complex permutations of guardian–ward and father–daughter relationships across two generations, both centred on the same authoritarian man. He first—without Day's design—finds himself in love with his flighty 18-year-old ward, then a generation later eventually allows himself to romantically rescue and recognize their daughter, previously spurned because of her mother's adultery.

biblical story, when the little boy is transferred to his adoptive
mother after he has been living with his wet-nurse—the wet-nurse
who, in reality, is the mother who had had to abandon him.[14]
A chubby, curly-haired blond boy stands between two mothers,
unsure but not visibly unhappy; seated on the right is the richly
colourful figure of the princess, robed in red and orange, welcoming
her little son; behind, on the left of the picture, half in shadow and
looking down at him, is the mother waiting to give him up—or pass
him on. She keeps her hands together as though not to pull him
back or clasp him, and she is also being given money, the wages for
her nursing, by a bearded man to her left. She just about smiles.
The moment is meant to be associated with the return of the Hospital's foundlings from their infant and toddler years in the country
to the welcoming, adoptive Hospital which will be their home for
the next few years. It vividly portrays a boy who has not one but
two devoted mothers: one who has given him her early love and the
other who is in a position to give him the best of everything, including her affection. Moses' mother is also a figure for the contemporary
Foundling mother who gives up her baby because she has no means
to care for it; the biblical parallel exalts her, as exemplary and piti-
able rather than culpable or inadequate. It was out of necessity that
Moses' mother exposed—and now again hands over—her baby.

The painting of Moses with his two mothers suggests no conflict
between the women; the boy is in transition from one to the other,
or shared between the two. Both of them will have been his mother,
and both have given him life—one by birth and then feeding, the
other by saving and rearing him. The only man in the picture is to
one side, in a subordinate but supportive role; it is as if the whole of
the boy's upbringing is in the hands of women. The Exodus account
of Moses' beginnings brings out this aspect even more. It is the
midwives who are ordered to kill the sons born to the Hebrews, and
who fail to, defending themselves on the grounds that Hebrew
babies are born too quickly, before they can get there.[15] The

---

[14] The picture is now on display in the Court Room of the Foundling Museum in
Bloomsbury.

[15] The 1962 edition of *Peake's Commentary on the Bible* gives this claim a would-be
realistic justification, based implicitly on twentieth-century anthropological distinctions:

fortunate farming out of the baby to his own mother depends on the watchful help of his older sister, who appears at the opportune moment to suggest to Pharaoh's daughter that she could find a suitable nurse. Moses' mother has kept and hidden the baby for three months. The only significant part played by a man is that of the brutal ruler, demanding the death of the Hebrew children—and resisted by his own daughter as well as by the midwives.

'Moses Brought before Pharaoh's Daughter' places one of the Foundling Hospital's own rites of passage in an illustrious frame. It elevates the regular scene of each child's return to a royal level, as if bestowing the prestige of historical and biblical destiny on every small foundling boy or girl coming back from their country life. In reality, of course, the Hospital's children were not, like Moses, marked out by God or the Governors as leaders and prophets, or personally adopted by princesses. But they did move (around the age of 4 or 5) from relatively humble family dwellings to a grand building in the capital. And they were, like Moses, brought to their new home by an individual foster-mother. Even if she was not at the same time the real mother, as Moses' was, the association could only help to honour the place of the present-day nurses—just as the very choice of an Old Testament analogue brought significance to the moment experienced by all the Hospital children and their temporary mothers. Hogarth's painting endowed the common story of a mother or foster-mother relinquishing a child with the particularity and the value of a biblical narrative.

A picture painted more than a century after the Hospital's foundation shows another scene of exchange between two mother figures. This time what is presented is not an elevated comparison through a famous story but a realistic representation of another emblematic rite of passage in the Hospital's own practices. Yet the new picture clearly echoes the composition of 'Moses Brought before Pharaoh's Daughter', with the effect once again of harking back to the biblical scene, and also to what by the mid-nineteenth century was the historical prestige of Hogarth himself. In Emma Brownlow

'The midwives' excuse is substantiated amongst primitive peoples—with them birth is generally easier than with more civilized folk'; Matthew Black and H. H. Rowley (eds.), *Peake's Commentary on the Bible* (London: Nelson, 1962), 210.

King's 'The Foundling Restored to its Mother' (1858), the receiving mother is again on the right, and she is dressed in clothes that have shades of red and orange, though more muted than the colours of Pharaoh's daughter's robe in the earlier picture. This woman is not royal or exotic, but is the real-life Victorian mother who has come, open-armed, to reclaim the child she left with the Hospital. As in Hogarth's Moses picture, there is a second woman on the left who has brought the toddler along for the moment of restoration; she clasps her hand while looking fondly down at her. A third woman, slightly bent, warmly smiling, stands behind the reclaiming mother—perhaps *her* mother. There is also a man standing between the two principal women and behind a table, evidently responsible for the formal procedures of the occasion. Tossed on the floor, no longer required—it has served its purpose—is the official document given to the mother at the time of surrendering her baby to enable her to prove her parental identity. A wastepaper basket appears under the desk with more papers in it—perhaps to signify that other such happy returns have taken place, and that the uncomfortable official record kept by the mother in place of her baby can now be dispensed with.

In the Foundling Hospital's practices and its own mythology there were three scenarios in which an infant or child was handed over by or to a mother or mother figure. The first was the moment when the (birth) mother brought her child in; the second, when the foster-mother brought the toddler back from the country where he or she had been since infancy; the third, as in King's painting, if a mother came to take back the child she had left behind. The first of these scenes was a *sine qua non*, in effect the occasion of a baby's beginning life as a Hospital foundling. The second happened as long as the child did not die in the first few years. The third was the dream: the moment of recognition and reunion, with the mother's happy return, in better circumstances, to the place where previously she had had to leave her child behind. In practice, it happened very rarely.[16]

---

[16] Between 1840 and 1860, out of 834 infants admitted, 26 were reclaimed; figures are from the Hospital's records cited in Catherine Roach, 'The Foundling Restored: Emma Brownlow King, William Hogarth, and the Public Image of the Foundling Hospital in the 19th Century', *British Art Journal*, 22 September 2008, n. 30. The ratio is about one in 32.

By the time of King's painting, the restoration of child to mother (and mother to child) involved a fantasy not just of the mother's improved material situation, but of her moral improvement too. When the Hospital began, there had been no selection process based on criteria other than the baby's age and state of health. Admission, when granted, was not only anonymous but no questions were asked of the mother. The child might or might not be without a father; many married parents found themselves unable to support a new baby (and the same was true of the Paris hospital: destitution was not confined to women or girls on their own). But in 1763 a new admissions procedure of 'petitioning' had been introduced, which required that applicants make a case in writing. From 1801, illegitimacy became a formal requirement; from then on foundling children were identifiable in terms of their irregular parentage.

The painter Emma King, *née* Brownlow, was herself, in a sense, a later fruit of foundling beginnings. Her father, John Brownlow, had grown up in the Hospital (he arrived as a baby in 1800) and had stayed on to work in the office there. He eventually became its Secretary in 1847, and continued in that post until his retirement in 1872. Brownlow was an enthusiastic advocate and publicist for the institution which had been his life. As a person and as a writer about the Hospital he influenced Dickens, who honoured him by giving his name to Mr Brownlow, the genial old man who adopts Oliver Twist—originally a foundling. Emma Brownlow King carried on her father's work, promoting the virtues and values of the institution through pictures of its daily life and rituals. 'The Foundling Restored to its Mother' was the first of a set of four pictures commissioned from the foundling's daughter.

Emma Brownlow King's mid-nineteenth-century picture resonates with two novels published in the same period, in which a foundling figures. Three years after it was painted, George Eliot's *Silas Marner* (discussed in Chapter 7) might almost have had the title 'The Foundling Given to the Father'. A million narrative miles from the ordinary outcomes of nineteenth-century child abandonment, which was not uncommon,[17] the novel also moves away from the

---

[17] Eliot's first novel, *Adam Bede* (1859), is concerned with the story of the abandoning rather than (as in *Silas Marner*) the adopting parent. On *Adam Bede* in this connection

foundling fantasy story. First, by throwing the emphasis not on the child and its future but rather on what her arrival does for the one who becomes the parent: Silas's own life is transformed by suddenly finding himself a father. And second, by having the grown-up found-ling decide, when given the chance of transferring to the affluent milieu of her natural father, to stay with the lower-class father who has brought her up. The moral force of Eliot's story is all the more insistent for its implicit departure from the usual order of unhappy and happy narrative events in which a baby or child is miraculously raised, in both senses, for a superior destiny. *Silas Marner* is a new kind of foundling fairytale, in which gold-love is replaced by a girl-love, and miserable solitude by joyous fatherhood, through the for-mation of a happy-ever-after parental relationship.

In Emily Brontë's *Wuthering Heights* (1847), the story of the boy Heathcliff's finding is repeated in the recollection, long afterwards, of the housekeeper Nelly, a child herself at the time. She now tells the tale of that much earlier first telling of the tale, just after the event. Mr Earnshaw had returned to his family after three days away in Liverpool, sixty miles' walk each way, carrying back with him an unknown child. Questioned by his wife,

The master tried to explain the matter; but he was really half-dead with fatigue, and all that I could make out, amongst her scolding, was a tale of his seeing it starving, and houseless, and as good as dumb in the streets of Liverpool where he picked it up and inquired for its owner—Not a soul knew to whom it belonged, he said, and his money and time, being both limited, he thought it better to take it home with him, at once, than run into vain expenses there; because he was determined he would not leave it as he found it.[18]

The account is devoid of emotion: the picking up is not amplified by any mention of sympathy or personal urge. The boy is already so far gone out of ordinary human society that what he might have

---

see Josephine McDonagh, *Child Murder and British Culture, 1720–1900* (Cambridge: Cambridge University Press, 2003), ch. 5, and Rachel Bowlby, 'Versions of Realism in George Eliot's *Adam Bede*', *Textual Practice* 25: 3 (June 2011), 417–36.

[18] Emily Brontë, *Wuthering Heights* (1847), ed. David Daiches (Harmondsworth: Penguin, 1985), 78. Further page references will be given in the main text.

had (but does not) is not a parent but an 'owner'—someone to take charge of 'it', in a basic sense, rather than someone who might feel an affective connection to a child as his or her 'own'. Mr Earnshaw's decision to take responsibility is, again, not stated as such but assumed; the last sentence presents a pragmatic choice of one practical course of action over another. Much more than the scene of finding in *Silas Marner*, Brontë's version is also close to a possible historical reality: desertion on the streets of a large city.

This is not a finding of a foundling that is transformational for the adopting parent (who is already a father), as it is for Eliot's Silas Marner. But it has other emotional reverberations, as Heathcliff is introduced into a family in which his presence produces a violent reconfiguration of existing patterns of relationship. Mr Earnshaw presents him to his wife as 'a gift of God'—perhaps as if 'sent', like Silas's Eppie; but he adds immediately, 'though it's as dark almost as if it came from the devil' (77). The ambiguity of the child is confirmed in his naming. Nelly is absent for a while, an effect of his arrival; but when she returns, 'I found they had christened him "Heathcliff"; it was the name of a son who had died in childhood, and it has served him ever since, both for Christian and surname' (78). Heathcliff's acceptance is marked in the way that it is 'they' who have collectively chosen the name; and the boy is now 'him', not 'it'. He has been given a family name, and placed in a relationship of direct replacement to a family loss; but at the same time the neither-nor both-and name fails to integrate him fully into the social (and familial) norm.

Heathcliff's disruptive incursion has more effects on his (henceforth) siblings than on his *de facto* adoptive parents, who fade quickly from the book. His arrival generates a forever troubled family. But he is not the only person ambiguously placed in it. Nelly has described her own halfway position, sleeping over and able to play with the Earnshaw children because her mother had nursed the boy as a baby; one immediate effect of the 'gift' of Heathcliff is her own brief 'banishment' (78). When Mr Earnshaw left for Liverpool, his son and daughter had asked him to bring back as presents a fiddle and a whip—respectively; that the 'gift' he does come back with is neither of these only exacerbates Heathcliff's poor reception. But Nelly was also promised a present:

He did not forget me; for he had a kind heart, though he was rather severe, sometimes. He promised to bring me a pocketful of apples and pears, and then he kissed his children good-bye, and set off.　(77)

The pocketful does not materialize any more than the other children's gifts, but it is here, in connection with apples and pears for Nelly, who is not his own child, that the kind heart is named—the kind heart unmentioned when, shortly after in Nelly's story of his 'tale' of what happened, he took up a foundling boy.

5

Childlessness

Euripides' *Medea*

In *The Interpretation of Dreams*, at the end of a famous few pages about Sophocles' *Oedipus the King* and Shakespeare's *Hamlet*, Freud throws in a quick reference to another tragedy. He has just mentioned the similarity of the name Hamlet to that of Shakespeare's son Hamnet, who died when he was a boy. 'Just as *Hamlet* deals with the relation of a son to his parents', he says, 'so *Macbeth* (written at approximately the same period) is concerned with the subject of childlessness [*Kinderlosigkeit*].'[1] In that smoothly symmetrical 'Just as...so' ('*Wie...so*'), a great deal is taken for granted. It is as if by moving from the child's perspective to the parent's or parents' we might complete a whole picture in which the two sides balance each other and can be viewed in comparable terms. Parental feelings are the counterpart of children's feelings; there is an interdependence between the two, with the qualities and intensities of one side being of a similar order to those on the other.

Where there is a child, there is or has been a parent; that much is true. But also: where there is a child there are or have been parents, in the plural, and here lies the first of many discrepancies that break up the seeming reciprocity of the relation. Or take the reverse formulation: where there is a parent, or a parental couple, there is a child. This breaks down straight away in the very example given, that of childlessness. Parental feelings may be at their most intense in situations where in reality there is no child: whether because, as with Shakespeare's son, the child has died; or because there has

---

[1] Freud, *The Interpretation of Dreams* (1900), *Standard Edition of the Complete Psychological Works of Sigmund Freud*, trans. James Strachey, 24 vols. (London: Hogarth Press, 1955–74), iv. 266; *Gesammelte Werke*, 18 vols. (1951–87; Frankfurt am Main: Fischer Taschenbuch Verlag, 1999), ii/iii. 272.

never yet been one, though there has been a wish for one. The word 'childlessness' refers most often to this situation: not to losing children but to wanting them—or sometimes, neutrally, simply to not having them. The bizarre new adjective 'child-free' sufficiently indicates the normally negative charge of 'childless'. There is nothing like this in relation to childhood. No child has ever sought to be born (as adolescents are prone to point out)—or, for that matter, sought not to be born (wishing not to *have been* born is a different matter); whereas parenthood can be as much dreaded as desired. Childhood is a temporally bounded state, which ideally just passes, as the individual moves on into whatever forms their adulthood may come to take. But the ending of parenthood, through a child's death or its loss in other ways, has a quite different kind of significance from the natural sequence that is supposed to take the child beyond childhood. In its own ways, this may also be true of giving up a wish for parenthood: acknowledging, with pain, that it is not going to happen, and hopefully imagining a different life.[2]

Freud's sentence about the theme of childlessness in *Macbeth* remains just that: it is not developed further, whether in relation to that particular play or to any others. At this point in *The Interpretation of Dreams* he has just presented his revolutionary 'discovery', as he puts it, about what is not yet called the Oedipus complex but will later, under that name, become the twentieth-century myth that has completely taken over the understanding of Sophocles' play. Say 'Oedipus' now, and the first association will be to Freud and childhood, not to Sophocles or Greek legend: such has been the cultural power of Freud's new version of the myth. Yet at a very simple level, when we read Sophocles' play, there is nothing to be found directly about 'Being in love with the one parent and hating the other', which is how Freud introduces the section on Oedipus.[3] On the other hand, there is a great deal of material in the tragedy about parenthood, including and especially the pre-parenthood of either fearing or longing for the arrival of children who do not yet exist.

---

[2] Rebecca Frayn's novel about IVF, *One Life* (London: Simon & Schuster, 2006), imagines this transition as a kind of benediction given by an embryologist who had been (and still somehow is) endowed with 'celestial powers' (174).

[3] Freud, *Interpretation*, *Standard Edition*, iv. 260.

This is all the more striking as the feelings are those of two contrasting sets of parents, or rather not-yet-parents, both of which, in their utterly different ways, become the mother and father of baby Oedipus. Laius and Jocasta dread parenthood (because of the fear of what the baby that is born will do to his father and do with his mother) and go to the lengths of having their baby exposed to die. Polybus and Merope, Oedipus' adoptive parents at Corinth, welcome with open arms the baby who is brought to them after he has been saved from the death on the hillside his father had ordered.

I have summarized this contrast in terms of two couples with shared feelings in each case. In contemporary cultures, the co-subjectivity of the couple who long for a baby, the couple 'desperate' for a baby, is usually taken as read; less so, the feelings of the two parents in the opposite case, when parenthood is feared or avoided. In fact, the shared subjectivity of the two couples in *Oedipus the King* is not really clear from the play, where what we are presented with is Jocasta's long-afterwards account of what Laius did to the baby (her own feelings are left chillingly unvoiced). She is making a point, she hopes, about the uselessness of oracles, since this baby that was meant to do such terrible things in fact did not (and so, as she does not add, there was no need to kill it after all). Jocasta perhaps separates herself from her former husband by saying that it was he who had the baby exposed; there is no dual 'we' at this point. Similarly in the case of the Corinthian couple, it is the father who is fore-grounded; we hear nothing whatever of Merope's feelings. Polybus is imagined by the grown-up Oedipus to feel 'longing' for him, *pothos*, now that he is no longer at home; and in a very striking moment, when Oedipus asks how his father could have loved him so much when he was given to him by someone else, the messenger simply answers that 'His childlessness taught him.'[4]

Throughout his writings, Freud sidelines parents and parenthood in favour of his focus on the feelings of children, or on those of adults as ex-children. He is writing in a post-Romantic tradition in which childhood comes to be seen as a state of passionate intensity with irrevocably formative effects on the adult the child will turn out

---

[4] Sophocles, *Oedipus Tyrannus*, ed. Richard Jebb (1885; Cambridge: Cambridge University Press, 1927), lines 1023–4.

to be. But the modern emphasis on how 'the child is father of the man' (in Wordsworth's phrase) has turned attention away from the seemingly more obvious question of how the man is or is not father of the child—or of how the woman is or is not its mother. In fact it is remarkable that Freud, who habitually questions every stage in the would-be normal development of human sexualities and identities, never seems to ask how men come to want, or not want, or want not to be fathers; fatherhood is simply taken to follow from the arrival at adult heterosexual normality, if and when that happens. In the case of women, the question is raised, with the desire for motherhood represented as the substitute and compensation for an unattainable masculinity. This has the effect of denaturalizing the child-wish by making it a secondary formation: it does not follow automatically from female nature or female biology or, as we might say today, from hormones; and in the ideological contexts of Freud's time, this is surely a radical move. He also indicates that the wish for motherhood is not simple or wholehearted; it has its source in a conflict and protest (against not being a man). Subsequent developments, however, have greatly changed the conditions in which parenthood—for both sexes—has come to be imagined or imaginable. The differences have diminished between men's and women's relative positions in the social order. Parenthood may be desired and sought independently of a relationship with a prospective co-parent. Childlessness has become a much-heard topic of public discussion as well as a major field of medical research and invention and an international business, the so-called fertility industry.

In this changed context from that of a century ago, it becomes all the more interesting and noticeable that in Greek tragedy, and not just in *Oedipus the King*, the subject of parenthood, including 'the subject of childlessness', is constantly being raised, both as matter for reflection by the chorus and as an active element in the stories of the plays. Let us consider, to take one example, Euripides' *Medea*, which has the following passage, spoken by the chorus of Corinthian women:

And I say this, that those people who are without experience of children and have never had any are ahead of parents in happiness. Those who have no children, not having the experience of children being a delight or a trouble, as they haven't happened to have them, stay well away from many troubles. For those who do have the sweet growth of children in their home, I see them worn down by worry the whole time. First, about how to bring them up well, and how to leave the children enough to live on. And then as well as this, it is not clear whether they are labouring away for worthless individuals or good ones.

And I will say what is the absolute worst thing for all human beings. For suppose that they have managed to get hold of enough to live on, and their children have physically grown to young adulthood, and they have turned out to be decent people. But then suppose bad fortune happens like this: along comes death and vanishes into Hades, carrying off the bodies of the children. What use is it then for gods to cast on men this most painful of griefs, as well as the others, grief on account of children?[5]

The capsule twentieth-century banalization of all this would have to be 'Kids! Who'd 'ave em?'—which now perhaps appears as a version of Desdemona's parent, near the beginning of *Othello*, wailing 'Who would be a father?'[6] Set in its own time, the passage is among other things a poignantly realistic evocation of the riskiness of early life and the material difficulties of having children. With great good luck—if they do not fall by the wayside through illness or because their parents cannot find the means to support them—the children may make it through to young adulthood, to *hèbè*. There are economic and emotional anxieties all the way. The kind of person the child will become is another matter of chance. This outcome is not, as it would be now, set in any likely relation to the quality of parenting or other aspects of the environment; or, for that matter, to an idea of natural inheritance, the parental or family stock. (But a notion of continuing family characteristics does sometimes figure in tragedy, for instance when Phaedra, in Euripides' *Hippolytus*, attributes her misplaced desire for her stepson to the predilection for inappropriate loves among the females of her family: her sister Ariadne's ill-fated relationship with the abandoning Theseus and, a little more potently, her mother Pasiphaë's fling with a bull.)

[5] Euripides, *Medea*, ed. Denys L. Page (1938; Oxford: Oxford University Press, 1976), lines 1090–115. Further line references will be included in the main text.

[6] Shakespeare, *Othello*, ed. E. A. J. Honigmann (1997; London: Thomson, 2006), Act 1, Scene 1, line 162.

But the point to stress most in this passage is its division of people into those who have and those who have not experienced the powerful feelings of parenthood. Motherhood and fatherhood are not distinguished (elsewhere in the play, they are, in Medea's famous proto-feminist complaints about the condition of womanhood[7]). Parenthood is the source of emotions that are both painful and constant. There is the unique pleasure of a home filled with the 'sweet growth' ('*glukeron blastèma*') of children, but this is counterweighted by the unremitting anxiety, and by the ever-present possibility of death, a child's death being 'the worst thing' that can befall anyone. Nonparents are exempt from these extremes of emotional experience.

There is irony here too, in that Medea is on the verge of deliberately bringing about this final grief that is marked out as the worst possible human life-event, the death of children. She will kill her own two sons to avenge herself on their father for taking another wife (whom she also kills): 'He shall never again in the future see alive the sons he got from me, nor will he have a child from his new bride, since that bad woman must die a bad death through my poisons [*pharmakois*]' (lines 803–6).

It is Medea's ultimate weapon against Jason's desertion of herself, which earlier—by his old servant or tutor, gossiping with Medea's old nurse—had been put like this: 'You have only just realized that everyone loves themselves more than their neighbour...since their father does not love these boys because of his marriage [*eunè*]' (lines 85–8). The self-pleasing new passion, the servant suggests, has taken Jason away from his children as well as from his first wife and first love; Medea's murder of the boys is designed, cold-bloodedly, to bring him back, too late, to his love for his children where she cannot bring him back to his love for herself. She will make him suffer for having imagined that what he feels for his new woman does away with what he has ever felt for his sons (never mind their mother).

The various speculations and strategies play on both the separability and the overlapping of several types of feeling on the part of a parent: those relating to their children, to their co-parent, and to a lover or spouse—who may be, but in this case is not, the same

---

[7] The speech concludes: 'I would rather stand three times in the battle line than give birth once'; Euripides, *Medea*, lines 250–1.

person as the co-parent. Connected with these confusions is the distinction, here marked as a likely hierarchization, between erotic and parental love. The servant attributes to Jason a forgetting of his love for his boys in the heat of the new erotic moment. Later, Medea's extreme revenge in effect does the same thing: her response is that of the slighted lover, the lover who was once at the same time the 'mother-of-his-children', but whose new position as the woman rejected for another woman leads her, like Jason himself, to go back to the priority of the sexual bond before that of the co-parents: the lover and the mother have been separated out, where once they could seem like one and the same. In another such separation, she can kill the children as the children of her faithless lover, but not as the children she loves (or rather, not as the children that 'they', the co-parents, have loved and raised together, as a pair). In the process, her own love for her children (and dread of their death) is put to one side, or put out of reach. Jason is made to come back to his paternity, and in the form of what the chorus describe as the ultimate horror of losing your children. How Medea lives with that same situation, when she has done it herself, or done it to herself, is not described: she is last seen heading off in a kind of helicopter, a genuine tragic *deus ex machina*, to find sanctuary in Athens.

Until the invention of reproductive technologies, the birth of a baby was always preceded by sex.[8] Until reliable contraception, heterosexual sex involving a woman in her childbearing years always included the risk or possibility of pregnancy. Contraception brought about a preliminary practical separation of the erotic from the procreative, and now, from the other direction, new reproductive technologies have separated the procreative from the sexual. This seems to answer to an old fantasy. In the *Medea* we find Jason ranting, against Medea's own rage: 'Mortals ought to have children

---

[8] The birth of Louise Brown through *in vitro* fertilization in 1978 is usually thought of as marking the beginning of the period of the new technologies; but before that, artificial insemination had existed for an indefinite period. In the middle of the twentieth century, 'artificial human insemination' was the subject of a special inquiry commissioned by the Archbishop of Canterbury. This recommended (but did not lead to) the criminalization of (what was not yet called) donor insemination; insemination with a husband's sperm was permissible. See *Artificial Human Insemination: Report of a Commission Appointed by His Grace the Archbishop of Canterbury* (London: SPCK, 1948).

some other kind of way, and the female species should not exist'
(lines 572–3). The prompt for this thought is that Medea—like all
women—has overreacted with her sexual jealousy. Everything's
fine, says Jason, when the sex and marriage, the *eunè*, are fine; but
if anything goes wrong with that, all hell breaks loose. Ergo, why
can't we make babies without women, without the problem of
female sexual passions? In the *Hippolytus*, a similar sentiment is
uttered by the young man who is disgusted to find that his stepmother, Phaedra, mother of two children with his father, is madly
in love with him:

Zeus, why did you settle on earth such a false and bad thing for mankind
as women? If you wanted to sow a race of mortals, then it wasn't from
women that you should have provided this. Instead, men should have put
down as payment a weight of gold or iron or bronze in your temples and
prayed for the seed of children, each according to his means, and then they
could live as free men at home, without females.[9]

In both cases, the advocacy of single-sex procreation is based on a
repudiation of the women and their disturbing feelings—for Jason,
their jealousy, and for Hippolytus, their sexuality *tout court*, which he
finds repulsive in general, not just in relation to his stepmother. The
other parent, in this case the female parent, appears as an inconven-
ience at best—though it is true that Hippolytus hardly sounds any
more keen on fatherhood than he is on sex: he attributes the reproductive wish to Zeus.

From another point of view, Hippolytus' hyperbolical scenario
may sound not unlike a kind of means-tested IVF, with the paternal
petitioners laying out gold or other currency according to what
they can afford, and going to a special temple—read hospital or
clinic—to set about getting their baby. In *Medea*, Jason's rhetorical
outburst takes on a much more realistic application than Hippolytus',
because there is an important subplot that is actually to do with a
medical remedy for infertility. Not far into the play, when Medea
is formulating her plan of action and revenge, a visitor to Corinth
turns up. This is Aegeus, the king of Athens, who has just been to

---

[9] Euripides, *Hippolytos*, ed. W. S. Barrett (1964; Oxford: Oxford University Press,
2001), lines 616–24.

consult the oracle about his childlessness—as characters in Greek
tragedy not uncommonly do (another case starts the main plot of
Euripides' *Ion*). Medea's own questioning of Aegeus about his
problem is quite detailed:

MEDEA: Why did you go to consult the oracle?
AEGEUS: In search of the seed of children—so that I could have
    children.
MEDEA: My god—so you have been living out your life childless up
    till now?
AEGEUS: I am childless through some unlucky chance.
MEDEA: Do you have a wife, or are you not married?
AEGEUS: Yes, I'm married.
MEDEA: So what did Apollo have to say to you about children then?
AEGEUS: Words more sophisticated than for a human being to figure
    out.
MEDEA: Is it permissible for me to know what the god's oracle was?
AEGEUS: Certainly, as it really needs an intelligent mind.
MEDEA: What oracle did he give? Tell me, if it is allowable for me to
    hear.
AEGEUS: Not to unloose the foot of the wineskin...
MEDEA: Until you do what or until you arrive where?
AEGEUS: Before I get back to my homeland. (668–82)

It transpires that Aegeus is planning to visit a male friend, Pittheus,
on his way back to Athens. He thinks Pittheus may have some
helpful interpretative advice. But in the meantime, Medea, his new
confidante, has other ideas. She tells him her own sad story—that
her husband has left her for another woman and she has been
ordered to leave Corinth by Jason's new father-in-law—and she asks
him to let her come to Athens. In return, she will offer him a private
treatment:

You don't know what a find you've got here. I will stop you being childless
and will get you to seed the birth of children. I know drugs [*pharmaka*] like
that. (716–18)

Medea is extremely definite in what she says, using the straight
future tense without ifs and maybes, and starting off by telling him
how he doesn't know how lucky he is: he has come to the right
person. She has the knowledge and, more precisely, she has the

medicine. And so they strike a deal: fertility treatment in return for unconditional right of residence. Aegeus has no idea that the banished Medea will be a multiple murderer if and when she arrives in Athens. There is also an irony, never voiced, in the fact that Medea the genius child-maker will, by the time she gets to help Aegeus make babies, have killed her own two children; and almost the same word, *pharmakoi* or *pharmaka*, is used for these drugs as for the poison that kills the new bride.

Reading these scenes now, in the light of the contemporary issues of assisted reproduction, a number of features stand out. First, that childlessness is an ordinary theme: it is spoken about and solutions for it are sought. In our own culture, treatment for infertility is now a very big medical field—and a vast global business—and it attracts a great deal of media attention. But this is quite a new phenomenon. Until relatively recently, infertility was not a prominent subject of medical research or public discourse (the private can never be known, and must be infinitely variable). It came to be so in the later twentieth century, especially following the beginning of IVF.[10] The second noticeable thing is that it is the men who go to the equivalent of the fertility consultant, the oracle, and that the problem is assumed to be theirs in some quasi-biological sense. Aegeus essentially wants to improve his sperm quality (the Greek word, *sperma* or seed, is the same). But there is nothing proto-feminist about this emphasis. The dominant (though not the only) model of reproduction at the time was one in which the mother had no seed-equivalent, no gamete of her own, as she does with the egg; her womb was simply the nursery for the baby that the father's seed implanted. Aegeus speaks of himself as childless, *apais*; it is his own misfortune, and a wife is just one of the necessary conditions for overcoming it (there is no issue about defective wombs, either). This makes it all the more interesting that in the chorus's description of the differences between parents and non-parents, there is no distinction between mothers and fathers: the parents are neutrally parents, both in their having of children and in their rearing of them. A further

---

[10] For a powerful study of the development of treatments for involuntary childlessness through the twentieth century, see Naomi Pfeffer, *The Stork and the Syringe: A Political History of Reproductive Medicine* (Cambridge: Polity Press, 1993).

striking aspect of the Aegeus and Medea exchange is that the remedy is a combination of the medical and the magical—with drugs, special drugs, which are sure to work. The cure is to be administered by a woman, and it is part of an economic exchange, a *quid pro quo* or payment in kind in which Medea will get her asylum in return for her extraordinary services. On both sides, the price is high, and this adds to the value of what is being offered and expected—a phenomenon that often seems to operate in contemporary reproductive medicine too. But in today's world there is also the specific issue of commodification, whereby parenthood becomes in this respect comparable to any number of other consumerly 'options'; on the websites of clinics and surrogacy and donor agencies it appears as a uniquely satisfying goal.[11]

There is also a suggestion of oriental powers and expertise. Medea is not a Greek; she is from the east. She has esoteric knowledges which are suspect in Greek terms, but which for all that are known and believed to work. In 2009 the *Observer* magazine had a feature about a Chinese fertility doctor, a woman, practising in London, whose success rates using TCM (Traditional Chinese Medicine), including acupuncture and special herbs, were far above those of other fertility clinics at the time. This doctor, according to the evidence of the article, was also gaining increasing respect among more mainstream practitioners. She is Medea without the menace.[12]

In Greek tragedy, as now, childlessness is anything but a silent subject, but the childlessness for which remedies may reasonably be sought has changed out of all recognition. There are surprising and coincidental similarities to very recent real historical possibilities in

---

[11] Some versions of transnational adoption may carry the same consumerly associations. A Matthew Pritchett cartoon in the *Telegraph* perfectly captures the would-be comparability of babies to other purchasable goods. A man is sat at the computer, a wife figure looks over his shoulder at the screen; he says: 'I've either just done our weekly shop at Tesco, or I've adopted twins'. Part of the joke here is that the interchangeability of baby-commodities is not with anything remotely special but with a routine supermarket order. The copy I saw had no date, but must relate to the 2001 case of the Kilshaws, a British couple who bought American twins on the internet whose birth mother turned out to have sold them to another couple as well.

[12] Louise Carpenter, 'The Baby Maker', *Observer Woman Magazine*, 46, 25 October 2009, 16–23.

the picture of the would-be father going alone to get himself a child, whether a child for a marriage, as Aegeus does, or a child in order to avoid marriage, to avoid women and sex, as Hippolytus imagines doing. British tabloid newspapers and magazines love to light on extreme stories of single and double parenthood involving people who have succeeded in obtaining or having 'a child of their own', usually but not always gay in the case of men and aged in the case of single women. As one kind of historical constant, the example of Medea suggests that childlessness may have been the object of extreme or eccentric remedies since time immemorial—just as much, perhaps, in periods when it was not, as it is in our culture, a topic of public discussion. What is new today is the possibility that the wish for a child may be something set apart from any existing attachment, marital or otherwise. In *Medea* we see parental emotions being played out in relation to the bitterness that attaches to erotic relations that have been lost; just as the wish for a child may well— usually does, usually did—relate to an initial romantic tie. But there is also in *Medea*, embryonically, the chorus's categorical separation of the parental from the non-parental. And today, it is thinkable that individuals may want to form a parental tie, one-on-one, as a way of exploring a new and unique kind of relationship—as a distinctive lifestyle choice that is no longer assumed to be bound up with the making or continuing of a family centred on a man–woman couple, or any other kind of partnership. Now that new reproductive technologies can conceive babies in the absence of bodies, the historically unprecedented question arises of whether future family forms should or will retain a connection to the old conditions whereby children came from two parents, of two sexes, who once had sex.

6

A Tale of Two Parents

Charles Dickens's *Great Expectations*

Great Expectations is not known for its parental stories. But they are very much there, they are very odd, and they involve some curious precursors to the present-day possibilities of single people seeking parenthood. That these stories do not, as a rule, get noticed in Dickens's novel is indicative of the tendency for parental perspectives and presences to be missed or disregarded in relation to other stories that more readily summon attention.[1] We have all been children; perhaps, where there is a strong story of childhood emotions it is to this and not to other facets of a work that our interest is drawn, and parenthood, as in the real order of things, comes subsequent (in later life; on second reading).

On the surface, the enigmatic developments of *Great Expectations* are centred on Pip, the narrator of the story. He is the one whose childhood is marked by his encounter with the convict Magwitch, his involvement with the fabulous Miss Havisham and her daughter Estella, and then by his removal to London to be formed for the fulfilment of grand 'expectations' of undisclosed origin. Dickens evokes the feelings of a child who is powerless in the face of an assortment of tyrannical adults, from Magwitch, who appears in the opening chapter, to the frightening Miss Havisham who orders him to 'Play', to the affectionless, much older sister who is bringing him up, along with her gentle husband, Joe. The novel's world is seen through the eyes of this boy, as remembered by the somewhat

[1] For other examples of overlooked odd family scenarios in Dickens's novels see Holly Furneaux, *Queer Dickens: Erotics, Families, Masculinities* (Oxford: Oxford University Press, 2009), especially chapter 1.

chastened man of middle years who now recounts what has been his misdirected life (the unrelinquished aspiration for the love of the cold Estella who cannot love him back, the assumption that the benefactor who moved him to London was Miss Havisham, when in reality it was Magwitch). As such, *Great Expectations* has rightly been seen as a brilliant study of the emotions of childhood—for Dickens, involving more terror and impotence than Romantic wonder—in keeping with the nineteenth century's relatively new-found attention to that state and time of life (the novel was published in 1861).

But underneath and alongside the story of Pip's awaitings, greater and lesser, his childhood, and his ill-fated love, there are stories in this novel which are concerned with other kinds of expectation: not children's but parents'. (As if to acknowledge this, there is currently a British company called Great Expectations which chirps on its homepage: 'Hello, welcome to Great Expectations and congratulations if you are newly pregnant'; it sells maternity wear.) These parental stories are not at the forefront of *Great Expectations*, but they are there, and they stand out more now, I think, in relation to the changed circumstances and norms of parental seeking in the twenty-first century.

It would seem reasonable to suggest that before our own time, parenthood was not much of a plot-pusher, in literature or in life: it happened or it didn't, and parents took back seats in relation to the driving force of the child and subsequent adult's story, leaving the parents behind him. The child appeared as unique and central, charged with any number of possible and fascinating futures; whereas parental characters flatly fulfilled a pre-scripted part, fixed and secondary, their role being simply to enable (or else to inhibit) the young person's development. But now parenthood has moved from being a back-story, a necessary but unspectacular prequel before and behind the child's story, to becoming, potentially, a fore-grounded, front-of-house story in its own right. Previously, parenthood might figure in the child or the adult's search for identity—Who are my parents? Who was the father?—but now there is a forward direction, as parenthood comes to be commonly imagined as a significant life choice or life ambition, bound up with the identity and desires of the prospective parent or parents; one element, and perhaps at a given stage the major one, in a personal *Bildungsroman*. A parent is something to be! And crucially, whereas in its classically uneventful mode, parenthood was almost always bound up with the initial existence of a couple—some kind of attachment, whether lifelong or night-long, to a co-parent—the new parental stories need have no such mooring or starting point. A child of one's own can be, quite simply, a child that is just my child and no one else's.

Great Expectations offers a nineteenth-century fictional version of what is nowadays a frequent, not an exceptional story of the child as a 'seekling' for the parent. It features two separate instances of unmarried, unattached adults, acting on their own behalf, who go out of their way to become parents, with huge and idiosyncratic emotional and financial investment in their adopted children.[2] The first of these is Miss Havisham, the woman whose life came to a stop when she was jilted on the morning of her wedding. Miss Havisham gets herself a girl 'to rear and love'—Estella.[3] The second seeking parent is Magwitch, the transported convict, who uses the money he has made and inherited in Australia to transform the life of the boy who helped him on the marshes—Pip.

Nor are these the only adoption stories in the book. Adoption is actively sought by Miss Havisham and Magwitch for their own purposes; but (and this is a regular feature of Dickens's novels) there are many other scenarios of adoption—so many, in fact, that the

[2] For a reading of the novel in relation to adoption which concentrates on the experience of Pip and Estella, rather than on their parents, see Marianne Novy, *Reading Adoption: Family and Difference in Fiction and Drama* (Ann Arbor: University of Michigan Press, 2005), 109–14. Adoptions by single people in England and Wales in fact constituted a significant proportion of the total in the years that followed the Adoption Act of 1926. 'unmarried women, and men, generally middle-class, could and did adopt children, with legal sanction after 1926, setting themselves up publicly as unmarried parents'; but after further legislation in 1949, 'Adoption by single people became difficult and rare'; Pat Thane and Tanya Evans, *Sinners? Scroungers? Saints? Unmarried Motherhood in Twentieth-Century England* (Oxford: Oxford University Press, 2012), 42, 99. Sometimes the adopting parent was in fact the birth mother or (more rarely) father, which gave both child and parent a legal status, instead of the child being officially nobody's (*filius nullius*) for purposes of inheritance.

[3] Charles Dickens, *Great Expectations* (1861), ed. Margaret Cardwell (Oxford: Oxford University Press, 1994), 396. Further page references will be given in the main text.

unusual situation is rather the one in which a child lives with both its birth parents. This is just about true in the case of the Pocket family; though the parents, if present, are not strong on parenting: 'I saw that Mr and Mrs Pocket's children were not growing up or being brought up, but were tumbling up' (184). And it is only fully actualized at the very end, with the two-child family of Biddy and Joe Gargery—in effect a second family for Joe, who has earlier been the most loving of stepfathers to Pip. At the start of the novel the primary family is this nucleus of Pip, Joe, and Joe's wife, an unchoosing adoptive mother who has taken on the upbringing of her small brother on the death of the parents of both of them. In the same village is Biddy, the 'girl next door' figure whom Pip will spurn, and who will end up, happily, with Joe. Biddy lives with her great aunt: 'she was an orphan like myself; like me, too, had been brought up by hand' (43). In addition to these informal kinship adoptions, in which a child is raised by other members of their family than the parents because the parents have died, a number of households consist of an adult child and a widowed parent: Clara Barley and her father; the clerk Wemmick and his 'Aged P.'; Mrs Brandley and her unnamed daughter—'The mother looked young, and the daughter looked old' (296)—who are joined by Estella as a kind of paying guest. Like Biddy before her great-aunt's death, Wemmick and Clara Barley are in effect carers for their very old fathers (delightful in one case, a drunken control freak in the other).

Amid this general population of disparate types of family, Miss Havisham's famous household arrangements are already so peculiar that their inclusion of an adopted child may escape notice as being perhaps one of its less eccentric features. This is yet another of the adoptive family set-ups in the novel—and one of the two extraordinary sought adoptions on the part of wealthy adults. Both Miss Havisham and Magwitch have or had personal expectations in their adopting, and both are led to articulate these at a much later stage in the presence of their grown adoptive children.

In a characteristically Dickensian way, the two adoptions turn out to be intimately entangled in ways unknown to either parent or, for most of the novel, to either child: eventually Pip discovers that Estella's father was Magwitch. This closeness makes Miss Havisham and Magwitch something like secret co-parents—a mother and a father who are unaware that they have a child in common. Or even two: it is not just that Miss Havisham becomes the mother of Magwitch's daughter, but also that Magwitch adopts the boy who has grown up alongside Estella, regularly going round to her house. The ironies are compounded by Pip's assumption, over many years, that it is Miss Havisham who is secretly his own adopting parent, funding his change of social status—'She had adopted Estella, she had as good as adopted me' (229)—when in fact it is Magwitch, the man who is really Estella's father, although she never knows it. Overseeing both adoption narratives, to the point that Pip knows him as 'my guardian', a further parental figure is Mr Jaggers, the consummately successful criminal lawyer.

Magwitch and Miss Havisham have certain perversities, parental and otherwise, in common. Both are over-hungry, in relation to their children or their food almost interchangeably; in both cases they want too much, or can't get enough. Miss Havisham has a 'greedy look' (232)—or worse, 'a ravenous intensity that was of its kind quite dreadful' (237). After Magwitch's arrival at Pip's lodgings in London, 'He ate in a ravenous way that was very disagreeable, and all his actions were uncouth, noisy, and greedy' (327). Miss Havisham wildly feeds as she roams the house at night; the first meetings with Magwitch, when Pip is a small boy, involve his frantic consumption of all the 'wittles' that Pip can provide and procure. Both these unsociable eaters have also undertaken their adoption projects in part as a kind of revenge. By creating a gentleman Magwitch will outdo his nemesis, the higher-class Compeyson; Miss Havisham—according to Herbert Pocket—has 'brought up' Estella 'to wreak revenge on all the male sex' (175), no less. (The man who jilted her turns out—of course, this being a Dickens novel—to have been none other than this same Compeyson.) Pip then interprets the behaviour he witnesses in the same way: 'I saw in this, that Estella was set to wreak Miss Havisham's revenge on men' (298). Estella has been trained as a sort of professional man-eater, a centre of men-wrecking excellence.

Leaving aside these idiosyncrasies of attitude and behaviour, both Magwitch and Miss Havisham have actively sought (and, for that matter, bought) their children, rather than finding themselves parents in more passive or ordinary ways; and both of them at different points articulate their sense of their parenthood and their reasons for seeking out a child—a particular individual in one case (Magwitch's Pip), and a general 'girl' in the other. Magwitch, who has illegally returned from Australia specifically to see him, shows up late one night at the adult Pip's London address, and the man of expectations is confronted with the most unexpected and unwanted of declarations: 'Look'ee here, Pip. I'm your second father. You're my son—more to me nor any son' (315). However far along in the series of possible Pip-fathers Magwitch might be—it could be said that he is the third, not the second, following his stepfather Joe as well as the actual father who is dead—Pip does, against his own first 'aversion' (338), come to accept or recognize, in relation to him, the place of a son, responsible for the welfare of a parent. In his turn, he adopts as his father this man who has unilaterally made him a more-than-son.

Magwitch's claim is to the achievement of a quite specific parental project: 'Yes, Pip, dear boy, I've made a gentleman on you! It's me wot has done it!' (315). In part Magwitch sees his 'son' as a piece of property, to the extent that the gentleman state is purchasable (with clothes, with appropriate living quarters, with the personal mentoring of Matthew Pocket and his son Herbert). Magwitch describes to Pip how he would say to himself, to parry the imagined taunts of 'them colonists', 'If I ain't a gentleman, nor yet ain't got no learning, I'm the owner of such. All on you owns stock and land; which on you owns a brought-up London gentleman?' (317). But at the same time as he lays stress on Pip as a paid-for possession, there is an altogether different dynamic at work. His saying he owns him seems to be a way of asserting his rapture at what he believes his money has been able to do for both of them: Pip has become a gentleman, and he has become a father to one. And beyond even the pleasures of gentleman-making, Magwitch is also almost in love with his image of Pip, who thereby becomes a sort of perfect virtual child: 'When I was a hired-out shepherd in a solitary hut, not seeing no faces but faces of sheep till I half forgot wot men's and women's faces wos like, I see yourn' (315). Between the 'solitary' shepherd and the unique face in an unpeopled continent, Pip represents a very particular kind of only child: he is in effect the only boy in the world.

But Magwitch fervently needs not only to own, and to love, at a distance, but to 'make myself known to him, on his own ground': hence the life-risking (and in the end, life-forfeiting) illegal return from Australia. The own and the known go together. Magwitch is compelled to get Pip to recognize him for the father he wants to have been to him. To make himself known in this way is a vital, a life-and-death part of the project: bodily co-presence involving the communication of his identity as father (or second father). He needs Pip to acknowledge him for what he has done, what he has made of him: 'Well, you see it *was* me, and single-handed' (316), the one and only parent to match the one and only child.

Miss Havisham's parental story is told very differently, even though she, even more than Magwitch, has brought about a dramatic change of social place for her adopted child: Pip comes from a respectable village family, but Estella's background is the criminal underclass. In Miss Havisham's case, the money she may have put into Estella's elevation is not at issue. As a wealthy brewer's daughter, Miss Havisham has never lacked, still less earned, financial means; the sense of what newly made money can do, so primary to Magwitch's conception of his project, plays no part for her. Her adoption of Estella as her future heir is also partly to spite the assortment of sycophantic relatives who hang about waiting for her to die. There seems to be no particular mystery or ambiguity attached to Estella's position, either for herself or for anyone else. Her adopted status is known to all; more than once she addresses or refers to Miss Havisham as 'Mother by adoption' (300, 359). Her surname is Havisham, as Pip verifies by questioning Jaggers on precisely this point (239); she appears to have all the normal expectations of a daughter of the family, and is even sent off to a finishing school abroad.

Late in the novel's time, Miss Havisham, now full of regrets at the miserable results of Estella's emotional formation ('What have I done?' she keeps repeating), gives a compressed narrative of how and why she came to adopt her, with the help of the lawyer Jaggers:

I had been shut up in these rooms a long time (I don't know how long; you know what time the clocks keep here), when I told him that I wanted a little girl to rear and love, and save from my fate. (396)

The three very different objectives are precisely stated: rearing, loving, and saving from having the same story as herself. Implicitly, a girl is specified because only a girl is comparable enough to Miss Havisham herself to have a different 'fate'. There is no mention of making (or not making) her a lady, which happens as though as a matter of course.

Magwitch boasts of having 'made' Pip a gentleman; Miss Havisham is less concerned with making Estella a lady than with cultivating a particular kind of love-proof personality. Estella subsequently complains that she has been shaped according to a perverse agenda of emotional education, whose effects she is now powerless to undo: ' "You must know," said Estella, condescending to me as a brilliant and beautiful woman might, "that I have no heart" ' (235). This programmed heartlessness was meant, however, to have one exception. Miss Havisham reproaches her daughter with being unfeeling to her—'You cold, cold heart!' Estella retorts that 'I am what you have made me' (300). Much later, when Pip's and Estella's lives have both gone wrong, Miss Havisham will come to blame herself, at the novel's last minute acquiring 'an earnest womanly compassion' and declaring to Pip that 'I stole her heart away and put ice in its place' (395). There is no disagreement about the psychological mechanism, one that recurs in other Dickens novels.[4] A heart is there at the outset, but it can be removed by experience or negative training. Estella comes out with a clear analysis of, and protest against, her own formation by Miss Havisham who, like Magwitch with Pip, has 'made' her according to a definite plan.

The two adoptions can be compared in several other ways. To begin with, they are almost poles apart in geographical terms: Magwitch adopts at an Antipodean distance, while Miss Havisham

---

[4] Another Dickens woman who is aware of no longer having a heart and knows what happened to it is Dombey's second wife, Edith Granger: 'Oh mother, mother, if you had but left me to my natural heart when I too was a girl—a younger girl than Florence—how different I might have been!'; *Dombey and Son* (1848), ed. Peter Fairclough (1970; London: Penguin, 1985), 514. The remark is prefaced by Edith recalling to her mother how she has 'more than once' sat at the window when 'something in the faded likeness of my sex has wandered past outside'.

never budges from her English home. During their children's growing up, the two of them are like caricatural versions of the absent father and the constantly present mother. Magwitch is never anywhere near Pip, and indeed his identity is unknown to his 'son'; but Miss Havisham is like a grotesque embodiment of a literally 24/7/365 stay-at-home mother: she never ever goes out of the house. In other respects, of course, she is not quite the model of maternal domesticity, and it is perhaps doubtful whether her establishment, with its drapings of dust, and food decades past its decay-by date, would have passed the home visit reports of twentieth-century social workers checking her out as a prospective adopter. A client assessment is evidently not something that Jaggers considers to be part of his remit, omniscient as he is. It is he who lets slip at one point that curious detail of Miss Havisham's nocturnal eating: 'She wanders about in the night, and then lays hands on such food as she takes' (239).

There are also some similarities between the adoptions. Both parents have a clear idea of the sort of adult they want their child to become, and see a need to form him or her specifically for that end. Miss Havisham's rearing is personal: she herself has made the heartless Estella, or made Estella heartless. We never see exactly how she does it, although there are some very slight indications of her parenting practices. She tells Pip that initially she only wanted to 'save her from misery like my own', but that when Estella 'promised to be very beautiful, I gradually did worse, and with my praises, and with my jewels, and with my teachings, and with this figure of myself always before her a warning to back and point my lessons, I stole her heart away and put ice in its place' (395). It is as if the words and the things—'with my praises ... with my jewels ... with my teachings'—can be virtually interchangeable as forms of relentlessly repeated persuasion. Magwitch's rearing, while equally directed towards a specific outcome, equally designed to produce an offspring whose story will be the opposite of the parent's, is delegated. A gentleman's education is something he is unable to provide in any other way: he isn't qualified and he isn't there. In both cases, the child is meant to be for the parent what the parent has not been able to be, and these are obviously gender-differentiated goals: in Miss Havisham's case it is about avoiding a particular kind of love-destiny, and in Magwitch's it is about achieving a worldly status. But Miss Havisham's 'save from my fate' suggests a timeless female doom; whereas Magwitch's gentleman is cast into a modern narrative of social aspiration and upward mobility.

A further connection between the two adoptions is that both have recourse to an intermediary to do the business—and it is the same individual in both cases. After the sentences in which she speaks of what she sought in a child—'I told him that I wanted a little girl to rear and love, and save from my fate'—Miss Havisham provides the background to her approach to Jaggers:

> I had first seen him when I sent for him to lay this place waste for me; having read of him in the newspapers, before I and the world parted. He told me that he would look about him for such an orphan child. One night he brought her here asleep, and I called her Estella. (396)

Jaggers appears to have taken on each of Miss Havisham's two unusual commissions, first to wreck and then to rescue, with an agent's impartiality. But his delivery of the baby is almost magical in Miss Havisham's telling: 'One night he brought her here asleep.' This transitional sentence metamorphoses the indefinite type, 'such an orphan child', into the real 'her' who then becomes Estella through her naming by the woman who now becomes her parent. Jaggers's role in both this adoption and Pip's is pivotal, not to say miraculous. The man is famous. Magwitch says that the case involving his own wife established Jaggers's name, and Miss Havisham had read about him (incidentally, this casual mention of newspaper-reading is a tantalizing glimpse, the only one, of a Miss Havisham before her catastrophe, engaged with the outside world). Jaggers is invested with infallible powers: for both parents, he appears as the man who can get them their girl or boy—and he does. 'Well, you see it *was* me, and single-handed', as Magwitch says; but he immediately adds: 'Never a soul in it but my own self and Mr Jaggers' (316).

Yet for all his professional neutrality and distance, Jaggers is not, it turns out, without views about the job he is asked to do for Miss Havisham: he gives a lengthy statement of his private opinion on the matter, something he is not heard to do with regard to any other case. This comes up when Pip has been letting him know what he has discovered (and Jaggers himself is unaware of), that Magwitch is Estella's father; Jaggers refers to himself hypothetically and in the third person:

'Put the case that at the same time he held a trust to find a child for an eccentric rich lady to adopt and bring up.'

'I follow you, sir.'

'Put the case that he lived in an atmosphere of evil, and that all he saw of children, was, their being generated in great numbers for certain destruction. Put the case that he often saw children solemnly tried at a criminal bar, where they were held up to be seen; put the case that he habitually knew of their being imprisoned, whipped, transported, neglected, cast out, qualified in all ways for the hangman, and growing up to be hanged. Put the case that pretty nigh all the children he saw in his daily business life, he had reason to look upon as so much spawn, to develop into the fish that were to come to his net—to be prosecuted, defended, forsworn, made orphans, be-devilled somehow.'

'I follow you, sir.'

'Put the case, Pip, that here was one pretty little child out of the heap, who could be saved.'   (408)

This is a theory of almost statistically packed non-expectations, or negative expectations; the 'saving' of one from 'the heap' is an act of human redemption in the face of the dire effects of overpopulation ('their being generated in great numbers'). A single symbolic gesture comes to the rescue, against the odds of biology and criminality, and 'one pretty little child' is plucked from the swarming mass, the 'spawn', to be given a chance as against all the numbers whose lifespan is merely a passage from bare and brutal existence to 'certain destruction'. By comparison, Miss Havisham's wish to 'save' her girl from 'my fate' appears to come from a different universe entirely. In some aspects Jaggers's picture resembles the modern biology textbook, in which reproduction is represented as the one in a million chance success of the single sperm that gets to make a life. The difference here is that the lucky one is actively helped on its way, is 'saved' by deliberate and miracle-working intervention. The scenario is similar to contemporary techniques in which a doctor will indeed select and pick out a single, hopefully viable sperm with which to fertilize the precious egg.[5] Jaggers goes on to give the pragmatic reasons for why, in the particular case of the girl not yet Estella (her original name is never stated), the parents would be likely to consent: 'Give the child into my hands', as he says he would have said to the mother (408). He becomes the recipient and bearer of the little girl, taking her from the first to the second mother. Carrying out Miss Havisham's instructions becomes a matter of physically carrying and delivering the child, according to the commission.

By his own account, then, Jaggers is endowed with almost divine powers. He is able to give a different life to one single chosen child. At the same time this action is situated against the background of a violently anti-social picture of the human world, in which life for the 'vast numbers' aimlessly 'generated' has only the end of 'destruction'. Jaggers is not himself a parent. Nor, for that matter, is he a son (or a brother, or a husband): he is one of a very few characters in the novel—the villain Orlick is another—for whom there is no information given about their early history or any family they might have been part of. Such isolation, splendid in Jaggers's case, has the effect of enhancing his assumed powers to make or break. In this connection the provision of an ethical rationale of his own for the saving of a single child is very striking.

I have described Magwitch and Miss Havisham as two consciously choosing adoptive parents, each of them using the same lawyer to achieve their aim, and each with a sure sense of what they want for the child they have so deliberately taken to be their own. But the opening setting already involves Pip's first, *de facto* adopting parents, the gentle Joe and the punitive sister (her first name, Georgiana, the same as her and Pip's mother's, is given only at the very end of the novel). Technically a brother-in-law, Joe figures for Pip as a loving, companionate father; they are also buddies and allies against the arbitrary rages of 'Mrs Joe'. Towards the end, after the death of Magwitch, whom Pip has taken care of, it is Joe who nurses Pip through a long illness, and in spite of Pip's earlier abandonment of

---

[5] Intra-cytoplasmic sperm injection (ICSI) began to be used in the early 1990s as a remedy for generally low sperm quantity or quality.

him in the period when he still had his expectations and was turning his back on what Estella had mocked as his 'coarse' and 'common' identity (64). Joe is in many ways the moral centre of the book, a paragon of selfless devotion to others and honest pride in his work. He is both good father and good mother, 'strength with gentleness' (139), and he is also Pip's friend and confidant. When Pip's 'expectations' and thereby his imminent removal from home have first been announced, Joe spurns the money offered by Jaggers as Magwitch's agent: 'But if you think as Money—can make compensation to me—for the loss of the little child—what come to the forge—and ever the best of friends—'(139). Pip is Joe's irreplaceable 'little child'; and though no mention is made of the fact, it is significant that he and Mrs Joe have no children.

The goodness of Joe, unlike the fierceness of his wife, is given a specific aetiology, when he tells Pip the story of his own upbringing, with a mother who was always escaping from and then being forced to return to a violent and drunken husband. Pip is to understand that Joe's own father's failures as a father and husband have shaped his own conscious forbearance in the face of the shortcomings of his wife, and also reinforced his wish and willingness to do right by 'the little child'. In a proto-twentieth-century way, Dickens explores the influence of patterns of family behaviour on the next generation. Joe becomes Joe through seeking not to repeat the behaviour of his own father; but that behaviour is the determining cause of what makes Joe Joe as a parent (and husband). In general, *Great Expectations* tends to explain its characters, when it does explain them, by their rearing and their life experience, not by their birth. There is no sense of hereditary taint or virtue, and nor is the social milieu determining of what the baby born into it will later become if transferred to a different one. In particular there is no suggestion, beyond the social stigma that the revelation would entail, that Estella might be negatively affected by being her violent birth mother's daughter; instead, she has been formed by Miss Havisham in the way that Miss Havisham intended, and she herself sees her character as being entirely the wrongful making of her adoptive mother.

Pip says of Miss Havisham 'That she had done a grievous thing in taking an impressionable child to mould into the form that her wild resentment, spurned affection, and wounded pride, found vengeance in' (394). An entire theory is implied in this: both of the power of parenting to form a child, and of what makes a parent parent in a particular way or to a particular end. Rearing, in this theory, is what moulds a child, through the 'impressions' from its outside environment that mark its mind; and in that sense all children are adopted. They become what they become as a result of how they are emotionally shaped, consciously or not, by those who raise them, who may or may not have been also their natural parents.

Apart from Magwitch, who emerges as having been Estella's father, and actively—he is said to have been 'extremely fond' of her (401)—none of Estella's and Pip's birth parents are fleshed out with feelings for their children. Pip's family before his parents' death is not a subject of local story or of the novel's interest; instead Joe emphasizes how 'When I got acquainted with your sister, it were the talk how she was bringing you up by hand' (47).[6] It is almost as though, in marrying his wife, Joe's first motive was to cherish the child: to give him a loving parent. Estella's mother is the only birth parent to be in any way party to the adoption of her child, 'whom the father believed dead, and dared make no stir about' (408). Her relinquishment of the toddler who will become Estella is in effect forced upon her by Jaggers, in exchange for his defending her in court for the murder he knows she committed. Nothing is said of Estella's mother's response, in words or gesture, or of her thoughts (was she, as Magwitch is said to have been, 'extremely fond' of their daughter?). Molly's giving, or giving up, of her small child is passed over silently. Similarly we never hear anything of Magwitch's feelings about the loss—as he supposes—of his daughter, let alone about the possible relationship of that loss to his wish to attach himself to Pip as a second child of his own.

Miss Havisham's moulding to 'save her from my fate' has not succeeded in bringing Estella happiness (she goes through a loveless and abusive marriage), and that, together with Pip's own unhappi-

---

[6] Joe goes on: ' "As to you... if you could have been aware how small and flabby and mean you was, dear me, you'd have formed the most contemptible opinions of yourself!"

Not exactly relishing this, I said, "Never mind me, Joe."

"But I did mind you, Pip," he returned, with tender simplicity'.

ness, is the source of the eventual self-reproach for what she has actually and unintentionally 'done'. By contrast Magwitch, whose own adoption has almost equally unhappy consequences for his 'son', never has to confront the failure of the project to which he, like Miss Havisham, has devoted himself to gratify a fantasy of his own. Instead, Pip carefully keeps from the dying convict the knowledge that all the money he has saved to assure Pip's affluent future will necessarily revert to the Crown on his death, because of his return from Australia. Nor does Pip ever protest—as Estella does to Miss Havisham—against the gentlemanly education that Magwitch has given him, or thrust upon him. But in proudly rather than penitently proclaiming his influence, Magwitch uses the same language of 'doing' and 'making' that Miss Havisham and Estella apply to her formation. On the night when he comes to Pip's lodgings and reveals his part in his history, Magwitch recalls how he used to say to himself, ' "but wot, if I gets liberty and money, I'll make that boy a gentleman!" And I done it' (315).[7]

There is an even deeper failure that the two determined adoption projects have in common. Miss Havisham unwittingly causes Estella to live another ill-fated story of abusive love, with Bentley Drummle. Magwitch's raising of Pip is meant to give him a life far removed from his adoptive father's, but it also, uncannily, re-enacts what was done to Magwitch. Pip's transfer from one sphere of life to another, and away from the place where he was born, comes about without any agency on his part. For the young Pip it represents the fulfilment of the vague expectations set in motion by his frequenting of Miss Havisham and Estella, but it occurs with the same irresistible fatefulness as Magwitch's own capture and subsequent transportation. First, a companion of Magwitch's comes to check out Pip's origins, and then some time later Jaggers himself comes to inform Pip of his expectations and make arrangements for his removal to London and his new mode of life. Thus agents seek out Pip and take

---

[7] A comical counterpart to Magwitch in loudly asserting his role in Pip's social rise is Mr Pumblechook, the local corn merchant and uncle of some sort to Pip's family, who puts it about that he is Pip's 'earliest benefactor and the founder of my [i.e. Pip's] fortunes' (470), and declares, upon Pip's humbled return, that 'I would do it again' (471).

him away, just as they do with Magwitch. For all that he longs to give Pip what he himself has never had, what Magwitch actually does, from this point of view, is to give him a life sentence in a new world, just as had happened with himself. No different from the unquestionable absent authority of 'His Majesty's service' (30), which commands that blacksmiths must help in arresting convicts on Christmas Day, and sends its agents to capture them, Magwitch becomes the anonymous personage on whose behalf Jaggers is sent from London to track Pip down; Jaggers 'come arter you, agreeable to my letter', as Magwitch precisely puts it (317). Meaning to do the opposite, both Magwitch and Miss Havisham inflict an aggressive repetition of their own stories upon the children whom they adopt for a different life.

When I began to think about the proactive parents, the self-made parents, in *Great Expectations*, my idea was that this aspect of the novel was a small but significant sub-story (or rather two), behind the principal plotline. As I continued to think about it, I found that this double parental story kept growing to the point that it seemed to have pushed everything else in *Great Expectations* to one side: all I could now see was Miss Havisham and Magwitch and Jaggers beside them, driving the action, driving the whole of Pip's and Estella's lives. (I apologize, but not too much, for this monomania.) In Pip's case, both the actual expectations, the ones derived from Magwitch, and the delusional expectations, the ones he imagines to come from Miss Havisham, are derived from the two parenthood projects: the real expectations directly, and the mistaken ones because Miss Havisham wants to use Pip as part of her malign experiment in negative emotional training for Estella. Pip's narrative begins with the encounter on the marsh from which, ultimately, Magwitch's gratitude and gentleman-making scheme will emerge. And the day of Pip's first visit to Miss Havisham's house is singled out as having been, in biographical terms, the day without which his whole life would have been different (71).

Miss Havisham's adoption is worth attention, I have suggested, because of the peculiarity of its aims and the special method used to get hold of a daughter in the first place. But there is also the fact that the parenthood initiative is a move beyond the static, stalled world in which she has encased herself. We see the picture of Miss

Havisham stuck there with her clock at twenty to nine, her mouldy ever after wedding feast, and her journeys that go nowhere, round and round the room; and this image of life stopped and suspended is what we remember. But sending for an Estella was actually a definite break in that cycle, taking Miss Havisham back out into the 'world' from which she was 'parted', and henceforth requiring various kinds of organization—from the days of Pip and Estella's dreadful playdates to the timing and planning of schooling and boarding elsewhere. The adoption and raising of Estella undermines the general spectacle of Miss Havisham herself as living in a time-warp of her own: in this respect she has in fact re-entered the world. By getting herself a child, she has started a new story beyond the fatal wedding day, setting out to do something with another life. Like Magwitch, she has treated parenthood as a reason for living in this world and a compensation for her own disappointments. For both of them, parenthood has been a second chance: or a means of getting their 'own' back.

7

Finding a Life

George Eliot's *Silas Marner*

Great Expectations has a multiplicity of adoption scenarios that appear beneath the surface of the primary narrative of a boy who was himself adopted not once but twice: first by his older sister and then, in effect, by a transported convict whose money transforms his life. But these parental stories are not the obvious focus of Dickens's novel. In George Eliot's *Silas Marner*, published in the same year, adoption is clearly at the centre. And although, implicitly, her adoption does change the life of the toddler who is taken in, the novel is much more concerned with its effects on the man who becomes her father. Parenthood is the beginning of Silas Marner's 'new self', a rebirth for someone who had been up till then almost totally withdrawn from his local world and who had suffered the loss of the one thing, his accumulated 'gold', to which he was attached.[1] More than anything, this is a novel which morally urges the power of parenthood to give meaning to an individual life; it does this not only in showing what happens with Silas Marner himself, but also by the contrast with another father—the original father of the adopted girl—whose own life, after he has failed to 'claim' her, either to acknowledge her or to bring her up, is marred by childlessness with his wife. As in *Great Expectations*, there is no promotion of the superiority of 'natural' parenthood.[2]

---

[1] George Eliot, *Silas Marner* (1861), ed. Terence Cave (Oxford: Oxford University Press, 1996), 138. Further references will be given within the main text.

[2] Marianne Novy has pointed out how *Silas Marner* differs from classical adoption narratives in this respect, validating the adoptive parent over the birth parent, once found, by giving the (now adult) child the choice between them. See *Reading Adoption: Family and Difference in Fiction and Drama* (Ann Arbor: University of Michigan Press, 2005), ch. 5.

Sometimes natural family ties are offered as happy and functional, but this is not the novel's norm, and Silas Marner's unusual story serves as a kind of parable of what the unexpected and unconditionally accepted child—the 'found' child par excellence—can mean to the parent.

The 2-year-old girl who comes into Silas Marner's cottage on New Year's night is in effect a foundling. Out of the dark she appears, lighting up the life of a man of middle years ('not yet forty' (19), but old before his time)—who, at the point when the novel begins, has been living for some time as a semi-recluse near the village of Raveloe. He has cut himself off from human connection since leaving his home town as the result of a false accusation which led to his fiancée breaking off their engagement. Working as a weaver, he has stored up a large amount of gold, which has become the only object of his devotion, lovingly counted and handled every evening. The disappearance of this gold one night while he is out is a catastrophe which wrenches away what has been his only consolation and companion:

> To any one who had observed him before he lost his gold, it might have seemed that so withered and shrunken a life as his could hardly be susceptible of a bruise, could hardly endure any subtraction but such as would put an end to it altogether. But in reality it had been an eager life, filled with immediate purpose, which fenced him in from the wide, cheerless unknown. It had been a clinging life; and though the object round which its fibres had clung was a dead disrupted thing, it satisfied the need for clinging. But now the fence was broken down—the support was snatched away. (73–4)

Into this purposeless void there enters the child who will be called Eppie, her arrival as magically unexplained as the departure of the supporting gold.

Silas repeatedly represents the relation between the gold and the girl as an equation. In a minimal sense, she takes its place as an object of devotion. But much more than that, she offers a prospect of life that is incommensurable with the gold-acquiring concentration of his previous existence. She gives him a future, and a present that is sensually enjoyable:

The gold had asked that he should sit weaving longer and longer, deafened and blinded more and more to all things except the monotony of his loom and the repetition of his web, but Eppie called him away from his weaving, and made him think all its pauses a holiday. (124)

Through his daughter, Silas is able to live or relive an experience of awakening to life: 'As the child's mind was growing into knowledge, his mind was growing into memory; as her life unfolded, his soul, long stupefied in a cold narrow prison, was unfolding too, and trembling gradually into full consciousness' (124). Eliot's language brings out a Wordsworthian world of childlike wonder. But here, instead of a countervailing encroachment as 'Shades of the prison-house begin to close',[3] there is now, in later life, an opening out into freedom. The growth of the child is the growth and flourishing of the parent—the parent's second life.

Many times Silas describes the girl as having been 'sent' to him, a deliverance and a destiny. His adoption of her comes about without any premeditation, as a refusal of the proposal that she should be taken off his hands:

'No—no—I can't part with it, I can't let it go,' said Silas, abruptly. 'It's come to me—I've a right to keep it.'

The proposition to take the child from him had come to Silas quite unexpectedly, and his speech, uttered under a strong sudden impulse, was almost like a revelation to himself: a minute before, he had no distinct intention about the child. (113)

From this point on, Silas holds fast to the sense of himself as the rightful and single parent of the girl he calls Eppie. More than anything, this involves a commitment to all the tasks of childcare (something that Miss Havisham, who sought a little girl 'to rear and love', is never seen to engage in with Estella), and this goes together with a demand for exclusivity. He rejects Dolly Winthrop's offer of help: 'I want to do things for myself, else it may get fond o' somebody else, and not fond o' me. I've been used to fending for myself in the house—I can learn, I can learn' (120). His reasons combine, without

[3] William Wordsworth, 'Ode: Intimations of Immortality from Recollections of Early Childhood' (1807), line 67, in *Poems, Volume I*, ed. John O. Hayden (Harmondsworth: Penguin 1977), 525.

welding, the practical and the emotionally demanding. 'I can learn'—but also, I want her to love just me.

Learn he does—and the reader too, from a passage several pages long that details Mrs Winthrop's parenting tips. But Silas is adamant from the very beginning that the parent of Eppie is him, and him only. In a practical sense, becoming the child's father entails him adopting the role that would normally be a woman's. His first gesture, after he finds her lying on the hearth in his cottage, is to feed her with some of his porridge. He rejects the assumption that 'an old bachelor, like you' (116) could not possibly be thinking of looking after a small child. In fact Silas's occupation as a weaver becomes a kind of special qualification for his unusual role, as Dolly says:

'Why, there isn't many lone men 'ud ha' been wishing to take up with a little un like that: but I reckon the weaving makes you handier than men as do out-door work—you're partly as handy as a woman, for weaving comes next to spinning.' (128–9)

Silas is more an old spinster than an old bachelor. But if he sets out to be all things, both parents, to Eppie—'I want to do everything as can be done for the child' (122)—there is also a movement of identification: 'it's a lone thing—and I'm a lone thing' (116). His very first response, when he finds the golden creature, is to see her as being conceivably 'his little sister come back to him in a dream—his little sister, whom he had carried about in his arms for a year before she died, when he was a small boy without shoes or stockings' (109). This phantom memory of love and loss bears with it the physical closeness that will come to be Silas's life with his daughter, to whom he gives his sister's name.

Like Joe Gargery, Silas becomes both a nurturing parent and a brother to his adopted child; as well as being 'ever the best of friends, Pip!' as he often reiterates, Joe is technically Pip's brother-in-law. But the significance of the companionate parenthood that both Joe and Silas undertake is quite different. Joe from the start is fully integrated into his community, and remains so until the end amid all the vicissitudes of Pip's own separate life. Silas is on the outside: he has come from elsewhere, and other than through his work he has never sought to make himself part of the local world in which he has settled. For him, the new child comes to make him part of the village life from which he had previously been detached. Eppie enables his own growth, alongside hers; there is even a 'double baptism' (123) as though Silas, too, had only just arrived in this world; 'the child created fresh and fresh links between his life and the lives from which he had hitherto shrunk continually into narrow isolation' (123).

Eliot presents the arrival of Eppie in Silas Marner's life as unambiguously positive; it is the making of him, an unequivocally happy event. At the end of the novel, Eppie's wedding to Dolly's son Aaron Winthrop—with whom, in effect, she has grown up—is carefully marked as more a continuation than a break with the perfect harmonious domestic life that Silas and Eppie have led: Aaron will come to live with them, and Silas will not lose his daughter. But throughout the novel, Eliot reinforces the joyous, quasi-magical tone of the tale of Silas and Eppie by counterpointing the story of the man who, unknown to anyone in the village, was Eppie's first father.

At the beginning Godfrey Cass, the eldest son of the village squire, is in love with the suitable Nancy Lammeter, but has blighted his life by contracting a secret marriage to the mother of the baby who will later be Eppie. Of this Molly, little is ever said. She lives at a distance from Raveloe; she is addicted to opium (which eventually causes her death, the night she falls asleep outside Silas Marner's cottage); she apparently worked in a pub, since her mind is a 'poisoned chamber, inhabited by no higher memories than those of a barmaid's paradise of pink ribbons and gentlemen's jokes' (106). Molly is represented as the lowest of the low, the antithesis of the now unattainable Nancy:

Instead of keeping fast hold of the strong silken rope by which Nancy would have drawn him safe to the green banks, where it was easy to step firmly, he had let himself be dragged back into mud and slime, in which it was useless to struggle. He had made ties for himself which robbed him of all wholesome motive, and were a constant exasperation. (30)

Before the death of Molly (and the arrival of Eppie), Godfrey has borne his marriage and fatherhood not only as the impediment to

his marrying the woman he loves, but as the guilty secret he is sometimes on the point of confessing, but never does. Eliot then brings
the moral issue to a head through the crisis engendered by Molly's
death in the course of a journey that was meant to end in her own
declaration, to Godfrey's father, of her situation as the wife of his
son and mother of his child. The death of the unloved woman
releases Godfrey from the state of marriage, but confronts him with
the more focused and immediate dilemma of whether to admit his
relationship to 'the "tramp's child"' (118).

Eliot carefully presents all Godfrey's impulses as tending in the
opposite direction from Silas's; the actual father resists and rejects
what comes naturally to the man who has no connection with the
child. The contrast is made all the more starkly as Godfrey, like
Silas, experiences the toddler's arrival as like something supernatu-
ral. For him, though, it has the effect of breaking in upon the
courtship of Nancy in which he has been indulging at the New
Year's party:

> But when Godfrey was lifting his eyes from one of those long glances, they
> encountered an object as startling to him at that moment as if it had been
> an apparition from the dead. It *was* an apparition from that hidden life
> which lies, like a dark by-street, behind the goodly ornamented façade that
> meets the sunlight and the gaze of respectable admirers. It was his own
> child carried in Silas Marner's arms. That was his instantaneous impression,
> unaccompanied by doubt, though he had not seen the child for months
> past. (112)

Godfrey recognizes 'his own child', his back-street child—as her
mother's social class is merged into a metaphor of the dark and
'hidden' quarters of Godfrey's mind. The narrator states, indirectly,
that he has been, in modern terms, an absent father, and the lapse
of time adds to the shock of what is so indisputably a recognition.
But this absence is put the other way round, as the child's non-
existence in Godfrey's world.

There are two subsequent scenes, one the same night and one
years later, when Eppie is grown up, in which Godfrey and Silas are
set against one another as the two fathers of a now motherless child.
In the first of these scenes, Godfrey sees in Molly's death 'the sudden
prospect of his own deliverance from his long bondage' (115). The

child is an encumbrance for which he will make some minimum of provision: 'As for the child he would see that it was cared for; he would never forsake it; he would do everything but own it' (117). Godfrey refuses to 'own' his child in the confessional sense; Silas subsequently lays claim to her with an owning that verges on the proprietorial: 'she'll be *my* little un...She'll be nobody else's' (121).

Much later, the question of the father's 'owned' child is raised once again, after Godfrey has belatedly told Nancy, now his wife for many years, that he is the original father of 'the weaver's child'. This is the day when Godfrey will eventually come home to tell her that the remains of his long-vanished brother have been found, along with the long-missing gold that had disappeared from Silas Marner's cottage—and will also, at last, reveal the suppressed story of his early marriage and fatherhood. In the meantime Nancy is reflective. She is thinking about the history of her life and marriage, including a baby who died; Eliot gently generalizes her preoccupation as a result of a life that has been denied the outlet of motherhood:

This excessive rumination and self-questioning is perhaps a morbid habit inevitable to a mind of much moral sensibility when shut out from its due share of outward activity and of practical claims on its affections—inevitable to a noble-hearted, childless woman, when her lot is narrow.   (149)

Despite Godfrey's sense of 'deliverance' through Molly's death, and the wedding to Nancy he wished for, the further sequel of children has failed to occur—or occurred only in the form of loss. 'Was there not a drawer filled with the neat work of her hands, all unworn and untouched, just as she had arranged it there fourteen years ago—just, but for one little dress, which had been made the burial-dress?' (150).

Yet Nancy sees their childlessness as having been more her husband's loss than hers; her 'deepest wounds had all come from the perception that the absence of children from their hearth was dwelt on in her husband's mind as a privation to which he could not reconcile himself' (150). For women, in Nancy's theory, a husband can partly take the place of children in a way that is not symmetrically true for a man: 'a woman could always be satisfied with devoting herself to her husband, but a man wanted something that would make him look forward more' (150). This accords with what Eliot has emphasized as being the newfound future perspective given to

Silas by his own fatherhood of Eppie; it also extends the pragmatic attitude to domestic happiness put forward in the first phase of the novel by Nancy's older sister Priscilla, who is uninterested in marriage and intends to spend her life living with their father: 'thank God! My father's a sober man and likely to live; and if you've got a man by the chimney-corner, it doesn't matter if he's childish—the business needn't be broken up' (92).

Nancy's meditations partly turn on the two moments, precisely dated as four and six years before now, when Godfrey had mooted the possibility of their adopting a child. It is here that Eliot draws the narrative towards a broader discussion of adoption. In passing, there is a general authorial statement about changing social attitudes: 'Adoption was more remote from the ideas and habits of that time than of our own' (151).[4] The novel implicitly contrasts the situations of Nancy and Godfrey, a childless couple who might have sought to adopt, with that of Silas, who is made a father by the wholly unanticipated arrival of a child. Nancy's objection to adoption centres on what she regards as the wrongness of actively seeking to go against what has been ordained:

To adopt a child, because children of your own had been denied you, was to try and choose your lot in spite of Providence: the adopted child, she was convinced, would never turn out well, and would be a curse to those who had wilfully and rebelliously sought what it was clear that, for some high reason, they were better without. (151)

This rationale is striking in the way that it speaks of trying, of choice, of seeking, of the desire for children 'of your own'—all the

---

[4] Like others of Eliot's novels, *Silas Marner* is set in the past—at a time which is vaguely dated to 'the early years of this century' (4). Before the Adoption of Children Act of 1926, which established a legal framework for full adoption, adoptions in England most often took the form of ad hoc arrangements, usually but not always within families; the absence of records in such cases makes the history quite conjectural. A more formal system of 'placing' children for adoption through the mediation of agencies began to take shape in the 1920s; their work was one of the spurs to the passing of the 1926 Act, but informal adoptions continued to occur in the 1930s and during the war. See Jenny Keating, *A Child for Keeps: The History of Adoption in England, 1918–45* (London: Palgrave Macmillan, 2008), and Stephen Cretney, *Family Law in the Twentieth Century: A History* (Oxford: Oxford University Press, 2003), 596–627.

elements that are present in the formulation today of the predicament of the childless person or couple. Yet here they are raised in order to refuse their legitimacy, to the point of imagining a punishment in the 'curse' of the child who 'would never turn out well'. Even the rituals of remembrance for the baby who died must be deliberately abandoned, in case they should represent a protest against what has happened: 'she had suddenly renounced the habit of visiting this drawer, lest she should in this way be cherishing a longing for what was not given' (150).

In the conversation that Nancy recalls, Godfrey counters her argument about an adopted child turning out badly with the local case of Eppie: 'She has thriven as well as child can do with the weaver; and *he* adopted her' (152). The irony of Godfrey knowingly but unconfessedly referring to the child who is actually his is followed by the comedy of casual argument. Like Godfrey, Nancy makes an inference about adoption in general from a single case, but hers is at two removes, and placed under the rubric of social chitchat: 'Don't you remember what that lady we met at the Royston Baths told us about the child her sister adopted? That was the only adopting I ever heard of: and the child was transported when it was twenty-three' (152).

Godfrey's perspectives on his childlessness are very different from Nancy's. It is not just that he favours adoption—favours the seeking of a possible solution—nor even just that he harbours the secret he has so far still failed to communicate to Nancy, that he was Eppie's father. His guilt in relation to this, both the fathering and the failure to confess it, does cause him to imagine the present situation as something like Nancy's own sense of a punishment: 'His conscience, never thoroughly easy about Eppie, now gave his childless home the aspect of a retribution' (154). But more generally his attitude is contrasted with Nancy's supreme resignation to her losses. 'Meanwhile, why could he not make up his mind to the absence of children from a hearth brightened by such a wife?' (154). As for her, the good marriage is raised as a possible compensation, a different source for domestic fulfilment; but raised in the form of Godfrey's own impatience with his inability to take the children out of the picture, to cease to see and feel an 'absence'.

Eliot pursues this theme with a passage of extensive moral gener-
alization, linking Godfrey's mental state to the stage of his life:

I suppose it is the way with all men and women who reach middle age
without the clear perception that life never *can* be thoroughly joyous:
under the vague dullness of the grey hours, dissatisfaction seeks a definite object, and finds it in the privation of an untried good. Dissatisfaction, seated musingly on a childless hearth, thinks with envy of the
father whose return is greeted by young voices—seated at the meal
where the little heads rise one above another like nursery plants, it sees
a black care hovering behind every one of them, and thinks the impulses
by which men abandon freedom, and seek for ties, are surely nothing
but a brief madness. (154)

Like an unwanted lodger, the grandly personified Dissatisfaction is
brought into the house to be given its own place at the hearth and
then round the family table. In the first case, like Godfrey, Dissatisfaction imagines what the 'childless hearth' excludes, enviously flesh-
ing out the counter-scene of a returning father. But in the second
instance, surprising the sentence after a dash, without any kind of
contrasting connective, it jumps into a very different household,
reversing rather than supplying an image of parental fulfilment. First
the dissatisfaction of the childless hearth adds what is seen as missing; then the ostensibly happy scene is viewed as just a façade. Initially cute, with their 'little heads' and their natural growth, the
picture of the children suddenly goes into the negative, without
exception—'a black care hovering behind every one of them', so
that the number of children now becomes simply the multiplication
of troubles. Parenthood, finally, becomes not the long-anticipated
goal, nor even the monochrome dailiness of the 'grey hours' of
middle age, but a prison sentence—'men abandon freedom'—
brought about by a moment of madness. And this fatal passing folly
is not, as might have been expected, a yielding to love or lust; much
more soberly, and in full conformity with social propriety, it is what
happens when men settle down to 'seek for ties'.

Eliot's moral reflections at this point seem to take children or
their absence, an excess or a scarcity, as one trigger among any
number of others for dissatisfaction that is an age-related probabil-
ity—at least for those who have not yet acquired a capacity for

compromise in the form of 'the clear perception that life never *can* be thoroughly joyous'. But this passage is more like a moment of impatient aberration in a novel which otherwise quite intently examines many kinds of both large and small change that parenthood, or the denial of it, may bring. There is no question that Silas Marner's adoptive fatherhood is the making of him, the happy turning point in his life; and it is also made clear that the different distresses experienced by Godfrey and Nancy Cass in their not having children in practice take far more complex forms than a simple excuse for some general sense of middle-aged unhappiness.

The second exchange between Eppie's two fathers occurs in quite different circumstances from the first even though notionally there is still the same discrepancy between the natural and the adoptive father. On the first occasion, Silas was taking, and taking in the child not yet named Eppie, and Godfrey was failing to 'own' his relationship to her. On the subsequent occasion, many years later, Silas is the man whom Eppie has known as her father for almost all her life, and Godfrey is the alternative father come to take her away, and presenting his claims to her first as part of a would-be adopting couple, then for himself as the natural father.

Godfrey and Nancy go together to the cottage where Silas and Eppie live on the same Sunday that Silas's gold has turned up again, and with it the evidence that shows it was Godfrey's younger brother who stole it all those years ago. These buried secrets now come to light have prompted Godfrey at long last to tell his wife the now ancient story of his clandestine marriage—and how Eppie is really his child. The belated confession does not just bring out what had been suppressed. It is now a story about a girl who is 18 years old, and it is told to a Nancy who has lived without being a mother throughout her married life (and with the grief of the baby she lost), not to a younger, not yet married Nancy likely to be turned away by the news of a prospective husband's failings. To Godfrey's surprise, Nancy's response now—though she then admits that it might have been different at the earlier time—is to pledge herself retrospectively as the mother to Eppie she has not been able to be:

'And—O, Godfrey—if we'd had her from the first, if you'd taken to her as you ought, she'd have loved me for her mother—and you'd have been happier with me: I could better have bore my little baby dying, and our life might have been more like what we used to think it 'ud be.' (158)

The child whom Godfrey always saw as an obstacle to his life with Nancy might after all have been the compensatory gift that would have made parents of them—the role that she did fulfil for Silas. Nancy estimates what would have been Eppie's value, in making her a mother and supplying the nearest possible version of the happy future that she and Godfrey had imagined. Her quick enumeration of the lost compensations fits with the novel's careful computation of parental satisfactions and deprivations, with the primary example being the golden child 'sent' to take the place of the gold that has gone from Silas's cottage. Eliot spells out the equation one more time: it is on the very day that the gold has suddenly come back that Godfrey and Nancy go to the cottage to take Eppie away again.

Godfrey first makes his request in the form of an offer of adoption, implicitly connected to the new discovery that it was his brother who stole Silas's gold. Eppie will be given a better life:

'You've done a good part by Eppie, Marner, for sixteen years. It 'ud be a great comfort to you to see her well provided for, wouldn't it? She looks blooming and healthy, but not fit for any hardships: she doesn't look like a strapping girl, come of working parents. You'd like to see her taken care of by those who can leave her well off, and make a lady of her: she's more fit for it than for a rough life, such as she might come to have in a few years' time.' (162)

Addressed to the potentially relinquishing parent, the argument is the same one that would be relentlessly used to persuade unmarried mothers in the middle decades of the twentieth century that they should give up their babies for adoption. A parent who wants the best for their child would be selfish in refusing to place it in a higher social setting: the first parent is quickly cast in the role of a depriver, in relation to the superior provisions that their child could enjoy elsewhere; and 'It would be a great comfort to you in your old age, I hope, to see her fortune made in that way' (163).

Godfrey then proceeds to a second strand of what is still an adoption argument, dwelling on a different kind of deprivation—not in the current prospects for Eppie, but in the lives of himself and his wife. Material surplus is urged, along with a personal lack that Eppie could come to supply:

'Mrs Cass and I, you know, have no children—nobody to benefit by our good home and everything else we have—more than enough for ourselves. And we should like to have somebody in the place of a daughter to us—we should like to have Eppie, and treat her in every way as our own child. (163)

Eppie, not Silas, replies, on both counts: 'I can't leave my father, nor own anybody nearer than him. And I don't want to be a lady. I couldn't give up the folks I've been used to' (163). Eppie—who is, in reality, the daughter of a gentleman—refuses the social elevation offered with as much assurance as Pip's acceptance of the equivalent offer in *Great Expectations*; both novels firmly endorse the desirability of staying in the (lowly) position you grew up in.

Having failed so far, Godfrey now moves on to make his case quite differently, by declaring himself as Eppie's real father:

'But I have a claim on you, Eppie—the strongest of all claims. It is my duty, Marner, to own Eppie as my child, and provide for her. She is my own child—her mother was my wife. I have a natural claim on her that must stand before every other.' (164)

After a little while, the 'natural' claim on Eppie becomes Eppie's duty to 'your lawful father' (167), but the gap between nature and law is already half elided in this first declaration by the gloss on 'my own child' that justifies the father legally as the husband of her mother. Still, the stress on the lawful father accompanies a shift of emphasis away from positive suggestion—what Godfrey and Nancy can offer—to almost threatening demand. What Godfrey calls his 'natural claim' sets him, individually, against both Silas and Eppie (Nancy is no longer in the picture). The force of the claim is that it brooks no others: it is natural and therefore it 'must stand before every other'. Godfrey puts himself forward now as the one and only parent (in comparison with Silas) and also as the only person, parent or prospective parent or child, with a valid 'claim'.

The question of claims had entered into Godfrey's arguments with himself at the distant first stage of this parental debate, all the years ago when Eppie was found by Silas and recognized by Godfrey as his daughter. Then, he had reflected 'that he ought to accept the consequences of his deeds, own the miserable wife, and fulfil the claims of the helpless child' (115): the claims were the child's not the parent's. The later insistence on 'the strongest of all claims', as a father, still includes the two elements of recognition ('to own Eppie as my child') and an obligation to 'provide for her'. Both of these disparate functions are placed under the head of 'duty', which is thus inextricable from the overarching 'claim'.

Godfrey's demands are rejected by both Silas and Eppie with argument and feeling. The 'natural claim', if it ever was one, has in effect been invalidated by Godfrey's failure to make it from the outset:

'then, sir, why didn't you say so sixteen year ago, and claim her before I'd come to love her, i'stead o' coming to take her from me now, when you might as well take the heart out o' my body?' (164)

Without him spelling it out, Silas's image gives a different meaning to the 'natural' claim. Eppie has grown into being the vital part of his own self; with these two, there can be no differentiation between the claims of the child and the parent, since they are as one. Taking her from him, 'You'd cut us i' two' (165): they have no existence apart from one another. And Silas returns to the image of the child as a gift, while acknowledging that as the original father, Godfrey would have had the prior claim:

'God gave her to me because you turned your back upon her, and He looks upon her as mine: you've no right to her! When a man turns a blessing from his door, it falls to them as take it in.' (164)

Godfrey had first refusal—and refused.

Beyond his impassioned appeal to the double self that he and Eppie have become, Silas also recasts Godfrey's rhetoric about his paternal duty to provide for a daughter. He rejects Godfrey's idea that in living elsewhere, down the road, 'She'll feel just the same towards you' (165):

'Just the same?' said Marner, more bitterly than ever. 'How'll she feel just the same for me as she does now, when we eat o' the same bit, and drink o' the same cup, and think o' the same things from one day's end to another? Just the same? that's idle talk. You'd cut us i' two.' (165)

Silas does not present his fatherhood as the transfer or provision of means from himself to his child; instead, food and drink are a part of a fully mutual daily life, in which the two are merged in their thinkings and doings.

In the final stage of the tense discussion between the four people, Nancy comes back into view. Her opinion, unspoken, is given: 'She felt that it was a very hard trial for the poor weaver, but her code allowed no question that a father by blood must have a claim above that of any foster-father' (166). It is a simple reiteration of the argument of a natural claim over any other—one real father, above 'any' number of others; no mention of a marriage or a mother that might dilute or complicate the primary case. Silas's own assertion of the difference made by a lifetime of being, in practice, the father is reduced to the secondary status of 'foster-father'. But Godfrey then modifies his own line by adding in Nancy as a positive persuasion: 'And you'll have the best of mothers in my wife—that'll be a blessing you haven't known since you were old enough to know it' (166). Here Godfrey makes no distinction between the natural and the adoptive or foster-mother: for the purposes of asserting Nancy's future merits, there must be no distinction. Nor does motherhood lead to claims and rights, for either mothers or children; having a mother is a contingent 'blessing', a gift to a child, just as the child, in Silas's account, can be gift to the parent.

In many ways, the confrontation in Silas's cottage situates the four people present as two symmetrical couples, both of whom have lived and developed together over the past fifteen or sixteen years; Nancy and Godfrey were married the year after Eppie's arrival (and Molly's death). These two emerge more, not less, united than before from the effects of Godfrey's confession and their joint attempt to persuade Eppie to live with them; when they have gone back to their house there is a pause, after which:

At last Godfrey turned his head towards her, and their eyes met, dwelling in that meeting without any movement on either side. That quiet mutual gaze of a trusting husband and wife is like the first moment of rest or refuge from a great weariness or a great danger.   (168)

Eliot's image of the gestures of love, the peaceful return home, reinforces the symmetry between this married relationship and the bond between

Silas and Eppie which is also, on her side, 'till death us do part', and without any possible putting asunder: 'I'll cleave to him as long as he lives, and nobody shall ever come between him and me' (167).

Having settled Eppie so finally and forever with her father, Eliot perhaps has a little difficulty in playing the final scene. Eppie's connection to Aaron is not presented as having the passionate unconditionality of her attachment to her father. When he has mooted the possibility of their marrying, she asks her father for advice, reporting her own attitude as 'take it or leave it':

And you mean to have him, do you?' said Silas.

'Yes, some time,' said Eppie, 'I don't know when. Everybody's married some time, Aaron says. But I told him that wasn't true: for, I said, look at father—he's never been married.'

'No, child,' said Silas, 'your father was a lone man till you was sent to him.' (144)

Eppie supplied the place that might have been a wife's. And in the event, Aaron himself has proposed that Silas must live with them and that, Eppie says, 'he'd be as good as a son to you—that was what he said' (145).

By placing a wedding at the end, Eliot gives a conventional kind of fantasy ending to the novel, and works hard to get it to blend in smoothly with the unconventional fantasy of domestic happiness and personal redemption that she has developed up to that point. After the fulfilment of fatherhood has been so perfectly sent to him—or after fatherhood has been sent to him as his fulfilment—it cannot, in the terms of the novel, be once again sent away.

8

His and Hers

Henry Fielding's *Tom Jones*

The History of Tom Jones, a Foundling: the full title of Fielding's epic-length novel suggests that it might be much concerned with the before as well as the after of a boy's birth and abandonment; or that there might be scenes of pathetic intensity relating to a child's early years. But *Tom Jones* is very far from the emotional and ethical registers of Eliot's *Silas Marner*, even though both novels involve a foundling being found—at his home—and then adopted, by a single man who becomes its loving father. If *Tom Jones* has any moral intentions, it imparts them almost incidentally, in the course of characters' lives that seem unmarked by losses that would be matter for tragic weight in another generic context. In this novel the arguments Fielding makes implicitly about upbringing and illegitimacy occur quite casually, alongside Tom Jones's singular pseudo-heroic adventures.

Tom Jones came out in 1749 when foundlings were at the forefront of public consciousness, with the Foundling Hospital in London having opened eight years before (see Chapter 4). The title was bound to resonate with that ongoing contemporary story;[1] and within the novel, the Hospital is already established as part of the fabric of euphemistic banter. Of a pregnant girl: 'She was a little hungry, it seems, and so sat down to dinner before grace was said, and so there is a child coming for the Foundling Hospital.' This levity is corrected by Tom

[1] In the words of the historian Paul Langford, 'The ventures of this age which most completely caught the contemporary imagination were the Magdalen House [for the reform of prostitutes] and the Foundling Hospital'; *A Polite and Commercial People: England 1727–1783* (1989; Oxford: Oxford University Press, 1998), 142.

Jones himself, foundling *extraordinaire* (he is discovered, and brought up, in the most genteel of homes): '"Prithee leave thy stupid jesting," cries Jones. "Is the misery of these poor wretches a subject of mirth?"'[2]

Fielding had been a supporter of Thomas Coram's venture, and his novelistic contribution is shrewd and deliberate. In the figure of a housekeeper called 'Mrs Deborah' he mocks those who would blame the babies for the supposed sins of their parents, and also, in the portrait of Squire Allworthy, throws in a picture of a modestly decent man, with an affection for children but none of his own, who surely bears some likeness to Captain Coram himself. The opening chapter of *Tom Jones* plunges straight into what its title promises, with Squire Allworthy's unlikely discovery of a baby between the sheets as he is getting into bed one night. Summoned to the scene, the housekeeper is initially more shocked by her master's state of night-time undress than by the arrival of a newborn baby. Mrs Deborah launches into a diatribe against the immorality of the 'sluts' who produce and abandon 'these misbegotten wretches, whom I don't look upon as my fellow-creatures'; she proposes dumping the child outside the church-warden's door, where, since the weather is not bad, 'it is two to one but it lives till it is found in the morning. But if it should not, we have discharged our duty in taking proper care of it.' The baby should not be looked after, because that is the job of 'the parish', and doing so might lead people to think that Squire Allworthy is the father (35).

Mrs Deborah's stream of invective is put in its narrative place not by counter-argument but by Squire Allworthy's obliviousness to it: 'There were some strokes in the speech which, perhaps, would have offended Mr Allworthy, had he strictly attended to it; but he had now got one of his fingers into the infant's hand, which by its gentle pressure, seeming to implore his assistance, had certainly out-pleaded the eloquence of Mrs Deborah, had it been ten times greater than it was' (35–6). Fielding mocks the moralizing not just as inhumane but as irrelevant. While damning the mother of the found child, Mrs Deborah advocates a repetition of her abandoning act with less

---

[2] Henry Fielding, *Tom Jones* (1749), ed. John Bender and Simon Stern (Oxford: Oxford University Press, 1996), 667. Further page references will be given in the main text.

chance of survival and also with the satisfaction of a duty done. Meanwhile, Mr Allworthy's indifference to the content of what she is saying casts out her words as meaningless in the face of the emotional pull of the baby before him and the little moving hand which makes its own irrefutable case.

The tiny touching of the baby's finger is a moment of intimacy which wordlessly crowns Mr Allworthy's responses to the situation. He calls for help; without any pause he takes the practical and paternal decision to provide for the child in the shorter and longer terms. Mrs Deborah is instructed to 'call up a maid-servant to provide it pap and other things against it waked' (36): wet-nursing is a familiar service. 'Proper clothes should be procured for it early in the morning' (36). The rant against the 'impudence' of the baby's deserting mother in 'laying it to your worship' is answered by the thought that 'I suppose she hath only taken this method to provide for her child' (35), which the Squire duly sets about doing. Next morning he tells Bridget, the sister he lives with, that he has 'a present for her' (38) and then tells her the story of the finding of the baby; 'the good man...ended his narrative with owning a resolution to take care of the child, and to breed him up as his own' (38). Actually, though neither readers nor characters will know this for many hundreds of pages, it was Bridget who had a present for her brother. Like Moses' mother she has neatly devised a means to continue living with her own abandoned baby (though not to 'provide it pap'), without presenting herself as its mother.

Later, when Bridget marries and gives birth to another boy, also raised in the house, no distinction of rank is made between the two of them. Tom calls Mr Allworthy father, and he is referred to as his 'adopted' son.[3] Allworthy's 'benevolence' (37) is proved and illuminated by his response to Tom's arrival; speaking of another issue, he later says simply: 'it hath been my constant maxim in life to make the best of all matters which happen' (61). As a good eighteenth-century

[3] At the baby's christening (69) Allworthy is godfather, and gives him his own name, Thomas. This may, as Lisa Zunshine suggests, consolidate an intended association with Captain Coram—another Thomas, who both gave his own name and was godfather to many of the first foundlings at the London hospital. See Zunshine, *Bastards and Foundlings: Illegitimacy in Eighteenth-Century England* (Columbus: Ohio State University Press, 2005), 99.

philanthropic character, he lives by maxims. He is straight for-
wardly and pragmatically ameliorative, active but modest in
'making the best'.

Akin to this is the lack of narrative fuss over the far from small
'matters' which already have happened to Squire Allworthy. He has
had and lost four loved ones—'three children, all of whom died in
their infancy', and also his 'beloved wife'—five years before the
point at which the novel begins. 'This loss, however great, he bore
like a man of sense and constancy' (32). Such 'loss' can be sanely
borne. It does not destroy him and his life goes on, with no thought
of another family; 'he never intended to take a second wife' (59). So
even though, like Eliot's Silas Marner, the foundling's new father is
a man who has suffered in his own life prior to the baby's arrival,
Tom is never represented as a replacement or compensation for
what once was. His adoption is not a life-changing experience for
Allworthy; it is a duty cheerfully done. And whereas Silas's daughter
is a means of integrating her newfound and new-made father into
the community from which he has hitherto lived apart, Allworthy is
at the other extreme. As a magistrate and landowner he already
fulfils a morally leading role in his local world.

In other ways too, *Tom Jones* is a world as well as a century away
from the psychological and social concerns of *Silas Marner*, and this
is all the more evident from its touching on some of the same
issues. At the start of the novel, the relationship between a couple
called the Partridges is bound up with their childlessness; the word
is not used, but the wife's bad temper is hypothetically attributed
to 'a circumstance which generally poisons matrimonial felicity.
For children are rightly called the pledges of love; and her husband, though they had been married nine years, had given her no
such pledges' (72). This leads Mrs Partridge to be suspicious of
other women (and ultimately, to think that her husband is the father
of Tom, who is initially supposed to be the son of the Partridges'
servant, Jenny Jones). There is a parallel here with Eliot's story of
the foundling whose original father became the husband in a childless couple; but in *Tom Jones* the Partridges' story is presented as
simply the comedy of a carping wife and the 'tempest' that is sparked
by her jealousy. The pair make it up when 'something or other
happened before the next morning which a little abated the fury

of Mrs Partridge' (74); if Mr Partridge has not 'given' his wife a
baby yet, it is not—as the jealousy of other women might have
suggested—for lack of what a later century would call trying. It is
also—and again against later patterns of explanation—not attributed
to any failing on the part of her body rather than his.

Other points of correspondence and difference between these two
foundling novels bring out more aspects of the ways that they think
about parenthood. Silas's Eppie has questions about her unknown
parents, her mother in particular, and for her the story of how she
turned up is part of what she grows up with. But Tom is never
shown to be curious, let alone troubled, about his beginnings. The
absence of disturbance on this score applies also to his birth mother
Bridget, who carries off her official role as adoptive aunt without
ever giving a hint to the rest of the household, her son included, of
the real connection; the novel is not interested in exploring divided
or passionate feelings she might have had at the time of the birth or
subsequently. Mrs Bridget is seen to have an unexpected partiality
to the foundling child, sometimes at the expense of her legitimate
son; but beyond that there is no hint of special interest. She dies
when Tom is a young man, leaving a letter of confession to her
brother which does not reach its destination for several years and
several volumes more—but the delay in revealing the secret and its
existence in the first place are not, as they would be in a Hardy
novel, sources of fraught experience or further unhappiness. Apparently Mrs Bridget simply repeats her first love story: her second son
is conceived before her marriage to his father, Captain Blifil, who is
living in Allworthy's house, as the first father had also been (69). Her
falling for Blifil is simply treated as an age-related phenomenon, the
sort of thing that tends to happen with 'women about forty' (57).

There is some discussion of Mrs Bridget's maternal emotions
when she turns against her husband—'nay, to be honest, she absolutely hated him'—and the feeling is transferred onto her child: 'It
will not be therefore greatly wondered at, if she had not the most
violent regard to the offspring she had by him'; or put in other
words, 'she certainly hated her own son'. This hatred also appears
to motivate the contrary feeling for the other child: 'in his infancy
she seldom saw her son, or took any notice of him, and hence she
acquiesced, after a little reluctance, in all the favours which

Mr Allworthy showered on the foundling, whom the good man called his own boy, and in all things put on an entire equality with Master Blifil' (120). So the fondness for Tom is attributed not to an undisclosed mother-love, but to a combination of deference to her brother and animosity towards her husband, and therefore towards his son. Of course, this attribution of unmaternal motives for Mrs Bridget's preference for Tom over his younger half-brother also serves the narrative purpose of keeping her identity as Tom's real mother unsuspected by readers. Yet even so, it is striking that Fielding imagines Bridget Allworthy's positive or negative feelings for Tom to be fully directed by the vicissitudes of affection and hostility involved in her relations with their two fathers. In contrast, Squire Allworthy's powerful manifestations of love, his showering of favours on the foundling, appear as a spontaneous outpouring that has nothing to do with any of his other ties.

In Bridget's case, maternal affection is secondary to, and dependent on, her feelings for men— her now hated husband and the brother who is also, by adoption, the father of her first son. The same distinction is made in a story told in passing by a character called Harriet Fitzpatrick, in the context of her unhappy marriage:

I became a mother by the man I scorned, hated, and detested. I went through all the agonies and miseries of a lying-in (ten times more painful in such a circumstance than the worst labour can be when one endures it for a man one loves) in a desert, or rather, indeed, a scene of riot and revel, without a friend, without a companion, or without any of those agreeable circumstances which often alleviate, and perhaps sometimes more than compensate, the sufferings of our sex at that season. (514)

There is no thought that the child might itself 'more than compensate' for the sufferings of labour. Instead, the 'agonies and miseries' are almost entirely dependent on whether the absent husband is loved or else (said three times lest the point be missed) 'scorned, hated, and detested'.

On the other hand, just a short while after Mrs Fitzpatrick's dramatic narration, a quite different picture of maternal love slips in as one of a pair of self-consciously elaborate, pseudo-epic similes to illustrate the indifference to public emergencies when someone is faced by a personal crisis:

As a miser, who hath, in some well-built city, a cottage, value twenty shil-
lings, when at a distance he is alarmed with the news of a fire, turns pale
and trembles at his loss; but when he finds the beautiful palaces only are
burnt, and his own cottage remains safe, he comes instantly to himself, and
smiles at his good fortune; or as (for we dislike something in the former
simile) the tender mother, when terrified with the apprehension that her
darling boy is drowned, is struck senseless and almost dead with consterna-
tion; but when she is told that little master is safe, and the Victory only,
with twelve hundred brave men, gone to the bottom, life and sense again
return, maternal fondness enjoys the sudden relief from all its fears, and the
general benevolence which at another time would have deeply felt the
dreadful catastrophe, lies fast asleep in her mind.   (516)

The moral passage from the first to the second simile, from material
to parental passions, is like that of *Silas Marner*'s movement from a
miser's all-consuming love of gold, the loss of which is his own catastrophe, to a father's unconditional love for his daughter. The second
simile evokes a parental or maternal world which is severed from any
connection with other human concerns; it omits the miser's smiling
that he has been luckier than others. In the midst of the mother's
own 'sudden relief', all other causes for grief or pity sink beneath the
surface—'the Victory only, with twelve hundred brave men, gone to
the bottom'. As against the overwhelming extent of the mother's
involuntary indifference—twelve hundred lives versus one, but one a
one and only—Fielding carefully emphasizes the 'general benevolence' of her ordinary disposition, the feelings of wider sympathy only
for now, in this crisis, 'fast asleep in her mind'.

   In this simile of mother and child, set apart from the novel's story,
the existence or not of a father or husband or other offspring is not
important; only this one child is present to the parent in the time of
terror and then rescue. And in less dramatically focused forms,
almost all the significant family scenarios in the novel involve either
just one parental figure, or else some sort of co-parenting arrangement
in which a child is brought up alternately by two people. (Exceptions to this are in the lower classes: the Seagrim family, whose
daughter Molly is Tom's first love, and the impoverished Andersons,
who are helped by Tom despite the father's attempt to rob him.) In
the first category is the idealized sketch of the widow Mrs Miller,
who 'had been a most affectionate wife, and was a most fond and

tender mother' (617). She seems to combine the two qualities that might be divided between two different parents in another situation: 'For as this good woman had all the tenderness, so she had preserved all the authority of a parent; and as her indulgence to the desires of her children was restrained only by her fears for their safety and future welfare, so she never suffered those commands which proceeded from such fears to be either disobeyed or disputed' (620). Some sort of theoretical paragon, and not at all an object of Fielding's satire, Mrs Miller merits a textbook sentence of classically balanced clauses to show how she herself miraculously moves between the two poles of authority and indulgence. Their tenuous relationship is a constant theme of the proliferating educational philosophies of the period—and continues, with only slight modifications of terminology, to this day.

Other parenting situations involve now adult children who grew up moving at intervals between two households. The widowed Squire Western is the doting father of Sophia, Tom's long-term love and eventual bride; he and his sister Mrs Western ('Di' to her cousin, Lady Bellaston), who has no children of her own, have brought her up between them. At one point Sophia has spent over three years living with her aunt (143), and this is not just a single extended stay: 'I am sure, sister, you can't accuse me of ever denying to trust my daughter to you. She hath a lived wi' you a whole year and muore to a time, without my ever zeeing her' (746–7). Sophia refers to Mrs Western as 'a second mother to me' (296). Another instance of alternate guardianship is Jack Nightingale, the man about town whom Tom persuades to do the decent thing and marry his pregnant girlfriend, Nancy Miller. Nightingale grew up in his uncle's house as well as in his father's; as his uncle's godson, he 'had lived more with him than with his father' (681).

These situations of doubled upbringing, mentioned almost in passing, form the background to prominent disputes between the two parent figures in each case as to their principles of education; for all concerned this is a tenacious subject for argument. Squire Western treats his daughter with 'the utmost profusion of fondness' (257) and 'the most violent affection'. This parental excessiveness has affinities with Squire Allworthy's show of love for Tom, but it occurs in the context of a very different kind of social presence. Allworthy is an

exemplary public figure and a sweet-tempered man, whereas Western is mainly interested in hunting and otherwise consorting with
male company; the measure of Sophia's hold on him is that 'his
beloved dogs themselves almost gave place to her in his affections'
(172). He spars with his sister over the way that Sophia has been
brought up, which Mrs Western calls 'a foolish education, neither
adapted to her fortune nor her family' (799). After the girl has run
away from the marriage her father has set up with young Blifil, her
aunt delivers herself of 'the following consolation':

'it is all your own doings, and you have nobody to thank but yourself. You
know she hath been educated always in a manner directly contrary to my
advice, and now you see the consequence. Have I not a thousand times
argued with you about giving my niece her own will? But you know I never
could prevail upon you; and when I had taken so much pains to eradicate
her headstrong opinions, and to rectify your errors in policy, you know she
was taken out of my hands; so that I have nothing to answer for. Had I
been trusted entirely with the care of her education, no such accident as this
had ever befallen you; so that you must comfort yourself by thinking it was
all your own doing; and, indeed, what else could be expected from such
indulgence?' (483)

The presumption is that two mutually exclusive methods of education have been applied, each attributable to one of the two people
who raised Sophia; and the outcome which is her adult behaviour
will be the responsibility of one or the other of them, but not both.
As usual, the alternative parenting principles appear to come down
to the choice between 'indulgence' and restraint, with disputes
hingeing not on the validity of the alternatives, but on what counts
as enough or too little of either: 'Zounds! Sister,' answered he, 'you
are enough to make one mad. Have I indulged her?' (483). Parents
are deemed to have, and to argue about, a philosophy of educational practice, and the practice adopted is thought—at least in the
safety of a comic fiction—to be decisive in forming the subsequent
character of the child to which it is applied.

The second case of educationally sparring co-parents is that of the
brothers Nightingale, father and uncle to Jack:

Mr Nightingale, the father, instead of attempting to answer his brother,
contented himself with only observing that they had always differed in their

sentiments concerning the education of their children. 'I wish,' said he, 'brother, you would have confined your care to your own daughter, and never have troubled yourself with my son, who hath, I believe, as little profited by your precepts as by your example.' (681)

Quite independently of what happens to their children, arguing about education is almost a way of life and a way of fraternal relationship for these two: 'these brothers lived in a constant state of contention about the government of their children, both heartily despising the method which each other took' (866). This permanent stand-off between the two of them is not affected by the difference in their family situations. While Jack's father is widowed (like Western and Allworthy), the home of the other Nightingale is the only comfortable establishment in the novel to include both two parents and a child (three others have died). This marriage is praised with conscious exaggeration: 'With this woman he had, during twenty-five years, lived a life more resembling the model which certain poets ascribe to the golden age, than any of those patterns which are furnished by the present times' (679). The mother appears as co-parent, uncontentiously, of the remaining daughter, 'whom, in vulgar language, he and his wife had spoiled; that is, had educated with the utmost tenderness and fondness, which she returned to such a degree that she had actually refused a very extraordinary match with a gentleman a little turned of forty, because she could not bring herself to part with her parents' (679–80). But the wife is never heard of again, even in the fall-out when the daughter does what the novel's grown children generally do, whatever their education: she runs away to get married.

In the cases of Jack Nightingale and Sophia Western, childhood and adolescence involve going to and fro between different places and relations—an oscillation which is translated by these parental figures into educational alternatives, two mutually incompatible methods. The distance between the parental places and times goes along with a separation of educational precepts which is not connected to any falling out between the 'parents' over other matters. But as sibling pairs, they have long-standing and seemingly unshakeable relationships and this seems, in the logic of the novel, to make them naturally fit to be parental pairs. With the Nightingale

brothers, educational theory seems to be the topic of choice for a
sibling relationship that is sustained by the energy of perpetual dispute. With the Westerns, brother and sister, the tussling over Sophia
is based on the primacy of their own relationship: of his sister,
Squire Western 'stood more in awe than of any other human creature, though he never would own this, nor did he perhaps know it
himself' (745).

In both these sibling co-parenting set-ups, one of the two is the
father of the child. A related situation is that of Tom himself. Tom
does not move between two different households, but he is raised by
a brother and sister, one of whom eventually turns out to be his
natural parent (and one of whom is his adoptive father, from the
beginning). At one level, this fraternal parenting which is the novel's
norm might seem to represent its comic or semi-serious alternative
to marriage, which is frequently lampooned by various characters as
an obviously ludicrous social arrangement. Lady Bellaston refers to
'that monstrous animal a husband and wife' (721). The narrator
speaks of marriage—at least marriage in the olden days—as a form
of imprisonment for women: 'I have often suspected that those very
enchanters with which romance everywhere abounds were in reality
no other than the husbands of those days; and matrimony itself was,
perhaps, the enchanted castle in which the nymphs were said to be
confined' (529).

Squire Western's theory might lead to the conclusion that brothers and sisters make the best partners: 'He did indeed consider a
parity of fortune and circumstances to be physically as necessary an
ingredient in marriage as difference of sexes, or any other essential;
and had no more apprehension of his daughter's falling in love with
a poor man than with any animal of a different species' (261).
Squire Western's own marriage is sketched as a memory of mutual
hostility, in which 'Western at length heartily hated his wife' and
continues to do so long after her death, by imagining her pleasure
in any misfortune that occurs; and their daughter Sophia is involved
in this posthumously extended marital disputatiousness: 'These
invectives he was especially desirous of throwing forth before Sophia;
for as he loved her more than he did any other, so he was really
jealous that she had loved her mother better than him' (295). In this
triangle, it is the parents who vie for the love of the child—not, as

in the Oedipal situation which Freud would put forward, the child who wants the exclusive love of one parent and hates the other as a rival. The more comfortably sparring co-parental relationship with his sister provides Squire Western with a familial *modus vivendi* much preferable to his past marriage.

However volatile on the surface, brother–sister relationships seem mainly to represent an image of continuity and stability that is absent from the more contingent (and more recently started) relationships of lovers or married couples. But of all the types of relationship to be found in the novel, the ones represented as most extreme are those between parents and children. One chapter heading promises 'extraordinary instances of paternal madness and filial affection' (311). In fact the excessiveness—as the difference between madness and mere affection implies—is all on the paternal side in the 'instance' which ensues, that of Squire Western's alternation of impassioned paternal reactions:

her father treated her in so violent and outrageous a manner that he frightened her into an affected compliance with his will, which so highly pleased the good squire that he changed his frowns into smiles, and his menaces into promises; he vowed his whole soul was wrapped in hers...tears of joy trickled from those eyes which a few moments before had darted fire and rage against the dear object of all his affection. (314)

This is initially offered as an 'extraordinary' instance, but very quickly it seems to become the norm. The next paragraph makes parents, without distinction of sex, into a general type:

Instances of this behaviour in parents are so common that the reader, I doubt not, will be very little astonished at the whole conduct of Mr Western. If he should, I own I am not able to account for it; since that he loved his daughter most tenderly, is, I think, beyond dispute. So indeed have many others who have rendered their children most completely miserable by the same conduct; which, though it is almost universal in parents, hath always appeared to me to be the most unaccountable of all the absurdities which ever entered into the brain of *that strange prodigious creature man.* (314)

'Almost universal in parents', and yet both absurd and the least susceptible of explanation. Parental inconsistency is itself out of synch with any other human phenomenon, Fielding's narrator implies; it is as if being a parent makes people even more absurd and incomprehensible than they already are by virtue of being that odd thing which is human.

Squire Western eventually comes to rest as a devoted grandfather to Sophia and Tom's two small children: he is last seen declaring the 'tattling' of his toddler granddaughter to be 'sweeter music than the finest cry of dogs in England' (870). The 'extraordinary' but allegedly commonplace phenomenon of wild parental inconsistency is confined to a single illustrative episode, the declaration of its virtual universality then almost appearing as a contagiously over-the-top moment of narrative exaggeration. Yet parenthood itself—for both natural and other parents—retains a certain unwavering hold as a continuous focus of narrative interest, and one that goes deeper—insofar as there is depth in *Tom Jones*—than the treatment of love affairs or any other kind of attachment. Tom himself, for instance, jogs through childhood and young adulthood without seeming to suffer from any preoccupations about his own identity or his love life that might keep him back from whatever enjoyments are offered within the current episode. One true love (Molly Seagrim) is untraumatically, and only by implication, superseded by another, Sophia Western (the narrative forgets about Molly just as Tom apparently does).

At the end, the realization that Tom was the son of Bridget Allworthy, the woman who partly brought him up and the sister of his adopting father, occurs without any sense of a major shake-up in his understanding of who he is; nor has he ever been preoccupied with knowing where he came from. No emphasis is placed on the discovery that Tom's mother is of the same class as his adoptive (and, it turns out, his actual) family. This is not the world of Dickens's *Bleak House* where the revelation of Lady Dedlock's unmarried maternity is implicitly part of an argument against the prejudices and double moral standards of the culture. In Bridget Blifil, *née* Allworthy, *Tom Jones* also features a well-born unmarried mother, but she is not, like Lady Dedlock, seen as suffering from a guilty secret (or punished with subsequent childlessness). Fielding is didactic only in mocking the moralists like Mrs Deborah at the beginning. In the same vein, the prospect, earlier in *Tom Jones*, that the hero might accidentally have slept with the woman then thought to have been his mother, does not seem to bother either him or anyone else unduly, even though the word is proclaimed out loud: 'Incest—and with a mother!' (810).[4]

But if the general temper of *Tom Jones* is uncomplicatedly casual, the few moments of emotional intensity stand out all the more. One such moment occurs precisely in relation to the realization that Tom is after all, in reality, closely related to the Squire, who now recalls the long-ago scene of his finding the baby in his bed:

All who know me, can witness that I loved him as dearly as if he had been my own son. Indeed, I have considered him as a child sent by fortune to my care. I still remember the innocent, the helpless situation in which I found him. I feel the tender pressure of his little hands at this moment. He was my darling, indeed he was.   (817–18)

At no other point in the novel does any character evoke a distant, poignant memory in this way, or make an emotional connection of continuity or distance between past and present moments. But here, in a kind of fore-echo of Silas Marner's repeatedly emphasized belief that his foundling daughter was 'sent' to him, something of the same profound significance is given to Squire Allworthy's experience. For once, a small and telling moment, instead of vanishing in the wake of the next narrative turn, has taken on the momentousness of a long-held memory, evoked in the tiny detail of the hands: 'he had now got one of his fingers into the infant's hand, which by its gentle pressure, seem[ed] to implore his assistance' (35).

---

[4] Martin C. Battestin makes an eloquently intriguing case for the seriousness, at some level, of the presence of 'Incest!' in *Tom Jones*, linking it to the possibility of sibling sexual relations in Fielding's adolescence; 'Henry Fielding, Sarah Fielding, and "the dreadful Sin of Incest"', *Novel* 13 (1979), 6–18. See also Ellen Pollak, *Incest and the English Novel, 1684–1814* (Baltimore: Johns Hopkins University Press, 2003), ch. 5.

9

Placement

Jane Austen's *Mansfield Park*

Like *Great Expectations*, *Silas Marner*, *Tom Jones*, and the Moses story represented in Hogarth's painting, Austen's *Mansfield Park* is about an adoption—this one undertaken neither as a wish for individual parental fulfilment (*Great Expectations*), nor with that being the unlooked-for result (*Silas Marner*), nor because of a needy foundling (*Tom Jones*, *Silas Marner*). The adoption of Fanny Price by her aunts and uncle is pragmatically charitable: not so much rescuing the child (as with the foundling narratives) but helping out a relative (Fanny's mother) by taking a child off her hands. *Mansfield Park* is not passionate in parental emotions, whether adoptive or natural. In a proto-modern way, it considers the effects of class and place in moulding and educating a growing child's consciousness; its formatively enduring early attachments are those with sibling figures.

At the same time, like Jane Austen's other novels, *Mansfield Park* is centred on young people at or near the marriageable moment, and ends with the happy settlement of at least one union. It is also, partly, and also like other Austen novels, a kind of *Bildungsroman* for one at least of its female characters. First seen in childhood, Fanny Price is the girl whose life is followed in detail up to the point of her marriage, and she is also cast as one of the chief moral voices in the novel, sharing that privilege only with her soulmate and cousin and eventual husband, Edmund; it is through Fanny's eyes and consciousness, alongside the narrator's, that the novel's events are seen. In one way, Fanny is fairly single-minded throughout, never wavering from her devotion to the boy, then man, whom she loves—and eventually gets to marry. Here, there is no story, apart from the diversion which for most of the novel seems to be leading to Edmund marrying someone else, and the other diversion which is Fanny's assiduous pursuit by the someone else's brother, Henry Crawford. The novel puts Henry through so many transformations of character in the speculations of others that when he is finally revealed as irredeemably bad through his elopement with a married woman, one of Fanny's cousins, it is almost as if he might have independently walked out on the moral novel, giving up in the most dramatically decisive way on trying to appear to be good.

Alongside this mainline drama of love and marriage prospects, *Mansfield Park* also involves intermittent and ongoing discussion, both implied and expressed, of different patterns of parenthood and education. What makes the child become the adult they turn out to be? What is the relationship between the 'ties' or 'attachments' of early life and those that a person takes on or falls into in adulthood? As Marilyn Butler points out, education was the commonest of themes in the fiction of the time.[1] Fanny's position as an adopted child— from the age of 9 she is brought up with her mother's sister's children—provides a cue for reflection on the forming significance of different home environments and modes of parenthood.

At 18 Fanny is sent back to her original family in her native town of Portsmouth on an extended visit which is meant, from the point of view of her uncle, to function as an 'experiment';[2] hopefully it will teach her the value of her second home and the kind of advantageous marriage that is currently being proposed to her (with a man she does not love). But from the start, Fanny's adoption—her transfer from her initial place and home to another—had itself been represented as a kind of experimental project. It is not born out of any established or sudden desire on the part of the prospective parental figures to acquire a new child, or this child in particular; nor from any likelihood of abandonment or neglect on the part of the girl's existing parents. Instead it is set out as a sensible scheme of practical use to an overburdened family member: 'Let us send for the child' (43).

[1] 'Its beginning must have encouraged contemporaries to feel that here was yet another novel by a female about female education'; Marilyn Butler, *Jane Austen and the War of Ideas* (1975; Oxford: Clarendon Press, 1987), 219.

[2] Jane Austen, *Mansfield Park* (1814), ed. Tony Tanner (London: Penguin, 1985), 364, 404. Further page references will be included in the main text.

Lady Bertram's double imperative—a project to be shared between 'us', an order or invitation to be sent in a letter to Portsmouth—comes midway in the family conference that begins *Mansfield Park*. The upshot is that Fanny Price spends the second half of her childhood as part of her aunt and uncle's household, much superior to that of her own parents, growing up alongside her four cousins. There are three parties, three prospective parental figures, to Fanny's proposed transfer to a new place and a new, or at least an extended family. Lady Bertram—who never shows more decisiveness at any point in the novel than this one—is joined by her husband, Sir Thomas, and her sister, Mrs Norris. The project of bringing Fanny to live at Mansfield is not prompted by any sudden need, like parental death, or by any wish for a new child on the part of the prospective parents; nor does it have to do with a special singling out of Fanny herself. It comes about in response to a letter from the two women's long estranged sister, who married beneath her. Now on her ninth pregnancy, she is bringing up 'a superfluity of children' (42) on a low income and asks for any help that her sisters can offer. First there was a dispatch of 'money and baby-linen' from Lady Bertram, accompanied by 'friendly advice and professions' from Sir Thomas. But, 'within a twelvemonth', the idea of 'a more important advantage to Mrs Price' is mooted: that she 'should be relieved from the charge and expense of one child entirely out of her great number' (43). So the transaction has nothing to do with Fanny personally; she is simply 'the selected child' (45) out of a large set, in a process of moderate provision on one side, selective reduction on the other.

Given the multiplicity of children, and the multiplicity of willing guardians, the discussion about the girl not yet picked out as Fanny has none of the urgency that attaches to the moment when Silas Marner determines to take in the foundling who has been 'sent' to him, or the much later moment in the girl's life when her birth father and his wife, desperate to have a child, seek to adopt her themselves. Nor is there any of the individual intensity of need that occurs when Miss Havisham, in her own way, 'sends for' a little girl; or when Magwitch, at a distance, makes himself the maker and 'second father' of Pip the gentleman. The adoption of Fanny in *Mansfield Park* has nothing to do with the reciprocal rights or claims of parents and children, or with the desire of any one of the adults for a child who will be their own. The adoption of the sister's daughter is only imagined as a practical arrangement between several adults for lightening the burden on one of their relations—not as a potential emotional bond between substitute parent or parents and child. It is not about someone else acquiring or seeking a parental tie as a privilege, or about Fanny or any of the other children being thought of as in need.

Mrs Norris, who is a widow, does mention her own childlessness, but not as a cause of pity or regret; the circumstance simply has the effect of making her nephews and nieces the natural recipients of what would otherwise have been her small maternal largesse: 'Having no children of my own, who should I look to in any little matter I may ever have to bestow, but the children of my sisters?' (43). It becomes one of the novel's recurring jokes that in the event Mrs Norris, while continuing to proclaim her own generosity, never actually contributes anything to Fanny's maintenance; but that does not alter the point. 'Having no children of my own' is mentioned passingly and pragmatically, not painfully, as a situation with useful bearings on the present issue.

Sir Thomas raises two objections to the adoption project. One has the appearance of personal concern for Fanny's feelings: that there might be 'cruelty instead of kindness in taking her from her family'. But this is meant in relation to the change of social position that her removal would entail: 'a girl so brought up must be adequately provided for.' There follows some speculation as to the likely outcomes of Fanny's altered situation; there is a consensus between Sir Thomas and Mrs Norris as to the 'propriety...of providing for a child one had in a manner taken into one's own hands'— Mrs Norris's words. Either, and most probably—'ten to one'—she will marry; with the education and the status that she will have acquired, 'she has the means of settling well, without further expense to any body', as Mrs Norris puts it, in unashamedly economic terms. Or, failing that, as Sir Thomas continues, in quasi-contractual language, 'we must secure to the child, or consider ourselves engaged to secure to her hereafter, as circumstances may arise, the provision of a gentlewoman' (44): an unmarried Fanny would have the right to a lady's companion (and not, for instance, though this is not said, have to fall back on that sad occupation herself).

Sir Thomas's second concern is not stated in the same confidently legal terms. 'He thought of his own four children—of his two sons—of cousins in love, &c' (43). Mrs Norris breezily clears away the nervous allusiveness by spelling out the fear and then turning it on its head:

'You are thinking of your sons—but do you not know that of all things upon earth that is the least likely to happen; brought up, as they would be, always together like brothers and sisters? It is morally impossible. I never knew an instance of it. It is, in fact, the only sure way of providing against the connection. Suppose her a pretty girl, and seen by Tom or Edmund for the first time seven years hence, and I dare say there would be mischief.... But breed her up with them from this time, and suppose her even to have the beauty of an angel, and she will never be more to either than a sister.'   (44)

The sibling-like connection is both low-key—'never be more than'—and pre-emptive.

That Fanny does marry Edmund, one of these sons, that she is in love with him for most of her adolescence, and he is eventually in love with her, is perhaps less of an irony than the fact that the issue of quasi-incest is never touched on again—except, indirectly once more, in the context of other events which are seen to have violated the proper ordering of familial and erotic relations. After Maria Rushworth, formerly Maria Bertram, has run off with Fanny's persistent suitor, Henry Crawford, Fanny is overcome:

She passed only from feelings of sickness to shudderings of horror; and from hot fits of fever to cold. The event was so shocking, that there were moments even when her heart revolted from it as impossible—when she thought it could not be. A woman married only six months ago, a man professing himself devoted, even *engaged*, to another—that other her near relation—the whole family, both families connected as they were by tie upon tie, all friends, all intimate together!—It was too horrible a confusion of guilt, too gross a complication of evil, for human nature, not in a state of utter barbarism, to be capable of!   (429–30)

For Fanny, the transgressions implied by what Maria and Henry have done are the equivalent of incest. They break open the intricate arrangements of 'families, connected...by tie upon tie, all friends, all intimate together!' by making the wrong connection, the over-connection. It is the end of civilization—'utter barbarism'. Fanny cannot find adequate names for the dissolution of order that the elopement represents to her; with its 'horror' and 'guilt' and 'confusion', it is a tragic catastrophe, the end of the moral world as she knows it.

Meanwhile Fanny's mother—the revelation of the news occurs while Fanny is on her extended visit to her first family—has a different reaction: 'Indeed, I hope it is *not* true . . . It would be so very shocking!—If I have spoken once to Rebecca about that carpet, I am sure I have spoke at least a dozen times; have I not, Betsey?— And it would not be ten minutes work' (429). For Mrs Price, the domestic order that really matters is the perpetual preoccupation of small chores and slow servants. This kind of order takes precedence in her thoughts over any distant report of the 'shocking' behaviour of her relatives or their friends. Mrs Price's unconscious deflation of her daughter's elevation of the incident to the heights of a disaster is not presented as a correct estimation of the moral seriousness of what has happened. But in other respects the novel is anything but dismissive of concerns over household management: this is one of the cardinal issues around which the questions about parenthood and adoption come to revolve.

By the time of her return to Portsmouth in early adulthood, Fanny has become a fully formed Mansfield young lady, judging her own parents and their establishment by the standards of the superior outsider she now is. Seeing the difference between the two places consolidates her second identity, as if it had been the first: 'After being nursed up at Mansfield, it was too late in the day to be hardened at Portsmouth' (404).

The chapters describing Fanny's stay at her old home are full of details of the dirt and noise and crowding and bad manners that Fanny finds herself surrounded with; from time to time her thoughts surface from the chaos to summarize in clean abstract prose the 'contrast' that she perceives: 'The elegance, propriety, regularity, harmony—and perhaps, above all, the peace and tranquillity of Mansfield, were brought to her remembrance every hour of the day, by the prevalence of every thing opposite to them *here*' (384). There are withering sketches of her mother and father. Neither pays her much attention—a mark, to Fanny, not just of parental neglect, but of the general rudeness of their household compared with the considerateness of Mansfield manners.

With her mother, as her visit approached, Fanny had hoped that 'they should soon be what mother and daughter ought to be to each other'. This would make up for a remembered lack of that implied relationship which Fanny can now attribute to Mrs Price having been 'occupied by the incessant demands of a house full of little children' (366). But nothing has changed, except the daughter's self-appointed capacity for moral and social assessment. Fanny provides the social worker's home report from hell. Her mother is deemed or damned by her daughter as

a partial, ill-judging parent, a dawdle, a slattern, who neither taught nor restrained her children, whose house was the scene of mismanagement and discomfort from beginning to end, and who had no talent, no conversation, no affection towards herself; no curiosity to know her better, no desire of her friendship, and no inclination for her company that could lessen her sense of such feelings. (383)

Lady Bertram is now the primary object of Fanny's daughterly love. When she is first reunited with her mother, there are 'looks of true kindness, and...features which Fanny loved the more, because they brought her aunt Bertram's before her' (371). Mrs Price is passingly affectionate, but no more: 'The instinct of nature was soon satisfied, and Mrs Price's attachment had no other source. Her heart and her time were already quite full; she had neither leisure nor affection to bestow on Fanny' (382). A maternal 'instinct of nature' is assumed, but assumed to be inherently limited, competing with other emotional and social demands. It exists in its own right, and by nature, but it is subordinate to a woman's other commitments. As an instinct it requires satisfaction, but a fuller 'attachment' would need more available personal inclination and more time. It is not a thing apart, but is inseparable from the daily life of existing domestic attentions and occupations: Mrs Price's 'full' timetable and 'heart', with no room in either for the addition of Fanny.[3]

[3] This model of a maternal instinct as present but of minor significance goes against Elisabeth Badinter's argument in *L'Amour en plus: Histoire de l'amour maternel ((XVIIème–XXème siècle)* (1980; Paris: Flammarion, 1981). Badinter thinks that the maternal instinct was invented as a definingly female quality and a mainstay of the ideology which confined women to a domestic role.

In the father's case, no expectation of special affection is mooted before Fanny's arrival, and none is found. Mr Price is the subject of a comedy sketch from the outset, when he arrives home with 'his own loud voice preceding him, as with something of the oath kind he kicked away his son's portmanteau, and his daughter's band-box in the passage'. Fanny, the daughter not seen for many years, 'sank down again on finding herself undistinguished in the dusk, and unthought of' (373). The reference that Fanny eventually provides for her father is as uncompromisingly negative as the verdict on her mother: 'he swore and he drank, he was dirty and gross. She had never been able to recal anything approaching to tenderness in his former treatment of herself' (382). When Henry Crawford visits, Mr Price does rise to a display of politeness in the role of 'an attached father' (395) to Fanny's beloved brother William; Henry's appearance equally elevates his wife to showing 'artless, maternal gratitude, which could not be unpleasing' (393). But these are exceptional moments. For the most part, because the family has been 'So long divided, and so differently situated, the ties of blood were little more than nothing' (418). As with Mrs Price's minimal maternal instinct, nature is easily outdone by other factors. The variable circumstances of geographical and social distance, maintained over time, have undone 'the ties of blood', now mentioned only as effectively non-existent.

Amid the social failings of her mother and father, Fanny herself takes on some remedial parental work in relation to her 14-year-old sister Susan, instructing her in the niceties of upper-class etiquette and getting her into reading with the help of a subscription to a circulating library. Susan's belated education is also Fanny's first independence. 'She became a subscriber—amazed at being any thing in *propria persona*, amazed at her own doings in every way; to be a renter, a chuser of books! And to be having any one's improvement in view in her choice!' (390–1). Like Fanny before her, Susan is singled out for separation from the detrimental Portsmouth ménage. The learning sessions are assisted by physical removal from the main domestic scene: 'By sitting together up stairs, they avoided a great deal of the disturbance of the house' (390). After this grooming from the advanced older sister, Susan is overjoyed to be invited to return with her to Mansfield. 'Visions of good and ill breeding, of old vulgarisms and new gentilities were before her; and she was meditating much upon silver forks, napkins, and finger glasses' (434). There is no disillusionment to follow this fantasy that sweeps from grand abstractions to the minutiae of dining-room etiquette. Eventually, when Fanny marries, Susan is there 'to supply her place' with Lady Bertram; 'she was established in Mansfield, with every appearance of equal permanency' (456). The 'place' of an adopted niece has now become fixed, with the need having shifted from that of the first to the adoptive mother—though no more attention than before to the individuality of the substitute (for the substitute) 'daughter'. Susan can be the new Fanny, just as Fanny could have been any one of Mrs Price's superfluity of children.

Nothing that is stated in *Mansfield Park*, whether by the narrator or by the characters, ever suggests that natural parents have a decisive role to determine the kind of adult that the child will become. On the contrary, the assumption is all on the other side; it is seen as quite obvious, in these developmental terms, that a Fanny transferred from Portsmouth to Mansfield at a still impressionable age will have profited from the re-education she received there. 'What would she have been if we had not taken her by the hand?' asks Mrs Norris. The implication is that Fanny's very identity has been made (or remade) by her being 'brought up in this family' (278); identity is not fixed at the beginning but is formed in relation to incompatible alternatives, what she is as opposed to what she 'would...have been'. At another point, Fanny's second formation is mentioned as if it were the only one, now standing as a defence against moving on. Edmund is counselling his cousin against her flat rejection of Henry Crawford, on the grounds that a change is bound to take time and effort:

the man who means to make you love him...must have very up-hill work, for there are all your early attachments, and habits, in battle array; and before he can get your heart for his own use, he has to unfasten it from all the holds upon things animate and inanimate, which so many years growth have confirmed, and which are considerably tightened for the moment by the very idea of separation. I know that the apprehension of being forced to quit Mansfield will for a time be arming you against him. (344)

In Edmund's theory of how a woman is successfully wooed, a suitor cannot simply add himself on to the 'array' of existing ties; he has to actively, even aggressively undo them in order to 'get your heart for his own use'. A little later, Fanny will summarize and translate this into her own protest against Henry's abruptness: 'How was I to have an attachment at his service, as soon as it was asked for?' (349). The prospective husband has before him a labour of numerous individual unfastenings from separate 'holds' that are currently 'tightened' in defence against his incursions. The 'attachments, and habits' are many and multifarious, and they encompass 'things animate and inanimate', separate but unspecified. These links and routines have come to be natural; they have been established over 'so many years growth'.

Edmund is referring here to Fanny's ties to Mansfield; her previous home is not alluded to. In the same way, Fanny's uncle appears, for Henry Crawford seeking to ask permission to marry her, 'to stand in the place of her parents' (314), in a precise native version of the legal guardian, *in loco parentum*. Yet only a little further on, when the visit to Portsmouth is mooted, Fanny is sent all the way back to the earlier place and people that had been obliterated or overlaid by the growth of all the subsequent Mansfield 'holds'. In this second account it is the ties already lost, long lost, which return and themselves seem to take the place of the present ties threatened by Henry's attack. It is with Portsmouth not Henry that, in her first joyful reaction to the news of the visit, she falls in love·

Had Fanny been at all addicted to raptures, she must have had a strong attack of them, when she first understood what was intended, when her uncle first made her the offer of visiting the parents and brothers, and sisters, from whom she had been divided almost half her life, of returning for a couple of months to the scenes of her infancy, with William as the protector and companion of her journey.   (364)

All the detailed attachments to Mansfield that Edmund mentioned vanish from sight without any effort, and Fanny's first world is brought back as the one from which she has been put asunder, 'divided almost half her life'. Where the loss of Mansfield was described quite abstractly as 'things animate and inanimate', here there are first and foremost 'parents and brothers, and sisters'. Now

it is Mansfield, unnamed, that is negatively cast, as the source of
what Fanny endured in being violently taken away from her home:

> The remembrance of all her earliest pleasures, and of what she had suffered
> in being torn from them, came over her with renewed strength, and it
> seemed as if to be at home again, would heal every pain that had since
> grown out of the separation. To be at the centre of such a circle, loved by
> so many, and more loved by all than she had ever been before, to feel af-
> fection without fear or restraint, to feel herself the equal of those who sur-
> rounded her...!   (364)

It is this fantasy of coming back home to a central place in the full-
ness of love which is torn down by the reality of her parents' indifference and that of most of her siblings when Fanny does go back;
the failings of Mr and Mrs Price both as civil human beings and as
Fanny's parents are brought out more by their disappointment of
Fanny's great expectations at this point. In the end, when Fanny
marries Edmund, she can be thoroughly installed in the place of a
good daughter for Sir Thomas and Lady Bertram; the marriage
functions almost as the confirmation of her full adoption into the
second or extended family, and the visit home also makes possible
her confident repudiation, now by her own adult choice and judgement, of 'the scenes of her infancy'.

By the time of its conclusion, then, *Mansfield Park* firmly endorses
the priority of nurture and cultural environment to 'the ties of blood'.
Fanny is what she becomes through the beneficent influence of her
second family (though it helps the narrative logic that the two families
are also connected as relations, so that Fanny in one sense is simply
restored to the gentility and wealth that her mother let go in marrying below her class). Informal adoption, in Fanny's case, enables the
effects of removal from one family environment to another to be
shown; and the mildly experimental air of this is amplified by the
novel's second case of quasi-adoption, which is that of Henry Crawford and his sister Mary. Like Fanny Price these two have spent the
second part of their childhood in the home of an uncle and aunt,
following the death of their parents. These surrogate parents are
sharply and succinctly sketched. Both of them are at once strong and
selective in their feelings for their charges, who implicitly make up for
what is unharmonious in their own relationship. '[T]hough agreeing

in nothing else', the narrator tells us, Admiral and Mrs Crawford 'were united in affection for these children, or at least were no farther adverse in their feelings than that each had their favourite, to whom they showed the greatest fondness of the two. The Admiral delighted in the boy, Mrs Crawford doated on the girl' (73–4). No separate account is given of the faults of the wife, who is dead by the time the Crawfords come to Mansfield, though she is included in Fanny and Edmund's shared condemnation of the negative 'effect of education' on the new neighbours: 'Yes, that uncle and aunt!' (275). The Admiral is declared to be 'a man of vicious conduct, who chose, instead of retaining his niece, to bring his mistress under his own roof' (74). The question of Henry's character, often debated in the course of the novel, is regularly tied to the influence of this uncle whom Henry defends as having been 'more than a father to me', a super-paternity then glossed as indulgence: 'Few fathers would have let me have my own way half so much' (299). When Henry is going through his period of ardent courtship of Fanny, his choice of object is proof to Edmund that he is after all 'unspoilt by his uncle' (347). The parent makes the man, for better or worse. When worse, the bad influence can even be represented as a form of infection: his sister praises 'the advantage to you of getting away from the Admiral before your manners are hurt by the contagion of his, before you have contracted any of his foolish opinions' (299). She uses a language of inevitable transmission from parent to child, but the bad blood is not biological, or not directly so (as with the Bertrams, one of the adopting couple is related, but not the other).

The background story of the Crawford siblings, adopted by an uncle and aunt just as Fanny is, seems to add weight to the novel's more general point about parenting. The adoption scenario reinforces the argument that it is the immediate cultural environment that forms the child. And here that argument is focused entirely on one parent, the uncle who is 'more than' a father—not, as in Fanny's case, on a broader picture of 'attachments, and habits' or else, at Portsmouth, of 'parents and brothers, and sisters'. The stories of Fanny and the Crawfords seem to uphold the theories of environmental influence that are intermittently articulated, and it is true that the general narrative perspective, as much as Fanny's own, roundly endorses a differentiation of Mansfield and Portsmouth in which Mansfield mores are self-evidently superior. Formed, or re-formed, by Mansfield, Fanny becomes its true daughter, and her shining success as a good Mansfield product is reinforced by Henry Crawford's failings as the product of the immoral Admiral.

But when we consider the many other offspring of the Portsmouth and Mansfield families, the outcomes are anything but consistent with the moral division that ought to follow from their upbringing in one or the other place. Of the four Bertram children, only Edmund is a paragon of virtue, properly matched to Fanny. The two daughters go wrong, the elder one spectacularly so (her elopement even makes it into the national press). The elder son, Tom, has to undergo a life-threatening illness in order to be rescued from 'the thoughtlessness and selfishness of his previous habits' (447). On the Portsmouth side, the bad outcomes that ought to be predictable from the noxious environment and indifferent parenting do not come about. None of the children, some of them in employment by the time of Fanny's visit, shows signs of going wrong; William is an Edmund before Edmund, the fraternal soulmate of Fanny's earliest years.

The Mansfield side of these stories is given some measure of explanation in the small accounts that are given of the Bertram children's upbringing, which is not the same as Fanny's because of the different treatment of her by the various parental figures. Sir Thomas is represented at the beginning of the novel as 'a truly anxious father' to his own children (55). He subsequently blames himself for Maria's transgression: 'Sir Thomas, poor Sir Thomas, a parent, and conscious of errors in his own conduct as a parent, was the longest to suffer' (446); the narrative supports Sir Thomas's own line of thought that there is a proper kind of conduct for a 'parent', who is thus responsible for any misconduct on the part of his children. Lady Bertram, who becomes like a mother to Fanny, and Fanny the most loving daughter to her, lolls about in a state of parental indifference with regard to her own girls:

To the education of her daughters, Lady Bertram paid not the smallest attention. She had not time for such cares. She was a woman who spent her days in sitting nicely dressed on a sofa, doing some long piece of needlework, of little use and no beauty, thinking more of her pug than her children. (55)

In the absence of their mother's active input, and with the imposition of her own, Mrs Norris is in effect the co-parent (with their father) of the Bertram daughters, blamed early on in the story for making them 'entirely deficient in the less common acquirements of self-knowledge, generosity, and humility. In every thing but disposition, they were admirably taught' (55). By the end of the story, after the scandal of Maria, the co-parent has become for Sir Thomas something like an intolerable spouse: 'He had felt her as an hourly evil, which was so much the worse, as there seemed no chance of its ceasing but with life; she seemed a part of himself, that must be borne for ever' (450). Mrs Norris in the end departs to spend her days with the disgraced Maria Rushworth, her most indulged niece in the past, as if there could be no more gruesome sentencing of either than to condemn them to continue their relationship as a permanent cohabitation. In a parallel dismissal, a second two-woman household is created to accommodate the other young woman the novel condemns: Mary Crawford. Mary's crime is ultimately no more than to have voiced inappropriately frivolous opinions at the time of the elopement scandal; but it is enough to find her guilty in the eyes of Edmund, her erstwhile suitor (who is therefore released to turn his attentions to Fanny at last), and she is packed off to live permanently with her half-sister, Mrs Grant.

Nowhere in *Mansfield Park* do the ties of 'blood' parenthood seem unconditional or even particularly strong (and the same is true of the correlative ties of sons and daughters to their natural parents); Sir Thomas Bertram, 'anxious' as a father, is probably the nearest to being an exception, and he is also the only parent in the novel who has a theory of what should be done in this position, criticizing his own parental performance both personally and generically: 'mismanagement' (448); 'a parent and conscious of errors in his own conduct as a parent' (446). Subsequent or surrogate parents may well show more emotional involvement with their charges than the original ones. Lady Bertram misses Fanny when she is away. Mrs Norris devotes herself to Lady Bertram's own daughters. The Crawfords' aunt (by marriage) and uncle give their respective adopted niece and nephew the 'affection' they do not give each other.

But if parent–child and husband–wife attachments are not compelling, sibling attachments are. Fanny's brother William's visit to
Mansfield is the occasion for a paean to this form of love, since

> even the conjugal tie is beneath the fraternal. Children of the same family,
> the same blood, with the same first associations and habits, have some
> means of enjoyment in their power, which no subsequent connections can
> supply; and it must be by a long and unnatural estrangement, by a divorce
> which no subsequent connection can justify, if such precious remains of the
> earliest attachments are ever entirely outlived.   (244)

This is the modern view of the power of first childish love, which for
Freud would be understood as the child's passion for the parents.
Here, the parents are not even mentioned; from the beginning, the
love is between the siblings, conveniently a boy–girl couple who
form already the prototype of later-life marriage. William and
Fanny indulge the fantasy, as they journey back to Portsmouth
together, of spending 'all their middle and later life together' in a
'little cottage' (369).

From this point of view, it is possible to look at Fanny's removal
to Mansfield as enabling the fulfilment of the wish to marry a brother
figure. Edmund is a second William: she partly grows up with him,
she loves him from the first. Although, on his side, the pattern is not
the same—he has had no equivalent affection for either of his own
sisters, and he is not initially disposed towards Fanny in the way that
she is towards him—his eventual falling for his cousin is linked to
the same emotional logic of the resilience of existing long-term
attachments. Edmund has been disappointed in his love for Mary
Crawford; he eventually comes to the conclusion, in relation to
Fanny, that 'her warm and sisterly regard for him would be foundation enough for wedded love'. The slowness of this realization is a
feature, sometimes, in cases of 'the cure of unconquerable passions,
and the transfer of unchanging attachments'. The passion for Mary
has been only a detour from the truer tie to the sister figure.
'[W]hat could be more natural than the change?' the narrator
arch-innocently asks (454).

10

At All Costs

George Moore's *Esther Waters*

One of the many ladies who employ Esther Waters during the first years of her son's life is a novelist called Miss Rice, who sits all day reading and is struck by the unfamiliarity, for her, of the story her servant tells her. 'She was one of those secluded maiden ladies so common in England, whose experience of life is limited to a tea-party, and whose further knowledge of life is derived from the yellow-backed French novels which fill their bookcases.'[1] The present novel, we are to understand, is not like these, nor is it like the novels that Miss Rice herself produces: 'her thoughts went back for a moment to the novel she was writing, so pale and conventional did it seem compared with this rough page torn out of life' (245).

Esther Waters was published in 1894. Like many writers at this time, George Moore boasts of the superior truth to 'life' of his own novel by loudly dismissing the 'conventional' literary novels it is not. Esther's own illiteracy, which persists throughout the novel despite one employer giving her lessons, and her immersion, with Miss Rice, in a world of books, seems to lend weight to Moore's wish to proclaim both the credibility and the extremity of his narrative. Esther Waters's world is meant to be a world that is not normally shown in proper literature, a piece of the 'rough' life—unrefined in both social and literary terms—that lies beyond the boundaries of genteel fiction. The promise of new and shocking literary, or less than literary territory, is also the selling point: Esther's story will

[1] George Moore, *Esther Waters* (1894), ed. David Skilton (Oxford: Oxford University Press, 1983), 204. Further page references will be given in the main text.

educate the novel's readers, who may be allowed to distance
themselves from the literary insularity of Miss Rice, but are still
presumed to be ignorant of lives like Esther's.

The radical charge of *Esther Waters* is to depict the struggles of a
working-class girl who has a baby out of wedlock and is determined
to keep it, on her own, and against all economic and social odds. In
the manner of other naturalist novelists of the period, Moore gives
meticulously precise details of exactly how much Esther can earn in
the various grades of servant; the practical difficulties and expenses
of getting a job in the first place; the prejudices in the way of
employment for a woman known to have a child. In the early years
of her child's life she just about earns enough to survive by working
as a wet-nurse for a lady while her own baby is farmed out to a
woman who has neglectful care of several children. The babies of
the lady's two previous wet-nurses both died; Esther gets out in time
to save her own when she realizes that this outcome is not only
likely but actively desired by her own employer (as she will then give
undistracted attention to the baby she is being paid to breast-feed).
This is a sharp exposé of the exploitation of poor mothers involved
in the practice of wet-nursing, a version of physical motherhood
which depends on the substitute mother having a child of her own.

For all her inability to read and write, Esther is shown as a
supremely articulate heroine, able at many stages in the novel to
voice a reasoned and passionate protest against the system that is
working against her simple desire and need to hang on to her child.
She is equally sharp when her boy's father reappears by chance and
wants to get back together with her (their son, by this time, is 8):

'I 'avent't time to 'ear all your rubbish. Now what 'ave you to say? Come,
get it out.'
    'There's the boy.'
    'Oh, it is the boy you're thinking of?'
    'Yes, and you too, Esther. The mother can't be parted from the child.'
    'Very likely; the father can, though.'   (207)

Within just this one nugget numerous possible divisions and connections are evoked: the differential relationship of mother or father to
a baby; the relative weight of a parent's connection to the child or
to the other parent; the existence of children as motive for maintaining

or, in this case, recommencing a relationship with the other parent. The father here, William Latch, is in a double bind: either he is at fault for giving precedence to his parental responsibilities over his love for Esther, or else—as has happened earlier—he is blamed for having neglected the child up till now:

If she'd only listen. She was prettier than ever. He had never cared for anyone else. He would marry her when he got his divorce, and then the child would be theirs. She didn't answer him, and her blood boiled at the word 'theirs.' How could Jackie become their child? Was it not she who had worked for him, brought him up? And she thought as little of his paternity as if he had fallen from heaven into her arms.   (202)

Esther's argument here is not about the primacy of the mother's bond over the father's, but about which parent, in practice, has supported and reared the child. Her postnatal work, nothing to do with her being a mother as opposed to a father, has retroactively transformed her baby into a case of parthenogenesis. The child's 'paternity' is of no account, because it is she who has 'worked for him, brought him up', not because it is she who is naturally his primary parent.

Moore's plotting of the novel cleverly undermines various standard narratives of romance and marriage, by including them in a different order. At the beginning of the novel, William and Esther have sex just once, after which Esther wants nothing more to do with him. He never knows of her pregnancy, and she never seeks him out after she has given birth to the child. William turns up again, post-marriage, to woo and then live with the woman who is also, as he learns, the mother of his child. He is also, at this point, in competition with another suitor, one Fred Parsons, and the difference between these two men appears for Esther—as if at the start of her life—as the choice between two possible future directions: one with the religious Fred, and the other as a Soho pub landlady. In this moment of decision and possibility, she sees herself as inexperienced; and sees the possibility offered as one that will show her, like a reader of a realist novel, a world that she does not know:

She had never seen much life, and felt somehow that she would like to see a little life; there would not be much life in the cottage at Mortlake; nothing but the prayer-meeting. She stopped thinking, for she had never thought like that before, and it seemed as if some other woman whom she hardly knew was thinking for her. She seemed like one standing at cross roads, unable to decide which road she would take.   (238)

In this disoriented experience of a choice, a real life-choice, it is as if the boy has disappeared. Esther is cast back to a situation she missed, of the young girl choosing between two men. But it is also the case that the new life henceforth, whichever of the two roads or men she might go for, will take her away from her emotional and practical preoccupation with parenthood.

The novel bears this out with some force. After she has gone off to live with William (who does get his divorce and does marry her), the son Jackie all but vanishes from the narrative, apart from a momentary acknowledgement, putting him second, that 'I've my husband and my boy to look to' (302). Some years and many chapters later it turns out from his mother's visit to her 'great tall fellow of fifteen' (359) that he has been at a boarding school of some unspecified kind, and he reappears, in person, at the very end, in time for his father's death and then, somewhat later, as a handsome soldier come to visit his mother. Apart from these instances, he is almost unmentioned in his absence, as the vicissitudes of the couple's doings take over the focus of the novel. The second chance of Esther's own new life has the effect of displacing the previous centre of her interest; but at the same time, it is true that the boy is simply getting older.

In some ways, then, *Esther Waters* reverses the usual story: instead of (by default) first no child, then marriage, then baby and parenthood, the sequence is rather: first baby and parenthood, then marriage to the father, then no child. This narrative oddness adds to the effect of Moore's social critique, as well as the shock he wants to inflict on his readers: all the proper elements are present, but they are out of order. Nor is the narrative one of a woman's irredeemable sexual fall. Esther has a baby, but is later given all the novelistic chances of a settled married life. Here too Moore does not operate a simple reversal of expectations, so that a downfall is not irretrievable. Instead, he continues the story past the moment of (redeeming) marriage, and ultimately leaves Esther literally back where she started, living with (and notionally working for) the woman who was her first employer, in a house that, like both of their lives, has much declined.

One of the results of Moore's mixing and stirring of familiar narrative elements is that both motherhood and fatherhood come to be scrutinized as matters of some contingency and infinite variability. When William appears halfway through his son's childhood, he has to become the boy's father: to adopt the role himself, but also to be accepted in it by both Esther and their son. The fragility of these many points of connection is highlighted by the simultaneous presence in Esther and Jackie's lives of a second possible father, the other candidate for marriage. As Esther confides to Miss Rice (who is no doubt gathering material for her own novel):

'He's been with me to see Jackie, and they both took to each other wonderful like; it couldn't 'ave been more so if 'e'd been 'is own father. But now all that's broke up, for when Fred meets William it is as likely as not as he'll think quite different.' (203)

In fact, it is not the meeting of Fred and William (which never happens) that breaks up the beginning bond between son and potential stepfather, but Jackie's own meeting with William. Unlike the reported introduction to Fred, the first encounter with the actual father is fraught with rivalry and separation:

She hated him to see the child, and to assert her complete ownership she clasped Jackie to her bosom without a word of explanation, and questioned him on matters about which William knew nothing, William standing by all the while like a stranger looking tenderly on his son, waiting for Esther to introduce them. (220)

Initially, the very statement that 'I'm your father' goes against what the boy thinks he knows: 'Father died before I was born; mother told me' (220). And Esther's exclusive claim, her single 'ownership' of her son, puts her in competition not only with the newly arrived father but also, in a gentler way, with his long-standing carer, Mrs Lewis, at whose house both meetings with prospective fathers take place. She presents herself and Esther as in effect Jackie's co-parents up to that point:

I 'ope, sir, we've brought 'im up to your satisfaction; we've done the best we could. He's a dear boy. There's been a bit of jealousy between us on 'is account, but for all that we 'aven't spoilt him. (221)

Subsequently, in the one vignette of the late-formed nuclear family, a mild trouble over the separate strength of the different parent–child ties is again evoked: ' "You will come, won't you, mummie? I shan't go to sleep till you do." Esther and William both laughed, and Esther was pleased, for she was still a little jealous of his love for his father' (251–2).

Mrs Lewis, Jack's second parent until the addition of William, is never heard of again (except for one passing moment when Esther, without William, is on the way to visit her but misses the train); the narrative does not concern itself with her, or with 8-year-old Jackie's reactions to the sudden change in his family situation. But up to this point, at least since his removal from the murderous 'baby farm', Mrs Lewis has been Jackie's constant carer, with his mother visiting them in Peckham as and when she has a few Sunday hours of her own. 'Keeping' her baby, for Esther, has meant in practice not having him with her but paying for him to be brought up by another woman (and this will continue after her marriage to William, when Jackie is sent away to boarding school). Her very determination to keep him alive, to provide him with sustenance, requires their physical separation (and her delegation of round-the-clock rearing to another woman). Without any other choice, Esther has been a provider at the expense of living with her child—a situation that Moore documents with the brutally precise figures of Esther's wages and hours in relation to the amount that she pays Mrs Lewis. It is her box, not her boy, that accompanies her when she departs from Miss Rice's house to begin her new life with William and their son (246).

The same distinction of parental functions is raised in relation to the newfound father who, from a position of relative affluence, offers at least 'maintenance' (231) if Esther refuses his proposal of marriage:

'If you won't, I can only say I am sorry; but that shan't stop me from paying you as much a week as you think necessary for Jack's keep and his schooling. I don't want the boy to cost you anything. I'd like to do a great deal more for the boy, but I can't do more unless you make him my child.' (236)

To 'make him my child' is a gift that Esther may bestow, or not—and not, for instance an obligation that is William's by virtue of his biological paternity, which is not in question. Economic provision—what Esther has been struggling to maintain up till now, at the cost of actually living with the boy—is presented as a simple benefit, one that is separable from the fuller adoption of Jack becoming his child through his marrying her or living with her.[2]

Although William's paternity is not offered as an unassailable argument for him to become Jackie's father in practice, it comes into play in relation to his rival, now potentially demoted in the eyes of the child who knows he has another father: 'Jackie would never take kindly to Fred as a stepfather, and would grow to dislike him more and more;…it would end by his going to live with William, and his being led into a life of betting and drinking' (232). For Fred, whatever his best intentions, there would be no control over Jackie's affections:

'But think if we was to marry. As like as not I should have children, and they'd be more in your sight than my boy.'

'Esther, I promise that—'

'Just so, Fred; even if you loved him like your own, you can't make sure that he'd love you.'

'Jackie and I—'

'Ah, yes; he'd have liked you well enough if he'd never seen his father. But he's so taken to his father, and it would be worse later on. He'd never be contented in our 'ome. He'd be always after him, and then I should never see him, and he would be led away into betting and drink.' (242)

Again, the fear of the dissolute life that William's influence might produce is voiced—but the danger is now associated not with Jackie's living with his father, but the opposite.

Moore cleverly uses the two possible husbands and fathers to point up a choice or uncertainty in relation to the child. Esther's

---

[2] Under the terms of the Bastardy Laws Amendment Act of 1872, it was possible for single mothers to apply through the courts for maintenance to be paid by their child's father. Unlike the situation in other European countries, a child in England who had been born out of wedlock could not be legitimated by its parents' subsequent marriage until the passing of the Legitimacy Act of 1926. See Stephen Cretney, *Family Law in the Twentieth Century: A History* (Oxford: Oxford University Press, 2003), 530–3, 547–51.

difficulty of deciding between the two men representing two possible
futures is echoed by what she imagines to be her son's; but in his
case, the alternatives carry the possibility of future resentment and
revision (the present choice is not his). Like Henry James's young
heroine in *What Maisie Knew* (discussed in Chapter 11), which
appeared just three years after *Esther Waters*, Jackie suffers from a
multiplication of possible parents, in his case sudden. In Moore's
scenario, the boy goes from having no fathers at all to suddenly
having two (who must battle it out for his mother's choice and his
own affection). Meanwhile the same alteration viewed as the provision of a husband for his mother simultaneously has the effect of
depriving him of another mother, the woman who could say of
herself and Esther that 'We' have brought him up.

At the end of the novel, after William's death, Moore takes Esther
all the way back to the place where she appeared at the beginning,
walking up the road from the station to start work at the big house
on the Downs west of Brighton. As she recalls her first meeting with
William, there is an echo of the ending of Dickens's *Great Expectations*, when Pip finds himself back at Miss Havisham's decaying,
untended house and encounters there an Estella whose own life has
been as unhappy as his. Here, Esther becomes the companion as
much as the servant of her first employer, the two women finishing
in the same place as solitary mothers living for the brief returns of
their absent adult sons. Jack comes to see Esther at the very end,
and there is also a passing visit from Mrs Barfield's own son.

In bringing Esther all the way back to her first setting out, this
ending seems in one way to cast doubt on the substance of all the
intervening years. Esther is as she was, a penniless and unconnected
woman on her own. In the years of her absence she has had and
raised a child, and she has been married and lost a husband. The
son is grown—and gone; Esther has gone back to a life of mildly
religious activity (both she and Mrs Barfield are members of the
Plymouth Brethren). With Jack, Esther has gone through the full
generational story of a passionate maternal love that gradually loses
its all-consuming urgency as the child grows up.

At the beginning of her motherhood, spurred by the fear for her
baby's health, she had walked out on the establishment where she
has been a wet-nurse and crossed London with the determination

'to save him from Mrs Spires'; everything else, the house and the place, falls away: 'The intensity and the oneness of her desire seemed to annihilate time, and when she got out of the omnibus she walked with a sort of animal-like instinct straight for the house' (152). The birth of the boy is preceded by a distressing hospital labour, with peering indifferent medical students—'they talked of the plays they had seen, and those they wished to see' (123)—and 'a scream from Esther' that leads to the specification of the pain-relieving drug of choice: 'I shall administer chloroform' (125). These details take readers inside the reality not just of a labour but of a contemporary maternity ward; and much is made of Esther's struggle to get herself registered for a place at Queen Charlotte's Hospital.[3] But after the birth, when the baby is brought to her, the emotional register sets Esther in a completely new world:

> Its eyes were open; it looked at her, and her flesh filled with a sense of happiness so deep and so intense that she was like one enchanted. And when she took the child in her arms she thought she must die of happiness. (125–6)

Moore strikingly conveys an experience of Madonna-like worship: 'She could not sleep for thinking of him, and the night passed in long adoration' (126).

Esther's love for her child is presented as a form of passion that is beyond comparison with any other relationship she has known: 'A sudden imagination let her see him playing in the little street, waiting for her to come home, and her love for him went to her head like madness, and she wondered at herself; for it seemed almost unnatural to love anything as she did this child' (178). The feeling gathers all the more power from its prompting by the most painfully practical of predicaments: at this point, Esther is once again out of a job, and elaborately repeating the calculation whereby with a salary of 'eighteen pounds', 'she could do very well', whereas 'sixteen

---

[3] This 'lying-in' hospital had its beginnings in 1739. It was unusual in admitting unmarried women (although only for a first baby); other maternity hospitals in the period might even include this restriction in their names (the Lying-in Hospital for Married Women was founded in 1749). An informational film of 1932, *Maternity: A Film of Queen Charlotte's Hospital* (made by Personal Films and available via the Wellcome Trust website, <www.wellcomecollection.org>) explicitly states: 'No unmarried mother is refused'.

pounds', the going rate for a maid-of-all-work, will lead sooner or later to the workhouse; between these two numbers, frequently repeated as Esther is forced to move from one employment to another, are the 'seventeen hours' of the daily work expected of her. When Jackie is 'waiting for her to come home', he is waiting where he lives, but not with his mother. And in the first months of Jackie's life, before she departs in rage and fear at the news of his illness, Esther is in the extraordinary position—emotionally intolerable but in practice the only one available—of being able to support her son only by living apart from him and giving her services as a wet-nurse to another baby. From the start, the intense love is marked by separation and longing. It is with two of her women employers, and also with her husband, that Esther knows the ordinary domesticity of a close relationship under the same roof, but these relationships—including the one with William—have none of the unconditional power of the connection to her son in his early years.

In removing the immediate material anxieties of Esther's life, the marriage to William seems simultaneously to set in motion the fading of her relationship to her son, who departs from the story just as he seems to be absent for most of the time from the marital home. There is no suggestion, however, that this is because William takes Jackie's place in Esther's affections; it is rather that the desperate quality of the initial exclusive relationship, when Esther was the only parent and had no resources, seems to diminish.

But even though it is unexpected, given the high hopes expressed for Jackie's future with his mother and father, this transition follows the expected progression of parent–child relationships, destined to lose their urgency as the child grows up. And in this regard, Esther's relationship with her boy is the only one of her close family connections that does in fact conform to the common emotional story, beginning with intensity and declining as he grows up. Of her other key relationships, the choice of marriage partner comes, as noted, some years into her motherhood (of a child of one of the possible husbands). There is also her relationship with her own first family—or families—which is detailed at the start of the novel, and which breaks off abruptly and permanently just when she becomes a mother. She is pressed, from her hospital bed, to give much of her meagre financial resources to fund her half-sister's fare for their planned emigration to Australia; it is this transaction which means that she will have to become a wet-nurse.

Moore's description of Esther's growing up makes a contrast between two phases, the first in her father's lifetime and the second after he dies (when she, the only child, is 10), 'and Mrs Waters found herself obliged to sell her business for almost nothing, and marry again' (23). The result is a stream of offspring, and a quasi-maternal role for the big sister, now side by side with her mother as a fellow carer of the children (and of her mother too):

This second marriage proved more fruitful than the first, children were born in rapid succession, the cradle was never empty, and Esther was spoken of as the little nurse. But her great care was for her poor mother, who had lost her health, whose blood was impoverished by constant child-bearing, and mother and daughter were often seen in the evenings, one with a baby at her breast, the other with an eighteen months' old child in her arms. (23–4)

Esther has to stop going to school, which is given as the reason for her never having learned to read and write (though she must be into her teens by this time); but the deprivation of her own later child-hood and education is also an early maturity, as she becomes a co-carer with and of her mother, and becomes her mother's confidante in the troubles of her marriage.

When Esther returns home having had to leave her job because of her pregnancy, her mother turns out to be pregnant too—'them babies allus coming' (96). But the levelling of the two generations is then suddenly curtailed when a half-sister comes to inform Esther in hospital that their mother has died, along with her baby, in childbirth—and to beg for her money to pay for the passage to Australia. None of the half-sisters and half-brothers figures again in the novel: they are gone from England and gone, it seems, from Esther's own consciousness. More strikingly, Esther's mother also vanishes from her thoughts as well as from the world. The coinci-dence of the loss of her closest relationship until then with the arrival of her baby throws the emphasis even more on both the isolation and the primacy of Esther's first bond with her own child—like nothing else in her life.

11

Between Parents

Henry James's *What Maisie Knew*

In Fielding's *Tom Jones*, one way of bringing up children is to move
them at intervals from one household to another, usually between a
parent's place and an uncle's or aunt's, with the different parental
figures enjoying their regular arguments over the proper methods of
education. This kind of arrangement is not presented as unusual, or
as a compromise. In Henry James's *What Maisie Knew* (1897), something similar operates, but to very different effect and for very different reasons; it is more recognizable as a precursor to the complex
separations of parents and places that happen in many contemporary
cultures. In *Tom Jones* the alternations go on (though this is not spelt
out) because one of the parents, the mother, is dead. In *Maisie* they
are initiated as a result of an acrimonious divorce case—at a time
when divorce was still very rare—in which the duality of parenthood
is starkly interpreted in the form of a fifty–fifty split. A child is divided
equally between her mother and father, in different places and one at
a time. At six-monthly intervals, Maisie is to move in turn between
the two households of Beale and Ida Farange; there ensues 'the positive certitude, bequeathed from afar by Moddle, that the natural way
for a child to have her parents was separate and successive, like her
mutton and her pudding or her bath and her nap'.[1] This, at the
almost beginning, is what Maisie knows, certainly knows, taken from
the rituals and orders of daily domestic life, and left her as a routine
model of parental practice by a now superseded nursery-governess.

---

[1] Henry James, *What Maisie Knew* (1897), ed. Adrian Poole (Oxford: Oxford
University Press, World's Classics, 1996), 24. Further references will be included in
the main text.

Maisie is subject to 'migration[s]' (26), as the narrative casually and beautifully puts it, both naturalizing the twice-yearly movements and drawing out the distance to the ends of the earth. Eventually, far away in time and place from the initial six-monthly displacements, Beale and Ida will come to substantiate this geography of flight quite literally, with far-flung plans to expatriate themselves. They are simply a 'disunited couple' (15). But these first parents are hardly ever seen or heard in the novel, or only heard of as absent— and not only during the periods when they are necessarily away from where Maisie is, but also when she is with them (or they are with her). Her father is out all night at 'the Chrysanthemum' or wherever—he 'never came 'ome at all', says the servant Susan Ash (111)—and her mother goes away on country house visits which take up not just the weekend, but most of the other days too.

The alternation between Maisie's two parents across long times may be one kind of rotation that the child comes to know as nature; but it is complicated by the supplementary figures who occupy various kinds of quasi-parental position. Servants and governesses for the day-to-day care and education of the child are normal enough in comfortably appointed homes in *Maisie*'s time, and change as the child's age changes. Moddle quickly fades into the past because, as Maisie understands, 'nursery-governesses were only for little girls' (24). But Maisie's two governesses, Miss Overmore and Mrs Wix, one belonging to each of her parents' establishments, quickly come to be bound up with her by attachments that in their intensity and their daily constancy far exceed those linking her to either parent. The contrast between these two women, and their own parental rivalry over Maisie, continue right up to the novel's indeterminate ending. The competition is fuelled and further complicated by the arrival, soon after their own, of a new husband for Maisie's mother, Sir Claude; he becomes the third of these surrogate parents and an object of adoration to both the women, as well as to Maisie herself.

From Maisie's point of view, which is the dominant and deliberate perspective of the novel, the idiosyncrasy of her position is that she is faced with a seemingly unlimited number of parental figures.[2]

---

[2] As Adrian Poole puts it, 'Maisie feels herself to be a kind of blank on to which all the grown-ups more or less casually and tenderly load bits and pieces of their plots'; *Henry James* (Brighton: Harvester, 1991), 99.

She can 'have' multiple parents in the way that parents can 'have', one after the other, multiple children. It is when the prospect of a stepfather first appears, in the form of an enticing photograph of her mother's new husband, that her reflections on the subject are set in motion:

Maisie lost herself in admiration of the fair smooth face, the regular features, the kind eyes, the amiable air, the general glossiness and smartness of her prospective stepfather—only vaguely puzzled to suppose herself now with two fathers at once. Her researches had hitherto indicated that to incur a second parent of the same sex you had usually to lose the first. (47–8)

This time, the irony proceeds not by presenting an exceptional arrangement as 'the natural way', but rather by presenting assumptions about what is natural as having been the object of Maisie's particular research. In historical terms, the discovery suggests a different kind of irony in its anticipation of what, in the later decades of the following century, would become an unremarkable situation in reality. Divorce and remarriage, in Maisie's time, were a rare combination of events, whereas remarriage following widowhood— the premise for Maisie's reference to losing the first parent—was common: second parents of the same sex were very often 'incurred' by this means.

The initially perplexing addition of a single supplementary father soon acquires a retrospective simplicity, as possible parents for Maisie appear from all directions. When one of the governesses, Miss Overmore, marries Maisie's father and becomes—like Maisie's mother before her—'Mrs Beale', a certain kind of symmetry is produced, as Maisie now has four parents, two on each original parental side, and for that matter two of each sex. But there are also, almost from the start, the claims and passions of Mrs Wix, for whom Maisie represents a replacement for a daughter who died. And then there is the succession—or simultaneous existence—of more or less specified lovers who move in and out of the lives of Maisie's first two parents. In what is perhaps the briefest of many episodes of passionate attachment to the image of a new parental figure, Maisie falls for the absent Mrs Cuddon (also known as the Countess) when her father takes her to her house. On one occasion Maisie and Sir Claude run into Ida, and Maisie asks who it is who is with her:

'Blest if I know!' said Sir Claude.
'Is it Mr Perriam?'
'Oh dear no—Perriam's smashed.'
'Smashed?'
'Exposed—in the City. But there are quantities of others!' (115)

Later, Maisie wonders 'Is it—*is* it Lord Eric?' and Sir Claude responds 'I think it's the Count' (116)—which in fact it is not: it is 'the Captain'. With this Captain, Maisie then enjoys an intimate tête-à-tête while her mother and stepfather argue away. The Captain may not be the Count, but the mistaken title fits with the constant interchangeability of adults in this novel, in relation to Maisie and also to one another. There is no Count, but the novel loses count of how many adults find or place themselves in quasi-parental roles in relation to Maisie, and implicitly asks what it means for someone to count as a parent, whether in their own eyes or in those of their putative child; it does so particularly through seeming to dispense with any sense of a natural or normal limit to the number of those who may do so. From quite early on, it ceases to be assumed that a child has two parents only; and by the same token the question of what it means to be a parent, to be taken for a parent, or to take oneself for one, is constantly being asked.

Maisie acquires two step-parents in addition to her birth parents when Sir Claude and Miss Overmore marry her mother and father, respectively. Each of these two individually is far more involved with Maisie than either Beale Farange or Ida. When Maisie is reunited with Miss Overmore (now her father's wife) after a long absence at her mother's, 'Mrs Beale fairly swooped upon her, and the effect of the whole hour was to show the child how much, how quite formidably indeed, after all, she was loved' (102). The predatory beginning, and the slight threat of 'formidably', more than hint at an aggressive need. Maisie is a required and desired object of the love this later parent seeks to envelop her in, just as she is also, at the beginning, a container for the opposite emotion emanating from her warring parents: 'The evil they had the gift of thinking or pretending to think of each other they poured into her little gravely-gazing soul as into a boundless receptacle' (22).

The novel's many scenarios of connection are full of seeming symmetries and parallels whose geometrical exactness only throws into relief the uncertainties of role and position that they provisionally clarify. Sir Claude and Mrs Beale regularly refer to the possible 'squaring' of their respective legal spouses in relation to Maisie, but other angles than right ones, and other numbers than four, are always emerging, which constantly frustrate the construction or establishment of this regular shape. Numerous couples or couplings emerge, whether between two adults or between one of them and Maisie; proposals are made and dropped for twos to become threes, or for one or more people to be discounted or discarded (by Maisie herself, or by one of her parental figures) with a view to producing some more permanent and happy construction. Miss Overmore, for instance, once she has been transferred from a home where she is indistinctly one of seven sisters, is initially cast as Maisie's new love, 'her first passion' (28), when she daringly crosses over, for Maisie's sake, from the maternal to the paternal house: 'She adored his daughter; she couldn't give her up; she'd make for her any sacrifice' (27). But Miss Overmore is then attached in a second couple to Maisie's father (making her 'Mrs Beale'), before beginning the relationship with her mother's second husband, Sir Claude, which will carry on until the end of the novel, bringing with it ever-changing or over-changing issues as to whether that couple's future is to be tied in with Maisie, or whether Maisie might instead be joined in a pair or a trio with either Sir Claude or Sir Claude and Mrs Wix.

Or, starting the same story from Mrs Wix: she first of all forms a new pair with Maisie that takes the place of Maisie's attachment to Miss Overmore, left behind at her father's; and for her, Maisie represents a return or reincarnation of the daughter she has lost. Later, Mrs Wix will confess to a passion for Sir Claude—'I adore him. I adore him' (221)—that mirrors Maisie's own, and has the effect of sealing rather than undoing the bond between these two: 'They had touched bottom and melted together' (222). Mrs Wix goes so far as to propose to Sir Claude that she and Maisie should live with him, and that she herself, to bring this about, should finish off what would otherwise be the impediment (or 'cloud') of Sir Claude's bond to the former Miss Overmore:

'Let me put in the two or three days—let me wind up the connexion. You stay here with Maisie, with the carriage and the larks and the luxury; then I'll return to you and we'll go off together—we'll live together without a cloud. Take me, take me,' she went on and on. (203)

In all of these many connections, with their various interrelations of compatibility and conflict, the question revolves of where Maisie is to put herself or be placed, and whether the adults' connections to her come before their connections to other adults. Sometimes triangular relationships figure as a threat (to a pair), and sometimes they are presented as a positive solution, or a happy hope. Maisie imagines living with Sir Claude and Mrs Wix, or with Sir Claude and Mrs Beale (the erstwhile Miss Overmore), and both of the other parties in each set-up entertain the same possibilities. Sir Claude, in disagreement with Mrs Beale, is of the view 'that they should either cease to be irregular or cease to be parental' (161). The 'regular' combination of the moral with the geometrical recurs through the lens of Mrs Wix's caricaturally corrective 'straighteners', the odd pair of glasses through which she portentously looks out at the situations about her. She constantly repeats and probes her dread that Maisie is lacking in what she calls 'a moral sense', in regard to the relationship between Sir Claude and Mrs Beale. But the irony of these trios is that they all conform to the most regular nucleus of family composition, a child and two adults—the basic *ménage à trois*. Sir Claude proposes to Maisie the other trio with its other rationale, the antithesis of Mrs Wix's:

'Of course it would be quite unconventional,' Sir Claude went on—'I mean the little household we three should make together; but things have got beyond that, don't you see? They got beyond that long ago. We shall stay abroad at any rate—it's ever so much easier and it's our affair and nobody else's.' (254)

Maisie begins as a 'shuttlecock' (22) in her parents' unhappy sport, to be batted to and fro, but as time goes on the game expands to encompass numerous other players and she herself joins in, taking an equal and decisive part in the 'choice' that she makes at the end, and making her own moves: 'We each have our turn!' (235). But the very proliferation of parental figures, and possible combinations, enables the novel to dismantle and expose all the props by which the continuities of development, and a demarcation between different modes of attachment, are normally upheld.

In many ways, *What Maisie Knew* reverses the (then) expected order of parental and romantic events: first the couple and then the child.[3] Here, it tends to work the other way round. Sir Claude and Mrs Beale (formerly Miss Overmore) each say that 'She has brought you and me together'—and Maisie reiterates, 'I've brought you and her together!' (59). Without her existence, and their separate attachments to her, they would never have met. The coming together, unparentally, unconventionally, of these two occurs as a kind of supplement, an after-event to the foundational ties to an existing child: 'What in the world's our connection but the love of the child who's our duty and our life and who holds us together so closely as she originally brought us?' (271). The same, at an earlier stage, is true of Miss Overmore's marriage to Beale Farange. Their relationship comes about through the governess's presence in the father's house (and her remaining there after Maisie has departed for her next period at her mother's). With Miss Overmore, she had 'conceived her first passion'; and that passion is then echoed, not preceded, by her father's own feeling for Miss Overmore: 'papa too liked Miss Overmore exactly as much. He had particularly told her so' (28). It is through Maisie, and the love of Maisie, that other couples come into being.

A passing instance of this—as if thrown in for confirmation, to add to the general pattern—occurs during Maisie's interview in the park with 'the Captain', one of her mother's many men. She never encounters him again, but the intimacy that momentarily establishes itself between them is like a microcosm of many of Maisie's other relationships with couples or halves of couples. Falling for him as the speaker of kind words about a mother of whom, up till now, she has only ever heard insults; and suddenly picturing a possible future or at least a departure with her and this new, and newly trusted man, she pushes him to declare that he loves 'her' (her mother)—'Of *course* I love her, damn it, you know!' (124)—and finishes by securing something that has the air of a promise of marriage:

---

[3] A comparable reversal of this order occurs in George Moore's *Esther Waters*, as described in Ch. 10, pp. 179–80.

And then supremely: 'You *do* love her?'

'My dear child!' The Captain wanted words.

'Then don't do it for just a little.'

'A little?'

'Like all the others.'

'All the others?'—he stood staring.

She pulled away her hand. 'Do it always!' (125–6)

The coupling of Miss Overmore and Beale in its turn becomes like a transitional relationship on the way to the subsequent joining of her with Sir Claude, and it is this pair, 'brought together' through Maisie, who become, both at odds and in concert, her active mother and father. In this regard, they might seem to have simply taken over from the first parents, forming as they do another couple, straight if not morally straight in Mrs Wix's sense: 'We stand absolutely in the place of your parents. It's their defection, their extraordinary baseness, that has made our responsibility' (258). Sir Claude is speaking in quasi-legal terms at this point: to all intents and purposes, they really have become Maisie's two parents, a role that is reinforced by their official positions as the legal spouses of Ida and Beale. Each of them is taking the place, quite neatly and symmetrically, of one of Maisie's parents. But whereas step-parents normally stand in for a parent of the same sex, whether dead or (in more recent times, and in this novel) alive, here that status has glided into another substitution: for the parent to whom they are married, not the one whose marital place they take. That different substitution also involves a change of sex: a woman takes over from the father and a man from the mother. But it is easy to miss this with Sir Claude and Miss Overmore (Mrs Beale Farange), since the result—in parental terms—is a regular pair: a mother and father, one of each.

Once this first instance of cross-substitution has been noticed, just about every maternal or paternal figure turns out to have traits of the other kind; here too it is as if there is a systematic reversal or dislocation of the straightforward perspective. Or rather, there is an exposure of the normal perspective, seeing only one at a time, as necessarily straightened or square. Beginning with Ida and Beale, it is she, not he, who is the champion billiards player, complete

with her cue. And it is Beale, not she, who becomes, with a succession of women, the kept man: 'he lives on other women!' (228),
Mrs Wix explains. Or more laconically, apropos of 'the Countess',
'She pays him!' (211). In the couple composed by Sir Claude and
Mrs Beale, it is she who 'swoops' like a predator and he who, several
times, is represented as naturally belonging in the parental roles of
the other sex: 'I'm an old grandmother,' Sir Claude declared. 'I like
babies—I always did. If we go to smash I shall look for a place as
responsible nurse' (58). So pleased is he with this self-description
that he recalls it many pages later, after Mrs Beale has praised him
for offering to bring over Maisie's things from the other house:

'There's a stepfather for you! I'm bound to say, you know, that he makes
up for the want of other people.'
    'He makes up for the want of a nurse!' Sir Claude laughed. 'Don't you
remember I told you so the very first time?'   (107)

Later, Maisie is seen in receipt of a piece of music called 'a "Moon-
light Berceuse"', sent her through the post by Sir Claude, her musi-
cal lullaby in the absence of himself the nurse, to be treasured by
her as being what he has called 'the real thing' (111).

    Sir Claude's self-identification as a *berceuse*, feminine and soothing,
goes together with a rueful commentary on the non-existence of
women with similar propensities. Speaking of his relation to Maisie,
Mrs Beale says:

'It's so charming—for a man of your type—to have wanted her so much!'
    'What do you know about my type?' Sir Claude laughed. 'Whatever
it may be I dare say it deceives you. The truth about me is simply that
I'm the most unappreciated of—what do you call the fellow?—"family-
men". Yes, I'm a family-man; upon my honour I am!'
    'Then why on earth,' cried Mrs Beale, 'didn't you marry a family-
woman?'
    Sir Claude looked at her hard. '*You* know who one marries, I think.
Besides, there *are* no family-women—hanged if there are! None of them
want any children—hanged if they do!'   (57)

Rejecting the insinuation of some unspecified 'type', Sir Claude
comes out with a label of his own, and then refuses Mrs Beale's
extension of this to a logic of marital likenesses. 'Who one marries'

is separate from, not continuous with, the role of the 'family-man'; and wanting children—the ones they have, like Maisie, or the ones they might have in a marital future—is implicitly something that only men do, not women. In this sense his marrying unmaternal Ida brought Sir Claude and Maisie together in much the same way that Maisie later brought Mrs Beale and Sir Claude together; and at the end of the story it is that couple, Maisie and Sir Claude, that for a while takes precedence (over Sir Claude and Mrs Beale, and over the possibility of other arrangements involving more than two). Escaping from the other women, who are left behind in the hotel where they have all ended up in Boulogne, these two almost, but not quite, take romantic flight to Paris.

Mrs Wix is probably the novel's only conceivable candidate for membership of the set that Sir Claude claims as empty, 'family-women'; and it is ultimately with her, and her alone, that Maisie returns to England. Mrs Wix has no husband or lover, and unlike Sir Claude or Mrs Beale, her fellow governess and female rival for Maisie, she never in the course of the novel becomes linked to anyone other than Maisie (her confession that she adores Sir Claude is neither reciprocated nor admitted to anyone but Maisie). Mrs Wix is unique among the adults with a connection to Maisie because she is herself (or has been) a parent, in a way that is fundamentally part of her identity and also of Maisie's instant understanding of who she is: 'What Maisie felt was that she had been, with passion and anguish, a mother' (29). Ida's delivery of Maisie to her new governess already sounds like the giving away of a daughter: '"Take her, Mrs Wix," she added...Mrs Wix took her and, Maisie felt the next day, would never let her go' (29). Nor does she; the close of the story dispatches them both back home to a *ménage à deux*.

For Mrs Wix, Maisie can represent a subsequent child to the daughter who had been 'knocked down and crushed by the cruellest of hansoms... "She's your little dead sister," Mrs Wix ended by saying' (29–30). Mrs Wix adopts Maisie from the beginning, with the promise of an unconditionally close attachment. Much later, as the two are seated together in the testing times at Boulogne, there is the moment when they are joined together, or when their separateness fades away: 'Their hands were so linked and their union was so confirmed that it took the far deep note of a bell...to call them back to a sense of hours and proprieties. They had touched bottom and melted together' (222). Mrs Wix declares the unconditionality of her love, which has led her beyond her own strong 'moral sense' (216–17), to the point that 'Now I know too much, too much!' (217):

'Have I lost all delicacy, all decency, all measure of how far and how bad? It seems to me mostly that I have, though I'm the last of whom you could ever have thought it. I've just done it for *you*, precious—not to lose you, which would have been worst of all: so that I've had to pay with my own innocence, if you do laugh! for clinging to you and keeping you.'   (217)

This parental passion has taken her consciously beyond the bounds of her own sense of right and wrong, and initiated her into a knowledge she never wanted. Doing it 'for *you*' then has the ambiguity of hovering between two opposite and now inseparable modes— between doing it on Maisie's behalf, or doing it in order to have her. Putting this negatively, as Mrs Wix does, 'not to lose you, which would have been worst of all', makes having and holding into a threatened state, one that is bound to precipitate unwonted and unwanted acts and experiences.

Mrs Wix's daughter, Clara Matilda, is the only child other than Maisie to be named in the entire novel; and she is dead on arrival in it, as if to emphasize this remarkable absence in a story that is centred on a growing child, and takes its own title from her. Maisie latches onto the tale of Clara Matilda (a tale of her death not her life); 'Somehow she wasn't a real sister, but that only made her the more romantic' (30). This leaves open whether a real sister is one who is alive, or one who has the same parent—or any other possible definition. In her romantic qualities, however, the unreal sister is matched by seven further sisters—to each other, though not to Maisie—who appear, again only in story, as part of what Miss Overmore brings to Maisie, who 'knew very soon all the names of all the sisters; she could say them off better than she could say the multiplication-table' (23). For Maisie, though, multiplication does not have to do—as it does many times over for all the Overmores— with numbers of sisters (or brothers). Instead, the non-existence of other children, let alone real siblings, in her world shows up all the more the numerous population of the category normally restricted to two: 'so many parents' (231). In the usual experience, a child may find a new brother or sister added to its world from time to time, but what Maisie knows transfers this experience to parents—ever more.

In the expected scheme of things, linear if not squared, a child's development takes it steadily towards the position of an adult, knowing enough; its ignorance of the world it comes into is set against a stable background in which adults have and know their place, in relation to one another and in relation to the children. But in this novel, not only is Maisie groping to find out where she is, or where to put herself, but the adults also are consciously seeking to find their place or places—both in relation to her and in relation to each other. There is a moment when Sir Claude and Mrs Beale, joyously together with Maisie, get jointly excited about the idea of going out and getting themselves an education; there is rapid talk of lessons, classes, courses, lectures, institutions, and subjects (109)—as if they all need to know, or are all on the same educational level, parents and child alike. In the event, the plans come to nothing, and Maisie 'was to feel henceforth as if she were flattening her nose upon the hard window-pane of the sweet-shop of knowledge', a determinate, delectable, and firmly inaccessible commodity (113).

The final scene, in the hotel at Boulogne, is played with all the passions of a tragic denouement: the last great act of a drama in which the protagonists' destinies must be decided once and for all. Verbal knifings, stabs, and 'a wild snatch' (271) circulate between the four characters, in the effort of sorting out who, in the end, will get who, at the cost of who else, and what are the 'relations'—a word of Mrs Wix's—that hold up the various pairs and trios or set them against each other. Speaking with the irony of someone who seems aware that they are all on their last pages, Sir Claude, the master of unceremonies, declares near the end: 'Will you be so good as to allow these horrors to terminate?' (273). Melodramatically, and for no obvious practical reason, the future pair that emerges at the end of it, Maisie and Mrs Wix, is rushed off to catch the boat leaving for Folkestone, in the same way that earlier the same day the chance of her going with Sir Claude instead, in a different couple,

had come to a head with the last-minute decision to take or not take
the train to Paris.

The power of this scene, perhaps partly because of its stagy
excesses of emotional violence, owes much to its surface resemblance to a conventionally dramatic end to a story, in which the
subject at issue is the choice of a marriage partner. Who will get the
girl? How will the couplings and uncouplings of likely lovers pan
out? Who will be left behind and who will be happy? As Maisie and
Mrs Wix sail away from the other two, there is even a faint reminder
of Dido and Aeneas. But when Maisie looks back (and Mrs Wix
doesn't), there is no funeral pyre—no sign at all of the one who
might have played the part of the lover, who might have had the
departing Maisie, or both of them, foremost in his mind. Unlike the
abandoned Dido, 'He went to *her*', Mrs Wix concludes; '"Oh I
know!" the child replied' (275).

This final declaration of knowing, almost the last words of the
novel, appears at one level to signify Maisie's completed initiation
into an adult world of sexual knowledge; 'the child' is precociously
aware of the adults' connections with each other, left to themselves.
Mrs Wix's response is most overtly along these lines: 'Mrs Wix gave
a sidelong look. She still had room for wonder at what Maisie knew'
(274). But the 'sidelong' here also suggests what will never be straightened out in Maisie's relations, 'mixed up' (134) as they have been
throughout her life without any of the usual order of family coordi-
nates. In the final scene, all parties seem to accept that Sir Claude
and Mrs Beale are now, *de facto*, *in loco parentum*: 'we stand absolutely
in the place of your parents', as Sir Claude had stated the matter to
Maisie, using the proper legal formulation.[4] Conventionally, these
individuals, replacing the parents, can further delegate educational or

---

[4] As Kevin Ohi says, 'The novel repeatedly thematizes being *in loco parentis* or more
generally, how a position in space ("place") constitutes an identity. A place, parenting
is a mode of exchange—of Maisie—that is itself exchanged'; 'Children', in David
McWhirter (ed.), *Henry James in Context* (Cambridge: Cambridge University Press,
2010), 120. Although the 'place' of the Latin formula may be less to do with space
than with a position (in relation to a child), Ohi is right to stress the interchangeability
of parental places in *Maisie*.

custodial responsibilities to a third party, Mrs Wix: this is one meaning of the closing separation of the four people into two pairs. From their 'place' they can send her away or move her on, two delegate parents appointing yet another—to make room for the couple that only through her being her parents' child they have become.

12

Parental Secrets in Thomas Hardy's
The Mayor of Casterbridge

The opening scene of Thomas Hardy's *The Mayor of Casterbridge* (1886) famously involves the unplanned sale, at a country fair, of a wife, plus girl toddler, by a young Michael Henchard who has had a few drinks. Twenty years on, at the time to which the narrative then jumps, Henchard has more than reformed and rehabilitated himself, rising from being an itinerant labourer to become the mayor of a substantial town, Casterbridge. Meanwhile the wife-purchaser or second husband, Richard Newson, has apparently died, and Susan, once the sold wife, decides to seek out her original husband. At this juncture she wonders—not for the first time—how or what to tell her now grown-up daughter about an early past in her life of which she is unaware:

A hundred times she had been on the point of telling her daughter, Elizabeth-Jane, the true story of her life, the tragical crisis of which had been the transaction at Weydon Fair, when she was not much older than the girl now beside her. But she had refrained. An innocent maiden had thus grown up in the belief that the relations between the genial sailor [Newson] and her mother were the ordinary ones that they had always appeared to be. The risk of endangering a child's strong affection by disturbing ideas which had grown with her growth was to Mrs. Henchard too fearful a thing to contemplate. It had seemed, indeed, folly to think of making Elizabeth-Jane wise.[1]

---

[1] Thomas Hardy, *The Mayor of Casterbridge* (1886), ed. Dale Kramer (Oxford: Oxford University Press, 2004), 24. Further references will be included in the main text.

Mrs Henchard's thoughts have sought confirmation in a vague memory of the well-known lines 'Where ignorance is bliss, | 'Tis folly to be wise'.[2] Still aphoristically familiar today, these words most often float free—as they do for Hardy's character—of their first poetic context, which has to do not with a learning of specific information about a personal past, but with foreknowledge of a general doom that is common to all. The speaker in Thomas Gray's 'Ode on a Distant Prospect of Eton College' (1747) is watching the boys on the playing fields, and reflecting that it is just as well that they do not know all the bad things, from illness to ageing to death, that the future necessarily holds in store for them. In her thoughts, Susan Henchard (or Newson) gives the lines a new application—still to a young person, seen by an older one, but now with regard to the way that a past that has already happened may, by being known anew, known in a different way, profoundly change the present (and the future). There is a past unknown which, if known, could spoil an otherwise happy life— just as Gray's unknown future would do to the present days of his schoolboys.

Hardy's use of Gray's lines is not about ends but about origins, and not about a general human (if not masculine) destiny, but about information relating to the history of one particular girl. And whereas Gray wittily concludes, from the perspective of maturity (or disillusion), that knowledge of a declining future is best not known, Hardy's point is at an entirely different emotional level. What is being suggested here, the danger of disclosure at a late age, is linked to a combination of folly and knowledge which threatens to give the knowledge the role of serious disturbance, going against what has become a second nature, or a developed identity. 'The ideas which had grown with her growth' is a lingeringly suggestive phrase, relating psychological and physical development in such a way that the two cannot be separated; and granting old-established 'ideas' a quality of naturalness which has nothing to do with their truth, verifiable or not.

---

[2] Thomas Gray, 'Ode on a Distant Prospect of Eton College', lines 99–100, in Roger Lonsdale (ed.), *The Poems of Gray, Collins, and Goldsmith* (London: Longmans, 1969), 63.

The same connection was forcefully made by the philosopher Jacques Derrida, in relation to just this issue and in just the terms that Hardy is drawing on, ideas—or belief—and growth. Derrida is responding to a question from the psychoanalytic historian Elisabeth Roudinesco about the significance of the new verifiability of paternity, via DNA testing. Roudinesco suggests that the availability of such tests only feeds a narcissistic fantasy of 'proven' fatherhood. Derrida, not contradicting, insists that fatherhood is something other than a matter of biological inheritance:

> The fantasy moves about, it gives movement from the moment when the father and/or the mother do *believe* they are the *authentic* 'parent' of that which is 'growing' in their home. We need to put some pressure, and more pressure, on the meaning of 'believe'. And of 'grow'. And of the growth of a belief. In this case and in others. There is a genetic fantasy: we love our children more than other people's because we project a narcissistic identification onto them: it's my blood, it's me. And the fantasy can be practically the same, or similar, with adopted children.[3]

Derrida's point is reinforced by the near-homonymic identity in French of growth and belief, *croître* and *croire*; here the sound replicates and seems to confirm both Hardy's and Derrida's semantic claim about the twinning and twining of the two.[4]

The secret in Hardy is marked as itself being part of the story. 'A hundred times she had been on the point of telling her daughter'—a hundred times that this not-said, not-spoken, has figured for the mother. Their life together has been, in part, the story of the non-telling of the story. On the parent's side, a secret has been kept and held: not just knowledge, but knowledge knowingly withheld, and (in this case) brought out over and over again

---

[3] Jacques Derrida, in Derrida and Elisabeth Roudinesco, *De quoi demain…: Dialogue* (Paris: Fayard/Galilée, 2001), 79.

[4] Compare the passage from *Mansfield Park* discussed above (pp. 170–1) which also addresses the difficulty of dislodging an established 'growth' of rearing influences: 'the man who means to make you love him…must have very up-hill work, for there are all your early attachments, and habits, in battle array; and before he can get your heart for his own use, he has to unfasten it from all the holds upon things animate and inanimate, which so many years growth have confirmed, and which are considerably tightened for the moment by the very idea of separation'; Jane Austen, *Mansfield Park* (1814), ed. Tony Tanner (Harmondsworth: Penguin, 1985), 344. The change

as something to be either kept back or imparted at last. Later on, in one of the crazily countless repetitions of this novel, Elizabeth-Jane will briefly live with another woman, Lucetta Templeman, who also fails to tell her that she once had a relationship with Henchard.

Elizabeth-Jane is described as 'an innocent maiden', not an ignorant one. But in fact, part of her own life's aim at this point is, at all costs, to make herself knowledgeable. On the very next page after the speculation about whether to make Elizabeth-Jane 'wise' there is her mother's dim recognition that she should be encouraged in her wish to improve herself by education:

The woman had long perceived how zealously and constantly the young mind of her companion was struggling for enlargement; and yet now, in her eighteenth year, it still remained but little unfolded.... She sought further into things than other girls in her position ever did, and her mother groaned as she felt she could not aid in the search. (25–6)

The relationship between the two kinds of knowledge, book education and family secrets, is made quite clear when Susan reflects that 'The awkwardness of searching for him [Henchard] lay in enlightening Elizabeth' (26). It is as if Elizabeth somehow senses the private enlightenment that is being withheld from her, is driven to investigate she knows not what, but is only able to pursue her researches in less sensitive directions. Elizabeth-Jane's ignorance is not bliss, because it knows itself as ignorance, even though she does not know of what in particular. Throughout the novel, we see her resolutely at work, passionately acquiring and studying all the books she can as she continues, elsewhere, to be the subject or object of various potential family disclosures and permutations. Some of the family knowledge that is revealed to her turns out to be false, or only half-truth—her mother's saying, for instance, that the man they are seeking, Henchard, is 'a relative'—and at one crucial point the falseness is unknown to the

---

in prospect here is one of habits, not facts of origin; but the language of growth and confirmation is the same, as is the acquired nature, in both cases, of what grows and is confirmed. Elizabeth-Jane could have known differently (and, as it happens, more accurately) about the parental past; Fanny Price's growing 'early attachments' are to what is in fact her second, adoptive family.

speaker himself, who is the bearer of a secret he does not know to be a cover, now, for another one.

This is the moment when Henchard, following his remarriage to Susan and Susan's death soon after, decides to tell Elizabeth-Jane that she is not, as she thinks, just his stepdaughter:

'Elizabeth, it is I who am your father, and not Richard Newson....I'd rather have your scorn, your fear, anything, than your ignorance; 'tis that I hate. Your mother and I were man and wife when we were young. What you saw was our second marriage. Your mother was too honest. We had thought each other dead—and—Newson became her husband. (114–15)

Henchard tells Elizabeth-Jane what he thinks is mainly the truth, but even so, it includes a lie or at least an elision: Henchard only sought out his wife, unsuccessfully, after having sold her. But the 'disclosure'—Hardy's own word—is substantiated by Henchard's promise of documentation and his assertion that it was he who 'gave you your name' (115), meaning her first name; he now persuades her, while she is still reeling from the revelation, to place an announcement in the local newspaper to say she is changing her surname to his. Henchard then goes off to search for the relevant documents, leaving his daughter alone to 'adjust her filial sense to the new centre of gravity'. On his side, Henchard congratulates himself on having secured 'the re-establishment of this tenderest human tie': 'Elizabeth was his at last' (116).

But then, with consummate Hardyesque irony, on the very same night he finds among his papers a letter from his wife which promptly overturns what he thought was his own knowledge of the parental connections. The letter reads:

My Dear Michael,

For the good of all three of us, I have kept one thing a secret from you till now. I hope you will understand why; I think you will; though perhaps you may not forgive me. But, dear Michael, I have done it for the best. I shall be in my grave when you read this, and Elizabeth-Jane will have a home [the letter is supposed to be read on her wedding day]. Don't curse me Mike—think of how I was situated. I can hardly write it, but here it is. Elizabeth-Jane is not your Elizabeth-Jane—the child who was in my arms when you sold me. No: she died three months after that, and this living one is my other husband's. I christened her by the same name we had given to the first, and she filled up the ache I felt at the other's loss. Michael, I am dying, and I might have held my tongue; but I could not. Tell her husband of this, or not, as you may judge; and forgive, if you can, a woman you once deeply wronged; as she forgives you. (117)

Apart from the obvious irony of the contiguity between the two mutually cancelling revelations—Henchard's to Elizabeth-Jane, 'I am your father', and now Susan's to him, 'She is not your daughter'—there is a smaller one concealed in the detail of Susan's letter being intended for reading only on Elizabeth's wedding day. For as Hardy has underlined, what Elizabeth represents to Henchard sounds like the kind of tie that would normally be associated with romantic marriage rather than with parenthood: the loved one is 'his' 'at last' rather than from the first. Also, the relationship is, in a sense, a chosen one, even while Henchard believes that he really is Elizabeth's birth father: chosen because it is his decision to tell her, and thus to initiate the making of the tie at all. And Elizabeth, like a bride, will change her name to Henchard's in recognition of her new condition. The new tie is marriage-like also in that Henchard seeks in the young woman something he might equally well get or seek from a wife: 'He was the kind of man to whom some human object for pouring out his heat upon—were it emotive or were it choleric—was almost a necessity' (116).

The couplings and triangulations of this novel are nothing if not Oedipal, with characters frequently coming to occupy more than one place in endlessly circulated and repeated configurations. In addition to the core trio of Henchard, Susan, and Elizabeth-Jane, cut across by the alternative husband- and father-figure of Richard Newson, there are two other characters, Donald Farfrae and Lucetta Templeman, both of whom enter into triple and dual entanglements, in the past and present of the novel, with both Henchard and Elizabeth-Jane. So overlaid with repetitions do all the relationships become that it can come to seem as if there may be no underlying truth of the matter at all: no primary secret or primary family unit. The hypothetical first family of Henchard, Susan, and Elizabeth-Jane has been dramatically supplanted in Henchard's present by the second family in which Newson is the father and Elizabeth-Jane is a different girl. And yet, it remains the case that Elizabeth-Jane—the adult Elizabeth-Jane who is Newson's daughter—was in effect given her name by Henchard: she was the replacement baby for the Elizabeth-Jane who had died and whose first name he chose, just as on the evening of the two revelations he gives her his surname as well.

Henchard's own distracting discovery from reading his wife's letter has the effect of imparting a new form of maddening ignorance to Elizabeth-Jane who finds, next morning, when she wakens prepared to treat him as her loving father, that he has overnight changed again: 'Of all the enigmas which ever confronted a girl there can have been seldom one like that which followed Henchard's announcement of himself to Elizabeth as her father' (121). Henchard is sent crazy by what he has learned, Elizabeth-Jane by what she has not been told, that she is in reality, after all and as before, the daughter of the man she grew up with and not of the one she now lives with.

These patterns of oscillation between seeming understanding and ignorance are not confined to the characters' experience; there are ways in which the narrative itself, in what it suggests and withholds, may replicate the processes of revelation and confusion that occur for Elizabeth-Jane. Here again is the moment when Hardy brings up Gray's 'folly-wise' lines:

A hundred times she had been on the point of telling her daughter, Elizabeth-Jane, the true story of her life, the tragical crisis of which had been the transaction at Weydon Fair, when she was not much older than the girl now beside her. But she had refrained. An innocent maiden had thus grown up in the belief that the relations between the genial sailor and her mother were the ordinary ones that they had always appeared to be. The risk of endangering a child's strong affection by disturbing ideas which had grown with her growth was to Mrs. Henchard too fearful a thing to contemplate. It had seemed, indeed, folly to think of making Elizabeth-Jane wise.

At the point when we read this, or first read this, we do not know that Elizabeth-Jane is a second Elizabeth-Jane, not Henchard's original daughter. The passage can be taken to refer to Susan not having told Elizabeth-Jane that her father was a man she has never met, not the one she grew up with; 'the true story of her life' appears to be the true story of Elizabeth-Jane's life. But then, as we later discover, Newson's fatherhood really is, after all, the true story of Elizabeth's beginnings, and it is the one she has always known. It would be no folly to tell her what she has always taken to be the truth. So is this passage, we might then wonder, an authorial mistake, something that, quite simply, Hardy failed to revise to make it consistent with subsequent plot developments he might not have worked out at the beginning? In fact, the passage makes sense after all if we read it instead, and in light of our subsequent knowledge of Newson's paternity, as Susan's unconfessed account of her marriage before meeting Elizabeth-Jane's father. 'The true story of her life' is the true story of Susan's life (although Hardy subtly hints as well at the interchangeability or comparability of mother and daughter, via Susan's thought that the 'tragical crisis' occurred 'when she was not much older than the girl now beside her'). What Susan has failed to tell Elizabeth-Jane is that she is illegitimate, and that her mother was legally married to someone other than her father.[5]

Formally, if not emotionally, the readjustment that readers have to make here is exactly like what has to happen with Elizabeth when she is given Henchard's three-quarters truth, as he then believes it, about him being her father and her mother's first husband. The novel taunts readers and characters alike with confusions of information and mistaken beliefs. Not only is it necessary to 'adjust... [the] sense to the new centre of gravity', but the new centre of gravity itself proves to be only provisional or temporary, there is no certainty that these are the facts, or that this is the right area to be looking for the truth in the first place. Thus an apparent issue of paternity turns out to be something different (if closely related), an issue of legitimacy; one seemingly questionable fact—the identity of a father—can cover the questionability of another, the marital status and history of a child's parents. 'Un secret peut en cacher un autre'—one secret

[5] This is why Susan Henchard mentions Elizabeth-Jane's husband in her letter to Michael: a husband might be indignant that his new wife was not from the proper, legitimate background he had assumed. But Susan does not at this point even raise the question of whether Elizabeth-Jane should be (or should have been) the first to be informed of her own history. She writes the letter to Henchard—for him to inform the husband, or not—and not to Elizabeth-Jane.

can hide another, as the French psychoanalyst Serge Tisseron, who has written extensively on the subject of family secrets, nicely puts it.[6]

Tisseron gives an illuminating account of the ways in which secrets can go underground only to re-emerge in distorted, unrecognizable forms at a later stage—typically in the second and third generation from the source. Or how one family secret, dimly sensed as such, may give rise to children with a tendency themselves—though they don't know why—to generate situations of secrecy, or a need for secrets. Tisseron objects to the use of the word 'transmit' in relation to the passage of secrets because, he argues, in this kind of connection no communication is ever straightforward or unidirectional. The play of the secret goes back and forth between the holders and those whom they tell, or partly tell, or fail to tell, in ways that they may not understand or suspect. Another message can be received from the one that was consciously meant; a secret may be guessed where the holder has said nothing that could be recognized as revealing. Tisseron shows how a secret is always more than an isolated particle, however out of reach it may seem to be. Instead, its effects may be glimpsed through what he calls the '*non-dit*': the things that families and couples don't say, the subjects of questioning and conversation that everyone, though they may not know why or consciously notice it, understands to be out of bounds. X is always marking the spot, even though the memory of what is hidden there may have disappeared long ago.[7]

---

[6] See Serge Tisseron, *Nos secrets de famille* (Paris: Ramsay, 1999). The sentence jokingly alludes to the warning signs that used to be placed at railway crossing points in France: 'Un train peut en cacher un autre'.

[7] When he was in his fifties, having previously thought he was an only child, the novelist Ian McEwan learned that he was in fact his parents' second son; the first had been given away in a wartime adoption when his mother was still married to a husband who subsequently died and who was not that baby's father. The parents subsequently married and then, some years later, had a second boy. Whether or not there is a connection, the author of *The Child in Time* (1987), about an infant suddenly taken away and a new baby born some years after, grew up, unknowingly, with parents to whom that had happend.

Another novel of Hardy's dramatically illustrates a failed attempt to bury a secret in this way. The title of *Far from the Madding Crowd* is another quotation from Gray, this time from the 'Elegy Written in a Country Churchyard'.[8] In the poem, the country churchyard really is peaceful, and so, for better and worse, have been the lives of those who lie in it. But just as Hardy dramatizes and intensifies the import of Gray's folly–wise lines, so his ironic title, and the events of the novel, bring right home to the village—and even to the churchyard itself—the 'madding' that Gray's 'Elegy' removes to the world of great men. Towards the end of the novel, the theatrical heroine Bathsheba, flamboyant and successful independent farmer, has succumbed to the seductive charms of Sergeant Troy, marrying him rather than one of two other long-standing suitors; Hardy says that 'the element of folly', though 'foreign' to her multifaceted nature, played its part in this.[9] Then, in her husband's absence, a chain of contingencies leads to a coffin containing the body of Troy's abandoned girlfriend, Fanny Robin, with that of her—or their—newborn baby, being brought to Bathsheba's own house. Gabriel Oak, Bathsheba's faithful and selfless admirer, endeavours to screen her from the knowledge of what had happened. He does this by an attempted erasure of what has been chalked on the coffin for the purpose of identification. 'The scrawl was this simple one, "*Fanny Robin and child*". Gabriel took his handkerchief and carefully rubbed out the two latter words, leaving visible one inscription "*Fanny Robin*" only' (350–1).

Bathsheba, however, has heard gossip and already has suspicions. She thinks, when she sees this, of asking Gabriel: 'If she were to go to him now at once and say no more than these few words, "What is the truth of the story?" he would feel bound in honour to tell her. It would be an inexpressible relief. No further speech would need to be uttered' (355). There would be, in twenty-first-century terms,

---

[8] 'Far from the madding crowd's ignoble strife | Their sober wishes never learned to stray; | Along the cool sequestered vale of life | They kept the noiseless tenor of their way'; Gray, 'Elegy Written in a Country Churchyard' (1751), lines 73–6, in Lonsdale (ed.), *The Poems of Gray, Collins, and Goldsmith*, 131.

[9] Hardy, *Far from the Madding Crowd* (1874), ed. Ronald Blythe (Harmondsworth: Penguin, 1978), 243. Further references will be included in the main text.

some closure with the disclosure, and this is what Gabriel, for the time being, and with the kindest of intentions, has denied Bathsheba, not seeing or guessing that she might already half know what he is seeking to protect her from. Bathsheba goes to Gabriel's cottage and hovers outside, but retreats without asking her question. Without the straight words that she expects from him, the ones that would set right the withholding of two words that he himself, unknown to her, has perpetrated, she then goes further, deciding to seek for visible proof by actually opening the coffin. It is during her contemplation of the two bodies that her husband returns; in remorse and rage, he denounces his actual, legal marriage, to Bathsheba, as a sham, and later pays for an extravagant headstone to be erected in the graveyard, on which his own name figures with Fanny's.

I think it would be difficult to find in Hardy's novels a single instance of a happy experience of parenthood, or the expression of a wish to have children. Over and over again, babies die, or their mothers die in consequence of childbirth, or unwanted pregnancies spoil the lives of young women and men. All these things, of course, were common enough occurrences in Hardy's real world, and perhaps, one could say, more the natural stuff of a novel's plot than stories of legitimate and healthy births and their unremarkable sequels. But no other novelist so relentlessly offers only the bleakest pictures of possible family lives; *Jude the Obscure*, in which the eldest of three children hangs them all, himself included, 'because we are too menny', is surely the most gruesomely shocking example of this.[10]

The Mayor of Casterbridge concludes with what is perhaps Hardy's nearest approach to a happy ending, in Elizabeth-Jane's belated marriage to her original suitor, Donald Farfrae; but only after he has previously married another woman, Lucetta, and she has died in childbirth in the wake of a miserable experience of public humiliation as the former lover of Elizabeth-Jane's father, or adoptive father—Henchard. The closing sentence of the novel grants Elizabeth-Jane 'unbroken tranquillity' in adult life, but its very last words contrast this with 'she whose youth had seemed to teach that happiness was but the occasional episode in a general drama of pain' (310). The movement is the opposite one from Gray's in the 'Ode':

---

[10] Hardy, *Jude the Obscure* (1896), ed. C. H. Sisson (London: Penguin, 1985), 410.

from youthful pain to moderate, precarious happiness, rather than from childhood bliss to the inevitability of adult decline.

The enigmas and discoveries of *The Mayor of Casterbridge* and *Far from the Madding Crowd* raise other questions, about the social history of family secrets and about the intersections between current ideologies and private experience. There is a reciprocal relation between adults' guilty withholding of what they know, and an ignorance on the child's side that is belied or covered over by 'the ideas that had grown with her growth'. There would be no disturbance unless what is not known already counts as shameful or in some way inadmissible to those who fail to let it be known. What figures in this way is variable historically and culturally. The last few decades, in particular, have seen momentous changes in the forms and subjects of family secrets and revelations, closely bound up with radical alterations in the likely or acceptable or typical kinds of couple, or family set-up. This can appear, from some points of view, as a process of progressive illumination, as former sources of secrets are no longer seen as knowledge to be kept hidden in the first place.

For instance, questions to do with legitimacy and with the priority of the union of two given parents have altered to the point that the motivations and reactions of Hardy's Victorian characters will soon be needing footnotes. In many western societies, the fallen woman and the stigmatized illegitimate baby have more or less disappeared as plausible characters; the 'unmarried mother' is no more—meaning that the term no longer has any ideological currency. In an earlier age, the pregnancy and probably the ensuing infant would be being kept well out of sight; today, the celebrity bump is a possible fashion accessory whose kudos is unrelated to the mother's marital status. Alongside the fading of the significance of legitimacy is the frequency and acceptability of serial couple relationships, marital or otherwise (that it makes little difference is part of the point). It is common not shocking for one or both parents to have had other children with another spouse, still living, before they formed the couple that produced this particular new child.[11] Today, there would

---

[11] The qualification is added because it was common and unremarkable enough in the nineteenth century too—when a previous spouse had died.

be no confession for Susan Henchard to have failed to make to
Elizabeth-Jane about her parents' non-marital union as such.[12]

Yet there is no reason to suppose that such seemingly enlightened
modern developments in the norms and possibilities of lifestyles and
lovestyles have put an end to secrets of origins; on the contrary, everything suggests that they have only generated new ones or reproduced old ones in revised forms. Thus the question of who is the real
father of a child is one that persists even if, with DNA, one kind of
scientific answer can be certainly given, and for the first time in
human history. (In fact arguably DNA testing just intensifies the force
of the old question, precisely because it does now have the possibility
of a certain answer: soap operas, talk shows, and popular journalism
run stories in which tests are taken and the revealing of the result will
function as a new kind of narrative moment of truth.)

In his thinking about infant development, Freud posited a
number of axiomatic origin questions that each child is thought
to come across and to try to answer in relation to its own capacities for understanding at the age it is at. Where do babies come
from?; What is the difference of the sexes?; And what is the intimacy of 'being married'? These questions were ones to which
straightforward answers from parental or other sources would be
unlikely to be forthcoming; where what counts as the straightforward answer from the grown-up point of view might be incomprehensible to the child at its current age; and where there is
anyway no one way of making stories out of the sexual something
which is never a matter of neutral knowledge. But today, the very
'facts' of reproduction, the 'facts of life' themselves, have changed
in ways that would have been unimaginable just a few decades
ago. As discussed in Chapter 1, there are new ways of beginning
a human life, in addition to what is now sometimes called the
'traditional' method. And there are new ways of knowing the differences, when the social and even biological distinctions between
a mother and a father have diminished. Linked to both changes

[12] It is true that Susan's being formally married to a man other than the one she
lives with would surely still be an occasion for secrecy and shame; but the present-day
normality of separations and divorces and the seriality of relationships that follows
from them means that such a situation would be differently improbable.

are newly acceptable kinds of parental set-up, such as gay parent-hood or chosen single parenthood, in which the child's arrival is bound to have involved at least one other birth or genetic parent beyond those who are going to bring it up. So the edges of live-able, normal knowledge about origins—the back-stories of each individual life—are in a state of mutation as well. What is enough or too much for children—and adults—to know or understand of where they come from? The question has always been there, but the new complications and multiplications of origin give it a dif-ferent prominence today.

The new technologies of assisted reproduction, along with the older one of sperm donation, are the source of much debate in relation to questions of disclosure. Is it necessary or desirable to tell a child it was conceived through IVF, when the gametes (the egg and sperm) came from both its intended social parents (and thus there were no 'donors' involved)? (Here there is a strange reversal of the age-old inseparability of conception and sexuality: instead of children's revolted pubescent realization that their par-ents must have had sex, here there is the differently weird poten-tial discovery that in this case, exceptionally, they didn't.) Or, who is the mother of a child who was gestated in the womb of one woman with her sister's egg, in order for the resulting baby to be raised by a third sister, unable to have biological children of her own?[13] Or, what counts as the place of origin for a child made with a donated egg from another country from that of the future parents, where the embryo was implanted in the mother-to-be, but who was born to that mother in her own native country? One of the curious aspects of the new technologies is that they often occur at these two extremes of too close and too far for comfort: either a genetic parent is in fact someone inside the family, but to be distinguished from the future mother or father; or else they are someone not only anonymous—there will be no name and the future parents will never have met them—but from another coun-try or even continent altogether. In the case of adoption, and

[13] See Sian Lewis, 'The Three Sisters Who Gave Birth to One Child', *Woman's Own*, 28 May 2007, 22–3. This was a much-shared story, also featuring in the *Guardian* and on BBC Radio 4 *Woman's Hour*.

increasingly with donor conception, it is now taken for granted that children should be told of their birth or genetic 'origins', not least for the practical reason of medical information: minimally, the right to know you are not your parents' or one parent's natural child.[14] In these cases it is also now considered reasonable for children to have the right to seek out their birth or genetic parents at a later stage—and similarly for original parents, or 'pre-parents', seeking to know their grown-up children.[15]

Any glance at a few of the websites either advertising reproductive services or giving information about them provides a sense of the turmoil of arguments here in relation to what it is proper or comfortable for children to know or to seek to find out. And in this matter of beginnings and origins, there is never, even in 'truth', one simple or single story. In the traditional scenario, after all, any baby has two parents, of two sexes, who come from different families if not places, and whose separate histories are very possibly as little known to each other, or in another sense to themselves, as they are to the child they beget. What is clear is that the likely or liveable stories of origin, what children or parents can tolerate or communicate as family tales, are no more stable or permanent or complete than other phenomena of other kinds of history—however much they may seem to be rooted in nature or in biology: in the well-known 'facts of life'. It seems clear too that there must be limits to what anyone can bear to know, as well as bear not to know, of the conditions of their existence: where they came from and who they are, however these matters are understood. Those madding limits or edges of secrets and partial stories are what Hardy's novels relentlessly dramatize.

---

[14] Graham Swift's novel *Tomorrow* (2007) is set (entirely) on the day leading up to what is to be a belated disclosure to twins of 16 that they were conceived by donor insemination.

[15] In Britain anonymous donation ceased to be possible in 2005. Children born through egg, sperm, or embryo donation now have the right to identifying information about their donors when they reach the age of 18. Donors cannot find out as much; they have the right at any point to know the number, sex, and year of birth of any children born as a result of their donation.

13

'I Had Barbara'

Women's Ties and Edith Wharton's 'Roman Fever'

The setting of Edith Wharton's short story 'Roman Fever' (1934) is consciously casual. Two wealthy American widows with 'time to kill' sit chatting through the afternoon, on the terrace of a restaurant in Rome, overlooking the ruins of the ancient city.[1] They have known each other off and on all their lives. Both have daughters who are at present out together, as they speak, with two eligible young Italian men; and the women recall their own courting days, also together, also in Rome. There is a risky edge to this talk because they had both been in love with the same man, and knew it at the time. One of the women had been engaged to him, and duly married him, yet it is she, Mrs Slade, who now asks herself, in relation to the other one, 'Would she never cure herself of envying her?' (17)—and who pushes the conversation forwards with further questions.

In its final pages, the story moves into high gear with the production, one after another, of three interlocking secrets from that earlier time. Mrs Ansley had received a letter from Delphin Slade inviting her to meet him one night at the Colosseum. The first thrust comes from Mrs Slade declaring that it was she, out of jealousy, who wrote that letter, in an attempt to trick her rival into a dangerous adventure. (Behind the stratagem lay the now repeated story of an old great-aunt who, by sending her out one cold night to the Forum

[1] Edith Wharton, 'Roman Fever' (1934), in *Roman Fever and Other Stories* (London: Virago, 1983), 10. Further page references will be given within the main text.

'because they were in love with the same man' (18), had caused her sister's death.) For Grace Ansley, this admission ruins the memory of 'the only letter I ever had from him' (21), and Mrs Slade's triumph seems to be confirmed. But then—return blow—Mrs Ansley reveals that the date did in fact take place (she replied to the letter). Mrs Slade recovers from this with difficulty:

'I oughtn't to begrudge it to you, I suppose. After all, I had everything; I had him for twenty-five years. And you had nothing but that one letter he didn't write.' (24)

With perfect pacing, Wharton then completes the series of revelations and reversals, ending the story like this:

Mrs Ansley was again silent. At length she turned toward the door of the terrace. She took a step, and turned back, facing her companion.
    'I had Barbara,' she said, and began to move ahead of Mrs Slade toward the stairway. (24)

'I had Barbara' is the clinching shock announcement. We take it to mean, as must Mrs Slade, that Delphin Slade was the father of Barbara Ansley, conceived that night of the meeting at the Colosseum. The scandalous information then appears to sort out several doubts and suspicions that Wharton has carefully planted during the course of the narrative. Mrs Slade envies Mrs Ansley her bright, 'dynamic' daughter Barbara and cannot understand how two such 'exemplary characters' as Grace and Horace Ansley could have produced her (16–17); she, meanwhile, is disappointed in her own too perfect Jenny. Grace had been ill after her late-night 'sight-seeing' (19) all those years ago, and she was 'married to Horace Ansley two months afterward' (22). If Barbara is now shown to be Delphin's daughter, then these anomalies seem to be cleared up: Grace was quickly married because she was pregnant, and Barbara is after all the daughter of the dynamic Delphin Slade.

    Grace Ansley's punchline—'I had Barbara'—rounds off the series of blows initiated by her ancient rival. A final detail appears to confirm that the relations between the two women have shifted, as Mrs Ansley, previously seen as the more timid and passive of the two, 'began to move ahead'. Thus the battle that has taken place this present afternoon seems both to repeat and complete the one that occurred a generation before. Then, Alida had taken the initiative in attempting to punish Grace for her interest in her fiancé. She had sent the fake letter that was meant to lead to a long, lonely wait at the entrance to the Colosseum, but in fact her action had the effect of bringing about exactly what she was seeking to avoid, a rendezvous between the two potential lovers. Today, unaware of what happened between Grace and Delphin as a result of her letter, Mrs Slade has been continuing to attempt to control the future. Her renewed jealousy of Grace is prompted by a 'prophetic flight' (17) in which she imagines Grace settled in grandmotherly contentment near her sparkling daughter's family. It is this fantasy—'Would she never cure herself of envying her?'— that sets off the conversational prod that is meant to humiliate Grace once more, but instead—and again as before—has the opposite result.

When the story is reread in the knowledge of what is revealed at the end, many phrases seem to take on a second, confirming meaning that did not appear the first time. One of the girls is described as a 'rare accident' (14). The two women are 'old lovers of Rome' (11). Grace's knitting collapses in 'a panic-stricken heap' (20); 'one, two, three—slip' (16) seems to point to a fall not a pattern. Violence is everywhere: in 'so purposeless a wound' (21), verbally inflicted, or in the 'time to kill', where the leisurely cliché now sounds openly murderous—time *to kill*. On the second reading, we see significance in the 'mutual confession' (13) that at first seemed only to refer to middle-aged women's regret at the dullness of their lives in comparison with their daughters'. Great-aunt Harriet, who had sent her sister out to her death, 'confessed it years afterwards' (18), just as Mrs Slade owns up to her own attempt to follow the great-aunt's example. Long ago, when she was the Ansleys' neighbour in New York, Mrs Slade had joked that 'I'd rather live opposite a speak-easy for a change' (12): belatedly, the speak-easy's double suggestion of transgression and confession has now turned the joke against her.

In going over the story again and finding hitherto unnoticed indications of what happened—the old story that the current story brings out—we are in the same position as the two women characters. They find themselves engaged in a process of reinterpretation and reconstruction as they go back over the events of twenty-five years before, as well as over their subsequent views of the other: 'So these two ladies visualized each other, each through the wrong end of her little telescope' (14). Each has partial and sometimes mistaken knowledge, and the present conversation causes the emergence of what had previously been hidden from both. Seemingly tangential elements in the narrative also suggest, the second time, the need for this kind of reappraisal of the situation, by readers and protagonists alike. Grace Ansley concurs with her companion's remark about the 'beautiful' view of the Palatine from where they are seated:

'It always will be, to me,' assented her friend Mrs Ansley, with so slight a stress on the 'me' that Mrs Slade, though she noticed it, wondered if it were not merely accidental, like the random underlinings of old-fashioned letter-writers.   (10)

On the second reading we know, as Mrs Slade has also found out, that there is more of a 'me' in Grace Ansley than had been imagined. She did not initiate, but she did go along with, the illicit tryst with Delphin Slade. Also, the very idea of the 'merely accidental' is discredited in this story: accidents happen not by chance, but in relation to particular designs and purposes that go wrong—both those in the past, and those in the present conversation. 'Like the random underlinings of old-fashioned letter-writers'? After the first reading, we know that in this story there need be nothing random or simply decorative about an old-time letter like the one that Alida Slade once signed with the initials 'D.S.'; nor are old-fashioned ladies, like Great-aunt Harriet, as innocent or haphazard in their ways as might be thought. Whatever the truth of the 'tradition' (18) of Harriet's youthful misdemeanour, as a tale it was effective both as a deterrent—'Mother used to frighten us with the story,' says Grace—and as an example to follow, as Alida then did when 'you frightened *me* with it' (19): Mrs Slade's characteristically conscious 'stress on the "me"'.

If the interpretation and use of stories is an issue within this one, there is also overt reference, by both characters and narrator, to confusions between different levels of language, making it difficult to know which elements are to be taken as central to a main story, and which as 'merely' metaphorical or accidental. 'Well, I mean

figuratively' (9), Barbara is heard to say to Jenny as the two girls
depart; 'figuratively' here refers to metaphorical knitting, which in
fact is what Grace will literally be doing on the next page, though
with additions of emotion and opulence that immediately detract
from the bare fact: 'Half guiltily'—one more phrase that resonates
differently on the second reading—'she drew from her handsomely
mounted black handbag a twist of crimson silk run through by two
fine knitting needles' (10). Sliding into suggestion, literal knitting
itself becomes ominous once more—'one, two, three—slip.'[2] In
New York, when their husbands were alive, Grace and Alida 'had
lived opposite each other—actually as well as figuratively—for
years' (12), the two would-be contrasting adverbs thrust into the
middle of an otherwise innocuous clause, and raising a question
about how, exactly, their meanings are to be understood. At one
point Mrs Ansley takes up her knitting 'almost furtively' and Mrs
Slade takes 'sideway note of this activity'—as though furtive or
almost furtive herself, but also, in this story, as a matter of mar-
ginal uncertainty: only in light of the later revelations is it clear
which gestures and which words need to be actively noted or interpreted. And at almost the end, when 'A stout lady in a dust-coat
suddenly appeared, asking in broken Italian if any one had seen
the elastic band which held together her tattered Baedecker' (23),
she seems to be both a crazy diversion, a trivial distraction from
the suspended drama, and also, equally, a comically allegorical
sideshow that embodies the unravelling—'broken' language,
broken guidebook—of previously settled stories of the ladies'
youthful past.

Whether trivially touristical or highly serious—as always, in this story,
both and either are possible—allusions to classical culture are scattered
throughout 'Roman Fever'. The letter from 'Delphin' proves oracular
in its production of a future event. The story's setting above the ruins
of Rome provides the backdrop for the emergence of long-buried stories, and for the gladiatorial violence of Mrs Slade/'slayed'. As in a
Greek tragedy, Mrs Ansley's face shows a 'mask' (20); at one point she

[2] In another way, the description of Grace's luxurious bag opens up metaphori-
cally onto the silky secret of something soft that must have been 'run through' at
different times by two penetrative instruments.

'looked straight out at the great accumulated wreckage of passion and splendour at her feet' (17). In its own minor key, the story could even be taken as a modern version of *Oedipus*. As in Sophocles' drama, what happens is not so much a new action as a conversation which, driving to its painful denouement, goes over ancient events, showing their significance to be quite different from what participants had imagined. Oedipus finds that a man he once murdered was his own father; that Polybus, the man he thought was his father, was not; and that Jocasta, the woman he married, was his birth mother. In 'Roman Fever', too, there is a revelation involving both illicit sexuality and mistaken paternity. The two families that 'actually, as well as figuratively' 'lived opposite each other' are in one sense the same family—more actually than 'actually' first suggested—conjoined by girls who turn out to have the same father. In 'Roman Fever', the attempt to ward off a feared event precipitates its happening; and so for Oedipus the fulfilment of the oracle that he will murder his father and marry and have children with his mother is enabled by the successive attempts, by his birth parents and later himself, to avert it (the newborn baby is exposed, and does not know his first parents; the young man flees those he wrongly thinks are his parents, and thereby encounters first Laius, his father, and then Jocasta).

To make such a grand comparison is perhaps to do an injustice to 'Roman Fever', a story without such classical or universal affiliations—or destinies—as Sophocles' *Oedipus*. For one thing, there is nothing at stake in the modern tale beyond the private concerns of two well-off, unoccupied women. In *Oedipus*, on the other hand, the inquiry which leads eventually to the discovery of Oedipus' other history, his 'true' identity, is initiated—by Oedipus himself—as a matter of social urgency: the city is suffering from a plague and the oracle has said that the person responsible for the pollution, Laius' murderer years ago, must be tracked down. The strong point of likeness between the ancient drama and the modern story is that in each, the action consists only of conversation and its accompanying emotions; words alone have the effect of changing the sense of the past and, thereby, of changing the characters' understanding of themselves and their place in the present time.

It would also be possible, in different ways, to look at 'Roman Fever' as a female version of the Oedipal paradigm. Freud adopted

Sophocles' drama as his literary template for thinking about children's—essentially, boys'—development to adulthood, from early years of incestuous longings and rivalrous hatred, out into the wider world of the cultural community in which the loss of their princely uniqueness—'His Majesty the Baby'—was compensated by the adult privileges of a life beyond the confines of the first family.[3] The girl had no comparable story; rather, in Freud's attempts to consider her different development, she ended up only—at best—a misfit, forever unconsciously seeking the masculinity of which she was deprived. Feminists since Freud's own time have regularly protested against this overt secondarization of femininity, but many too have understood the theory as a useful allegory of the complexities of women's psychological placement in a patriarchal society. In this context 'Roman Fever', written quite literally from the women's point of view, as Grace and Alida sit overlooking the valued remains of a violent masculine civilization, might seem to lend support to two different perspectives on women's lives in a modern but age-old patriarchal culture.

From the first point of view, Mrs Ansley and Mrs Slade have both lived the conventional feminine lives of girl, wife, mother, and widow; their identities have been primarily in relation to husbands secured, then lived with, then lost. Mrs Slade was proud to see herself admired as '*the* Slade's wife' (13). After the death of her husband and, prior to that, of their son, 'There was nothing left but to mother her daughter' (13), presented less as compensation for her losses (Jenny's, too) than as a poor third choice. '[N]othing left but...' also seems to echo the *ennui* which has led to the two ladies' spending the afternoon talking—the equivalent, on this particular day, of the third-choice outlet for unused energies. '[S]ometimes I get tired just looking—even at this,' says Grace; 'Her gesture was now addressed to the stupendous scene at their feet' (10). With nothing going on in their own lives—no one to tend—the women are jaded sightseers, and conversation is tediously time-filling, time-killing, before—and alongside—its secret violence.

---

[3] 'His Majesty the Baby' appears in Freud, 'On Narcissism: An Introduction' (1914), *Standard Edition of the Complete Psychological Works of Sigmund Freud*, trans. James Strachey (London: Hogarth Press, 1955–74), xiv. 91.

The differences she thinks she sees from her 'opposite' side cause Mrs Slade to rank herself and her marriage far above that of Grace and Horace Ansley, whom she dubs 'two nullities' (12); but it is also stressed that the two women's life stories have been virtually identical. They married, they had children, they 'lived opposite each other', their husbands died; now, '[t]he similarity of their lot' (13) has brought them back together. Their daughters are repeating or continuing the same old story of girls, in each generation, finding husbands. Within it, there are minor historical variations to do with local conditions and the degree of restraint placed upon the young ladies, but essentially the same one narrative which is likely to involve rivalry between two girls for the same man. Great-aunt Harriet is the most ancient version of this, and Alida takes it for granted that the same thing is going on between her daughter and Grace's right now.[4]

The lack of individuality that this entails is specified by Grace, in response to Alida's reaction to the mockery of the disappearing daughters:

'That's what our daughters think of us!'

Her companion replied by a deprecating gesture. 'Not of us individually. We must remember that. It's just the collective modern idea of Mothers.'　(10)

---

[4] In *Roman Fever: Domesticity and Nationalism in Nineteenth-Century American Women's Writing* (Columbus: Ohio State University Press, 2004), Annamaria Formichella Elsden argues that there is a distinct progression for each successive generation of women. Mrs Slade's handling of the waiters is Wharton's suggestion of how far (American) women have come since the nineteenth century. Their daughters' repetition of the old story is only in Mrs Slade's projection; today they are flying high above the 'bad air' of the old dangers of 'Roman Fever' (malaria). 'Even more than their mothers, Barbara and Jenny are able to take command of the foreign environment' (123); 'the accuracy with which Mrs Slade reads the situation and the poise with which she manipulates circumstances indicate her independence and efficacy and allow her to get what she wants' (122). It is certainly true that we are told nothing of Babs and Jenny's actual relations, whether with each other, their mothers, or their men—which leaves it entirely possible that there may be real differences from the previous generation. But we do know that it is Mrs Slade's own attempts to 'read' then react to situations, to 'take command' or 'manipulate circumstances', both in the past and in the course of the present conversation, that form the story of her failures.

Later, this suggestion of historical determinations is elaborated and corroborated in Mrs Slade's version of maternal Roman history:

'I was just thinking,' she said slowly, 'what different things Rome stands for to each generation of travellers. To our grandmothers, Roman fever; to our mothers, sentimental dangers—how we used to be guarded!—to our daughters, no more dangers than the middle of Main Street.' (15)

What looks like a semi-sociological objectivity in this account becomes less striking when it turns out that Mrs Slade is about to home in on 'the spice of attraction' (16) that drew girls out in their own generation. But still it remains true that both women think back through their mothers, and their foremothers' daughters, just as their focus today is on their own daughters' amorous adventures. This could be seen as further evidence of their subordination to the underlying patriarchal arrangements, in which mothers protect, more or less, and daughters escape, more or less, until the point where they settle down ready to repeat the story in a new form a generation later. But it also points to the other feminist perspective through which the female relationships of 'Roman Fever' might be considered.

For it could be said that far from being victims of men, collectively or individually, the women of 'Roman Fever' are the drivers of the plots; it is they, not the husbands or boyfriends, who control what happens. No men appear in the present scene of the story, apart from unidentified waiters of another class and nationality than the protagonists, whose role is no more than to let the ladies sit on through the afternoon. The young Italian men with whom the daughters are spending the day feature only as the presumed objects of the girls' predatory desires: 'if Babs Ansley isn't out to catch that young aviator—the one who's a Marchese—then I don't know anything' (16). In the past time that the conversation brings up, Delphin Slade and Horace Ansley are given purely reactive or passive roles. Delphin goes to the assignation with Grace because he receives her reply to the letter sent in his name. Horace appears in several dual situations with his wife—one of 'those two nullities'; 'two such exemplary characters'; 'just the duplicate of his wife' (12). Here he has no distinctive character and no masculinity of his own; they are two of a dull kind, he second ('duplicate') to her. At one crucial point he is engaged in a doubly passive situation, after Grace's unspecified 'ill-ness' when, according to Alida, 'As soon as you could get out of bed your mother rushed you off to Florence and married you' (22–3). Horace is merely the accessory groomed for a mother's swiftly prag-matic arrangement of a daughter's wedding; in fact he is not even mentioned, so that the marriage appears, syntactically, to take place between mother and daughter alone.

In this second view, it is women who call the shots, even if their sphere of influence remains that of the family and marriage.[5] From generation to generation, what takes place is a female negotiation over men. There is also the suggestion that despite appearances, the primary relationships of women are not with men so much as with one another. Babs and Jenny go around as a pair. Alida and Grace 'had been intimate since childhood' (12). They are introduced at the start of the story as a kind of dual subject:

From the table at which they had been lunching two American ladies of ripe but well-cared-for middle age moved across the lofty terrace of the Roman restaurant and, leaning on its parapet, looked first at each other, and then down on the outspread glories of the Palatine and the Forum, with the same expression of vague but benevolent approval. (9)

They move as one, they lean as one, and their expression is the 'same' one. 'Mrs Slade and Mrs Ansley had lived opposite each

[5] It is here that Wharton's perspective differs markedly from that of an earlier text, *Daisy Miller* (1878). Henry James's story focuses on a contemporary American girl whose uncautious behaviour in Rome, including a late-night visit with a man to the Colosseum, ultimately leads to her contracting Roman fever—malaria—and dying. Daisy is filtered through the perceptions of an observing American man who is fasci-nated, attracted, judgemental, and ultimately critical of his own prejudices. Daisy's point of view is never given; the story is rather concerned with the man's responses to a modern girl who assumes a freedom that ignores the conventions of sensible or respectable conduct. Wharton also uses the idea of Roman fever differently. In a previous generation—the Daisy Miller generation—Great-aunt Harriet's sister did die of it, but what Grace Ansley caught as a result of her Roman night out was pregnancy, initially represented as an illness only in order to conceal it. Within the story, it is historically distanced—'what different things Rome stands for to each generation of travellers. To our grandmothers, Roman fever...'. Malaria had, in fact, ceased to be the real danger it had been in nineteenth-century Rome. But Roman fever's title role makes it also function for Wharton's story like a catch-all, semi-euphemistic diagnosis of wayward sexual behaviour in young American women abroad.

other—actually as well as figuratively—for years': a cohabitation, figuratively if not actually, alongside their marriages. When, prior to the final exchange of secrets, the two fall silent, 'Mrs Ansley was slightly embarrassed by what seemed, after so many years, a new stage in their intimacy' (15). It is crucial, too, that the only declaration of love represented in the story is from woman to woman: the letter to Grace, purportedly from Delphin, that was written by Alida.

Division and rivalry are also part of this two-in-one, with the facing Upper East Side windows functioning like mirrors which both separate and join the two women as one and as two, self and image 'opposite'. There are also the metaphorical distorting telescopes through which 'these two ladies visualized each other, each through the wrong end'. 'You think me a monster!' Mrs Slade bursts out after confessing to her writing of the precious love letter; but then a few lines further down, reflecting on Grace's treachery in getting together with her fiancé: 'Wasn't it she who was the monster?' (22). Each woman projects onto the other the features dissociated from herself, or exaggerates the assumed differences that make them so conveniently contrastable and comparable, like their supposedly divergent daughters.

There is a further way in which the primacy of woman-to-woman relationships comes through as a buried possibility in this story. The closing 'I had Barbara' appears, initially, to be dramatic and euphemistic shorthand for 'Your husband was the father of my child'; it is a formally symmetrical riposte to 'I had him for twenty-five years' (24). In the context of what has been said about Barbara's unusual and emphasized *'edge'* and the doubt about 'where she got it, with those two nullities as parents' (12), the line's ultimate reference to paternity seems to explain a minor mystery as well as produce a personal scandal. Everything we have heard up to this point would suggest the likelihood of this other parentage, once it is mooted, while the whole argumentative force of the struggle between the two women seems naturally to come to an end with the decisive reversal.

But what Grace Ansley actually, not figuratively, says is that she had Barbara. She does not say she had sex with Delphin on that night—or that Delphin is Barbara's father. The simple meaning of her statement of motherhood escapes notice, is overlooked, because it is what we and they already know: sure, Grace had Barbara, Barbara is Grace's daughter.

Maternity is never in doubt; paternity has been, throughout the history of human story-telling, the question-generating status. This is what leads us as readers, and presumably Alida Slade as well (no reply is actually given), to interpret Grace's announcement as supplying new information, clinching the story with the utterance of an age-old species of female secret. And to all intents and purposes, it makes no difference whether Grace meant to speak more than her words or not, since the dramatic effect is exactly as if she had: 'She began to move ahead of Mrs Slade toward the stairway' (24)—end of story.

Yet if we look again at the evidence that the closing statement seems to support, it turns out that it too involves elisions. For if Barbara is Delphin's daughter, she remains, surely, Grace's as well. So there is still, in Alida's terms, a problem about how one of 'two such exemplary characters as you and Horace had managed to produce anything quite so dynamic'. Even more strikingly, no doubt is raised at all about the equally anomalous quiet daughter of 'the exceptional couple' (13), the Slades. Dull Jenny has not only come from '*the* Slade' (13), but from a mother known for her 'vividness' (14): more than Babs, she has two inexplicable parents, not just one. While we may go with the rhetorical flow of the final sentences, it does not, on closer inspection, sweep away the kinship questions that the story has explicitly raised (in the case of Babs) and, following the same logic, suggested (in the case of Jenny).[6] The story leads us to accept that a daughter should be 'like' her father or 'like' her parents. The missing connection, between her and her mother, could then be seen as the one surreptitiously supplied by 'I had Barbara'.

It turns out, then, that there may be more to the ambiguity of 'I had Barbara' than a formal point about narrative undecidability.

---

[6] My argument here is similar to Jonathan Culler's in relation to Sophocles' *Oedipus the King*. Culler points out that the claim more than once in Sophocles' tragedy that there were 'many murderers' of King Laius, not just one, is never disproved; rather, it is forgotten in the face of the compelling convergence of narratives which leads us, like Oedipus himself, to be convinced that the murderer was him; see 'Story and Discourse in the Analysis of Narrative', in *The Pursuit of Signs: Semiotics, Literature, Deconstruction* (London: Routledge & Kegan Paul, 1981), 169–87.

'I had Barbara', in its lovely literalness, says nothing about a father; instead it matches a desirable daughter against Mrs Slade's boast of having had 'him', that husband or father. There is no second parent in view: in the singular, 'I' had Barbara. In this sense the hidden victory of 'Roman Fever' goes to a same-sex bond, and to the connection of mother and daughter elided and downgraded by paternal kinship relations.[7]

Yet the opposition between the known, literal mother and the inferred and doubtful father may seem, from another point of view, too neat an affirmation of what is itself a classically patriarchal division. '*Pater semper incertus est*', as Freud puts it in his essay 'Family Romances', using the Latin legal phrase; and if the father is always necessarily uncertain, then the mother, at the other extreme, is superlatively certain, '*certissima*'.[8] This is the distinction that comes, Freud argues, to enter into every child's understanding of the relations between the sexes; and it is never abandoned, remaining as the basis of adult thinking.

Freud is individualizing a theory put forward by nineteenth-century anthropologists, who saw a crucial and progressive turning point in the move made by primitive cultures from matriarchal to patriarchal thinking; this is how he puts it himself, in *Moses and Monotheism*:

[I]t came about that the matriarchal social order was succeeded by the patriarchal one—which, of course, involved a revolution in the juridical condition that had so far prevailed. An echo of this revolution seems still to be audible in the *Oresteia* of Aeschylus. But this turning from the mother to the father points in addition to a victory of intellectuality over sensuality— that is, an advance in civilization, since maternity is proved by the evidence of the senses while paternity is a hypothesis, based on an inference and a premiss. Taking sides in this way with a thought-process in preference to a sense perception has proved to be a momentous step.[9]

---

[7] Dale M. Bauer sees equally transgressive implications in the primary interpretation of 'I had Barbara': 'Grace threatens the symbolic order of society by exposing the arbitrary assumption Alida makes about Babs's father, not to mention the assumption about Grace's respectability'; *Edith Wharton's Brave New Politics* (Madison: University of Wisconsin Press, 1994), 160.

[8] Freud, 'Family Romances' (1909), *Standard Edition*, ix. 239.

[9] Freud, *Moses and Monotheism* (1939), *Standard Edition*, xxiii. 113–14.

This vaunted cultural progress comes about because bodily evidence is replaced by intellectual evidence, logically consistent ('based on an inference and a premiss') but necessarily fallible (no DNA testing yet). It seems, at best, a shaky shift, confirming rather than cancelling the fragility of fatherhood as a category.

Read in its connotative sense, as we initially take it, 'I had Barbara' succinctly combines a patriarchal logic ('he's the father') with the maternal self-evidence ('I gave birth to her') that allegedly needs no proof. But it subordinates, as culture does, the obvious, 'sensual' side, within the closing logic of the story and the overt rivalry between the two women. In its maternal rather than paternal emphasis, 'I had Barbara' goes without saying and therefore doesn't *figure*: it is what is already known and is thereby passed over in the context of the other available meaning.[10] It is ironically apt, in this context, that the name Barbara originates in the feminine form of the ancient Greek word for the non-Greek, non-civilized 'barbarian' or *barbaros*. The barbarian was named for his (rarely her) incomprehensible language, sounding to Greek ears like a meaningless repetition ('bar...bar'); he had no place in the community defined by its *logos*: logic, reason, and language. What Grace Ansley 'had' was (in both senses) out of order—a wild child, as yet unassimilated to patriarchal civilization. Like any baby, but especially like any girl.

There are other tensions concealed in the phrase 'I had Barbara'. To begin with, 'I' is apparently 'I as opposed to you': you had him for all those years, but Barbara is what I had. But it is also, obliquely, a claim to maternal autonomy: 'I' not 'we'. Here both 'fathers'—the likely biological one and the one who raised her—are dismissed from having had Barbara. Only 'I' 'had' her, even if an illicit paternity is also being asserted. But what does it really mean, even for a mother alone, to 'have' Barbara, or to have 'had' Barbara? In this connection the simple statement of maternity opens out into more than one possibility. 'Having' a baby is what women do at the point of birth; it is the specific point of separation. But Grace has also implicitly 'had' Barbara for the twenty-five years that Alida 'had' Delphin; the

---

[10] See Barbara Johnson, 'Is Female to Male as Ground is to Figure?', in *The Feminist Difference: Literature, Psychoanalysis, Race, and Gender* (Cambridge, Mass.: Harvard University Press, 1998), 17–36.

daughter represents a long-term affective tie, begun but not defined by giving birth. 'I had Barbara' all that time: better than having had 'him', boy baby or husband.

When I first read and reread 'Roman Fever', decades ago, the less obvious because so obvious maternal meaning of 'I had Barbara' seemed to me interesting mainly because of the way it could be used to illustrate a narrative instability even in stories that seemed most tightly stitched together—actually as well as figuratively. 'One, two, three—slip': meaning was never as neatly knitted together, nor destinies and pasts so safely patterned or predictable, as they might appear. In this particular development, orderly in its own consciously dis-ordering fashion, a structuralist analysis such as was found in the earlier writings of Roland Barthes must now give way to a more deconstructive openness to the misfit elements in a text. At that time, in the 1980s, the theoretical emphasis was moving on, now allowing for movement and 'give' in the object of study as well.

A generation on from *that* moment, something else has happened to the solely maternal meaning of 'I had Barbara'. In light of developments occurring elsewhere than in theory, the statement has lost its apparent literal simplicity of contrast to an inferred, assumed, and disputable father. Today, single parenting can be seen and experienced as a positive choice, and many women are adopting children—for the most part daughters—on their own. Seeking to have a child of one's own is a quest that may well be separate from and set above the desire for any other kind of attachment, including to possible co-parents. So Grace Ansley's words acquire a different historical resonance, in relation to subsequent possibilities and patterns of parenthood, or of women having daughters. No 'prophetic flight' of Alida Slade's, fearful or fantastic, could have seen these changes on the horizon; today, they may give Mrs Ansley's closing statement about her past the surprising twenty-first-century gloss of an alternative future.

Afterword

To return, at the end, to Hogarth's painting of 1746, 'Moses Brought Before Pharaoh's Daughter', discussed in Chapter 4. In its place of exhibition, the scene taken from Exodus was meant to give symbolic significance and honour to a particular moment that occurred in the life of every Foundling Hospital boy or girl. Having spent their first years being fostered with a wet-nurse and her family, the children were brought back to live in London. The Hospital is like the grand, welcoming adoptive mother, Pharaoh's daughter, and the foster-mother is the woman who, in the biblical story, was both wet-nurse, appointed by Pharaoh's daughter, and, secretly, Moses' real mother.

The scene evokes many of the ambiguities and complexities of parental stories old and new. A small child is given, or given up, by one parental figure to another. There is a first and a second mother: birth and adoptive mothers, or else surrogate and intending, or in-determinately more than one of these on one or other side. There is a question about one of the women being the real mother and which one has the right or the duty to raise the child. The rearing is shared—one woman hands the baby over, her work done. Or the rearing is contested: both parents want to 'have' the child. The relin-quishing woman may be an employee handing back her charge to the wealthier woman who has had the means and the wish to avoid the work herself. Or she may be a birth mother who has no choice but to give her baby into other parental hands. (Moses' mother is both of these.) As a birth mother it may be she cannot keep it, or has not been allowed to keep it—or cannot bear to keep it. The receiving parent may be one who charitably gives a home to a child who might otherwise die. Or one who longs for children of her own. (Or both.) The child may be being moved from an impoverished environment to a comfortable one, or from a dangerous situation to a safe place of care. Or, a mother who has been a child's only carer in its early years may have reached the moment when it is time for him or her to enter a world apart from hers.

Taking away the particular image of the Moses story and a little boy in transition between two female figures, the scene also suggests other situations, both ordinary and exceptional, in which a child is handed over, from one parent to another, from one carer to another. It may show division or sharing, conflict or collaboration. One person gives up or gives back a child to another—for an hour, for a day or two, for the time being, or forever.

There always is, or was, or will be, another person or institution or social world in the life of the child, with whom or with which it has been or will be divided. With relief, with grief, or with pleasure; sometimes with all of these. There is never, once and for all, a child of one's own. Amongst the many meanings it suggests, 'Moses Brought before Pharaoh's Daughter' is a picture of letting go.

Bibliography

Articles from newspapers and magazines, referenced in footnotes, are not included in the bibliography. Biblical quotations are taken from *The Jerusalem Bible* (London: Darton, Longman & Todd, 1966), unless otherwise stated. Unattributed translations are my own.

Adie, Kate, *Nobody's Child: Who Are You When You Don't Know Your Past?* (London: Hodder, 2005).

Allen, Grant, *The Woman Who Did* (1895), introduced by Sarah Wintle (Oxford: Oxford University Press, 1995).

Appignanesi, Lisa, *All About Love: Anatomy of an Unruly Emotion* (London: Virago, 2011).

Archard, David, and David Benatar, *Procreation and Parenthood: The Ethics of Bearing and Rearing Children* (Oxford: Clarendon Press, 2010).

Arditti, Rita, Renate Duelli Klein, and Shelley Minden (eds.), *Test-Tube Women: What Future for Motherhood?* (London: Pandora Press, 1984).

Aristotle, *Ethica Nicomachea*, ed. I. Bywater (Oxford: Oxford University Press, 1894).

——*Ethics*, trans. J. A. K. Thomson (1955; Harmondsworth: Penguin, 1986).

——*Politica*, ed. W. D. Ross (1957; Oxford: Oxford University Press, 2008).

——*The Politics*, trans. T. A. Sinclair (Harmondsworth: Penguin, 1962).

Artificial Human Insemination: The Report of a Commission Appointed by His Grace the Archbishop of Canterbury (London: SPCK, 1948).

Asher, Rebecca, *Shattered: Modern Motherhood and the Illusion of Equality* (London: Harvill Secker, 2011).

Austen, Jane, *Mansfield Park* (1814), ed. Tony Tanner (1966; London: Penguin, 1985).

Badinter, Elisabeth, *L'Amour en plus: Histoire de l'amour maternel (XVIIème–XXème siècle)* (1980; Paris: Flammarion, 1981).

Bainham, Andrew, Shelley Day Sclater, and Martin Richards (eds.), *What is a Parent? A Socio-Legal Analysis* (Oxford: Hart, 1999).

Baraitser, Lisa, *Maternal Encounters: The Ethics of Interruption* (London: Routledge, 2009).

Battestin, Martin C., 'Henry Fielding, Sarah Fielding, and "the dreadful Sin of Incest"', *Novel* 13 (1979): 6–18.

Bauer, Dale M., *Edith Wharton's Brave New Politics* (Madison: University of Wisconsin Press, 1994).

Becker, Gay, *The Elusive Embryo: How Women and Men Approach the New Reproductive Technologies* (Berkeley: University of California Press, 2000).

Black, Matthew, and H. H. Rowley (eds.), *Peake's Commentary on the Bible*
(London: Nelson, 1962).

Boswell, John, *The Kindness of Strangers: The Abandonment of Children in
Western Europe from Late Antiquity to the Renaissance* (New York: Pantheon,
1988).

Bowlby, Rachel, *Freudian Mythologies: Greek Tragedy and Modern Identities*
(Oxford: Oxford University Press, 2007).

—— 'Versions of Realism in George Eliot's *Adam Bede*', *Textual Practice* 25: 3
(June 2011): 417–36.

Brontë, Charlotte, *Jane Eyre* (1847), ed. Margaret Smith (Oxford: Oxford
University Press, 2000).

Brown, Lesley, and John Brown, with Sue Freeman, *Our Miracle Called
Louise: A Parents' Story* (New York: Paddington Press, 1979).

Butler, Marilyn, *Jane Austen and the War of Ideas* (1975; Oxford: Clarendon
Press, 1987).

Chesler, Phyllis, *Sacred Bond: The Legacy of Baby M* (1988; London: Virago,
1990).

Corea, Gena, *The Mother Machine: Reproductive Technologies from Artificial Insemination to Artificial Wombs* (1985; London: Women's Press, 1988).

Cotton, Kim, and Denise Winn, *Baby Cotton: For Love and Money* (London:
Dorling Kindersley, 1985).

Cretney, Stephen, *Family Law in the Twentieth Century: A History* (Oxford:
Oxford University Press, 2003).

Culler, Jonathan, *The Pursuit of Signs: Semiotics, Literature, Deconstruction*
(London: Routledge & Kegan Paul, 1981).

Deech, Ruth, and Anna Smajdor, *From IVF to Immortality: Controversy in the
Era of Reproductive Technology* (Oxford: Oxford University Press, 2007).

Delaisi de Parseval, Geneviève, *La Part du père* (1981; Paris: Editions du
Seuil, 2004).

—— with Jacqueline Bigeargal (eds.), *Objectif bébé—Une nouvelle science: la bébologie* (1985; Paris: Autrement, 1987).

Derrida, Jacques, and Elisabeth Roudinesc, *De quoi demain... : Dialogue* (Paris:
Fayard/Galilée, 2001).

Dickens, Charles, *Bleak House* (1853), ed. Stephen Gill (Oxford: Oxford
University Press, 1998).

—— *Dombey and Son* (1848), ed. Peter Fairclough (1970; London: Penguin,
1985).

—— *Great Expectations* (1861), ed. Margaret Cardwell (Oxford: Oxford
University Press, 1994).

—— *Oliver Twist* (1838), ed. Kathleen Tillotson (1966; Oxford: Oxford University Press, 1999).

Donzelot, Jacques, *La Police des familles* (Paris: Editions de Minuit, 1977).

Dowrick, Stephanie, and Sibyl Grundberg (eds.), *Why Children?* (London: Women's Press, 1980).

Edwards-Jones, Imogen, *The Stork Club: One Woman's Journey to the Front Line of Fertility* (2006; London: Corgi, 2007).

Eliot, George, *Silas Marner* (1861), ed. Terence Cave (Oxford: Oxford University Press, 1996).

Elliott, Sue, *Love Child: A True Story of Adoption, Reunion, Loss and Love* (London: Vermilion, 2005).

Elsden, Annamaria Formichella, *Roman Fever: Domesticity and Nationalism in Nineteenth-Century American Women's Writing* (Columbus: Ohio State University Press, 2004).

Elton, Ben, *Inconceivable* (1999; London: Black Swan, 2000).

Euripides, *Bacchae*, ed. E. R. Dodds (1944; 2nd edn. Oxford: Oxford University Press, 1960).

——*Hippolytos*, ed. W. S. Barrett (1964; Oxford: Clarendon Press, 2001).

——*Ion*, ed. A. S. Owen (1939; Oxford: Oxford University Press, 1971).

——*Medea*, ed. Denys L. Page (1938; Oxford: Oxford University Press, 1976).

——*Phoenissae*, in *Fabulae*, vol. iii, ed. Gilbert Murray (2nd edn. 1913; Oxford: Oxford University Press, 1954).

Fauser, Bart, and Paul Devroey, with Simon Brown, *Baby-Making* (Oxford: Oxford University Press, 2011).

Fessler, Ann, *The Girls Who Went Away: The Hidden History of Women Who Surrendered Children for Adoption in the Decades Before 'Roe v. Wade'* (New York: Penguin Press, 2006).

Fielding, Henry, *Tom Jones* (1749), ed. John Bender and Simon Stern (Oxford: Oxford University Press, 1996).

Fisher, Kate, *Birth Control, Sex and Marriage in Britain 1918–1960* (Oxford: Oxford University Press, 2006).

Franklin, Sarah, *Embodied Progress: A Cultural Account of Assisted Conception* (London: Routledge, 1997).

Frayn, Rebecca, *One Life* (London: Simon & Schuster, 2006).

Freud, Sigmund, *Gesammelte Werke*, 18 vols. (1951–87; Frankfurt am Main: Fischer Taschenbuch Verlag, 1999).

——*Standard Edition of the Complete Psychological Works of Sigmund Freud*, trans. James Strachey, 24 vols. (London: Hogarth Press, 1955–74).

Frydman, René, *L'Irrésistible désir de naissance* (Paris: PUF, 1986).

Furneaux, Holly, *Queer Dickens: Erotics, Families, Masculinities* (Oxford: Oxford University Press, 2009).

Gieve, Katherine (ed.), *Balancing Acts: On Being a Mother* (London: Virago, 1989).

Girard, Christophe, *Père comme les autres* (Paris: Hachette, 2006).

Gosden, Roger, *Designer Babies: The Brave New World of Reproductive Technology* (London: Victor Gollancz, 1999).

Goulding, June, *The Light in the Window* (1998; London: Ebury Press, 2005).

Gray, Thomas, in Roger Lonsdale (ed.), *The Poems of Gray, Collins, and Goldsmith* (London: Longmans, 1969).

Gregory, Elizabeth, *Ready: Why Women are Embracing the New Later Motherhood* (New York: Basic Books, 2007).

Griffith, Edward F., *Modern Marriage* (19th edn. London: Methuen, 1946).

Hall, Ruth (ed.), *Dear Dr Stopes: Sex in the 1920s* (1978; Harmondsworth: Penguin, 1981).

Hardy, Thomas, *Far from the Madding Crowd* (1874), ed. Ronald Blythe (Harmondsworth: Penguin, 1978).

——*Jude the Obscure* (1895), ed. C. H. Sisson (1978; London: Penguin, 1985).

——*The Mayor of Casterbridge* (1886), ed. Dale Kramer (Oxford: Oxford University Press, 2004).

Haynes, Jane, and Juliet Miller (eds.), *Inconceivable Conceptions: Psychological Aspects of Infertility and Reproductive Technology* (Hove: Brunner-Routledge, 2003).

Hewlett, Sylvia Ann, *Creating a Life: What Every Woman Needs to Know About Having a Baby and a Career* (New York: Miramax Books, 2003).

Homer, *The Odyssey*, vol. i, books I–XII, ed. W. B. Stanford (2nd edn. 1949; London: Macmillan, 1974).

Houghton, John, *A Forever Family* (London: Faber, 2006).

Iacub, Marcela, *Le Crime était presque sexuel, et autres essais de casuistique juridique* (Paris: Flammarion, 2003).

——*L'Empire du ventre: Pour une autre histoire de la maternité* (Paris: Fayard, 2004).

——and Patrick Maniglier, 'Les Enfants de la ménopause', in Iacub and Maniglier (eds.), *Famille en scènes: Bousculée, réinventée, toujours inattendue* (Paris: Editions Autrement, 2003), 104–15.

Inchbald, Elizabeth, *A Simple Story* (1791), ed. J. M. S. Tompkins (Oxford: Oxford University Press, 1998).

Indichova, Julia, *Inconceivable: A Woman's Triumph Over Despair and Statistics* (New York: Broadway Books, 2001).

Jack, Florence R., and Rita Strauss (eds.), *The Woman's Book: Contains Everything a Woman Ought to Know* (London: T. C. & E. C. Jack, 1911).

Jacobson, Dan, *Time and Time Again: Autobiographies* (London: André Deutsch, 1985).

James, Henry, *Daisy Miller* (1878), *Daisy Miller and Other Stories*, ed. Jean Gooder (Oxford: Oxford University Press, 1985).

——*What Maisie Knew* (1897), ed. Adrian Poole (Oxford: Oxford University Press, 1996).

Johnson, Barabara, *The Feminist Difference: Literature, Psychoanalysis, Race, and Gender* (Cambridge, Mass.: Harvard University Press, 1998).

Jolly, Hugh, *Book of Child Care* (3rd edn. 1985; London: Unwin Paperbacks, 1986).

Kaim, Stéphanie, *Nous, enfants d'homos: Homoparentalité: Une génération témoigne* (Paris: Editions de la Martinière, 2006).

Kane, Elizabeth, *Birth Mother: The Story of America's First Legal Surrogate Mother* (San Diego: Harcourt Brace Jovanovich, 1988).

Keating, Jenny, *A Child for Keeps: The History of Adoption in England, 1918–45* (London: Palgrave Macmillan, 2008).

Klein, Renate D. (ed.), *Infertility* (London: Pandora Press, 1989).

Kohl, Beth, *Embryo Culture: Making Babies in the Twenty-First Century* (New York: Farrar, Straus and Giroux, 2007).

Laborie, Françoise, 'Les Intérim-mères (à propos des mères porteuses)', in Geneviève Delaisi de Parseval with Jacqueline Bigeargal (eds.), *Objectif bébé* (Paris: Autrement, 1994), 109–20.

Laqueur, Thomas, *Making Sex: Body and Gender from the Greeks to Freud* (1990; Cambridge, Mass.: Harvard University Press, 1992).

Layne, Linda L., 'The Home Pregnancy Test: A Feminist Technology?', *Women's Studies Quarterly* 37: 1–2 (Spring–Summer 2009): 61–79.

Lefaucheur, Nadine, 'De l'abandon aux retrouvailles en cinq tableaux', in Benoit Bastard (ed.), *L'Enfant séparé: Les voies de l'attachement* (Paris: Editions Autrement, 2001), 60–79.

Lesnik-Oberstein, Karin, *Reproductive Technologies and the Cultural Construction of Childhood* (London: Karnac, 2008).

McClure, Ruth K., *Coram's Children: The London Foundling Hospital in the Eighteenth Century* (New Haven: Yale University Press, 1981).

McDonagh, Josephine, *Child Murder and British Culture, 1720–1900* (Cambridge: Cambridge University Press, 2003).

McEwan, Ian, *The Child in Time* (1987; London: Picador, 1988).

McInerney, Jay, *The Good Life* (London: Bloomsbury, 2006).

Malthus, T. R., *An Essay on the Principle of Population* (1798), ed. Geoffrey Gilbert (1993; Oxford: Oxford University Press, 2008).

Mamo, Laura, *Queering Reproduction: Achieving Pregnancy in the Age of Technoscience* (Durham, NC: Duke University Press, 2007).

Melosh, Barbara, *Strangers and Kin: The American Way of Adoption* (Cambridge, Mass.: Harvard University Press, 2002).

Mill, John Stuart, *On Liberty* (1859), ed. Gertrude Himmelfarb (London: Penguin, 1982).

—— *The Subjection of Women* (1869; London: Dent, 1974).

Moore, George, *Esther Waters* (1894), ed. David Skilton (Oxford: Oxford University Press, 1983).

Moss, Brigid, *IVF: An Emotional Companion* (London: Collins, 2011).

Mundy, Liza, *Everything Conceivable: How Assisted Reproduction is Changing Men, Women, and the World* (New York: Alfred A. Knopf, 2007).

Musée de l'Assistance Publique de Paris [catalogue] (Paris, 2004).

Necker, Madame [Suzanne], *Réflexions sur le divorce* (Paris: Pougens, 1802).

Novy, Marianne, *Reading Adoption: Family and Difference in Fiction and Drama* (Ann Arbor: University of Michigan Press, 2005).

Ohi, Kevin, 'Children', in David McWhirter (ed.), *Henry James in Context* (Cambridge: Cambridge University Press, 2010), 115–25.

O'Neill, Onora, and William Ruddick (eds.), *Having Children: Philosophical and Legal Reflections on Parenthood* (New York: Oxford University Press, 1979).

Perrier, Nathalie, *Faut-il supprimer l'accouchement sous X?* (Paris: Editions du Rocher, 2008).

Perry, Ruth, *Novel Relations: The Transformation of Kinship in English Literature and Culture, 1748–1818* (Cambridge: Cambridge University Press, 2004).

Petchesky, Rosalind Pollack, 'Foetal Images: The Power of Visual Culture in the Politics of Reproduction', in Michelle Stanworth (ed.), *Reproductive Technologies: Gender, Motherhood and Medicine* (Cambridge: Polity Press, 1987), 57–80.

Pfeffer, Naomi, *The Stork and the Syringe: A Political History of Reproductive Medicine* (Cambridge: Polity, 1993).

—— and Ann Woollett, *The Experience of Infertility* (London: Virago, 1983).

Plato, *The Symposium*, ed. R. G. Bury (2nd edn. 1932; Cambridge: W. Heffer, 1972).

—— *Symposium*, trans. Robin Waterfield (Oxford: Oxford University Press, 1994).

Pollak, Ellen, *Incest and the English Novel, 1684–1814* (Baltimore: Johns Hopkins University Press, 2003).

Pollitt, Katha, 'When is a Mother Not a Mother?', *Nation*, 31 December 1990.

Poole, Adrian, *Henry James* (Brighton: Harvester, 1991).

Ragoné, Helena, *Surrogate Motherhood: Conception in the Heart* (Boulder, Colo.: Westview, 1994).

Raphael-Leff, Joan, 'The Gift of Gametes: Unconscious Motivation, Commodification and Problematics of Genealogy', *Feminist Review* 94: 1 (March 2010): 117–37.

Riley, Denise, *War in the Nursery; Theories of the Child and Mother* (London: Virago, 1983).

Roach, Catherine, 'The Foundling Restored: Emma Brownlow King, William Hogarth, and the Public Image of the Foundling Hospital in the 19th Century', *British Art Journal* 9: 2 (22 September 2008): 40–9.

Rousseau, Jean-Jacques, *Les Confessions* (1781), ed. Bernard Gagnebin and Marcel Raymond (Paris: Gallimard, 1973).

—— *Émile ou de l'éducation* (1758; Paris: Garnier-Flammarion, 1966).

Salomone, Jeanine, with Isabelle Léouffre, *Je l'ai tant voulu: Maman à 62 ans* (Paris: J.-C. Lattès, 2002).

Savage, Carolyn and Sean, *Inconceivable: A Medical Mistake, the Baby We Couldn't Keep, and Our Choice to Deliver the Ultimate Gift* (New York: HarperOne, 2010).

Shakespeare, William, *Othello*, ed. E. A. J. Honigmann (1997; London: Thomson, 2006).

—— *The Winter's Tale*, ed. Ernest Schanzer (London: Penguin, 1986).

Simmons, Christina, *Making Marriage Modern: Women's Sexuality from the Progressive Era to World War II* (New York: Oxford University Press, 2009).

Soloway, Richard Allen, *Birth Control and the Population Question in England, 1877–1950* (Chapel Hill: University of North Carolina Press, 1982).

Sophocles, *Oedipus Tyrannus*, ed. Richard Jebb (1885; Cambridge: Cambridge University Press, 1927).

Stanworth, Michelle (ed.), *Reproductive Technologies: Gender, Motherhood and Medicine* (Cambridge: Polity Press, 1987).

Stopes, Marie Carmichael, *Married Love: A New Contribution to the Solution of Sex Difficulties* (1918; 11th edn. London: G. E. Putnam's, 1925).

Strathern, Marilyn, *Reproducing the Future: Essays on Anthropology, Kinship and the New Reproductive Technologies* (Manchester: Manchester University Press, 1992).

Styles, John, *Threads of Feeling: The London Foundling Hospital's Textile Tokens, 1740–1770* (London: Foundling Museum, 2010).

Swift, Graham, *Tomorrow* (London: Picador, 2007).

Testart, Jacques, *De l'éprouvette au bébé spectacle* (Paris: Editions Complexe, 1984).

—— *L'Œuf transparent* (Paris: Flammarion, 1986).

Thane, Pat, and Tanya Evans, *Sinners? Scroungers? Saints? Unmarried Motherhood in Twentieth-Century England* (Oxford: Oxford University Press, 2012).

Thompson, Charis, *Making Parents: The Ontological Choreography of Reproductive Technologies* (Cambridge, Mass.: MIT Press, 2005).

Tisseron, Serge, *Nos secrets de famille* (Paris: Ramsay, 1999).

Tort, Michel, *Le Désir froid: Procréation artificielle et crise des repères symboliques* (Paris: Editions La Découverte, 1992).

—— *Fin du dogme paternel* (Paris: Aubier, 2005).

Tyler, Anne, *Digging to America* (London: Chatto & Windus, 2006).

Uglow, Jenny, *The Lunar Men: The Friends Who Made the Future, 1730–1810* (London: Faber, 2002).

—— *Hogarth: A Life and a World* (London: Faber, 1997).

['Warnock Report'] Department of Health and Social Security, *Report of the Committee of Inquiry into Human Fertilisation and Embryology* (London: HMSO, 1984).

Wedd, Kit, *The Foundling Museum* (London: Foundling Museum, 2004).

Wharton, Edith, 'Roman Fever' (1934), in *Roman Fever and Other Stories* (London: Virago, 1983), 9–24.

Winston, Robert, *A Child Against All Odds* (London: Bantam, 2006).

Wolf, Naomi, *Misconceptions: Truth, Lies, and the Unexpected on the Journey to Motherhood* (London: Chatto & Windus, 2001).

Wollstonecraft, Mary, *A Vindication of the Rights of Woman* (1792), ed. Janet Todd (Oxford: Oxford University Press, 1993).

Woolf, Virginia, *The Diary of Virginia Woolf*, 5 vols., ed. Anne Olivier Bell (1977–84; London: Penguin, 1979–85).

—— *A Room of One's Own* (1929; London: Panther, 1984).

Wordsworth, William, *The Poems: Volume One*, ed. John O. Hayden (Harmondsworth: Penguin, 1977).

Worth, Jennifer, *Call the Midwife: A True Story of the East End in the 1950s* (London: Phoenix, 2002).

Wright, Helena, *The Sex Factor in Marriage: A Book for Those Who Are or Who Are About to be Married* (1930; London: William & Norgate, 1933).

Yates, Richard, *Revolutionary Road* (1961; London: Vintage, 2009).

Zipper, Juliette, and Selma Sevenhuijsen, 'Surrogacy: Feminist Notions of Motherhood Reconsidered', in Michelle Stanworth (ed.), *Reproductive Technologies: Gender, Motherhood and Medicine* (Cambridge: Polity Press, 1987), 118–38.

Zunshine, Lisa, *Bastards and Foundlings: Illegitimacy in Eighteenth-Century England* (Columbus: Ohio State University Press, 2005).

Index